# Teachers Thinking, Teachers Knowing

# Teachers Thinking, Teachers Knowing

Reflections on Literacy and Language Education

Edited by

Timothy Shanahan
University of Illinois at Chicago

**NCRE** National Conference on Research in English

**NCTE** National Council of Teachers of English
1111 W. Kenyon Road, Urbana, Illinois 61801-1096

Manuscript Editor: Lee Erwin

Production Editor: Rona S. Smith

Cover Design: Pat Mayer

Interior Book Design: Tom Kovacs for TGK Graphics

NCTE Stock Number 50136-3050

Prior to publication, this manuscript was submitted to the National Conference on Research in English for critical review and determination of professional competence. This publication has met such standards. Points of view or opinions, however, do not necessarily represent the official view or opinions of the National Conference on Research in English.

It is the policy of NCTE in its journals and other publications to provide a forum for the open discussion of ideas concerning the content and the teaching of English and the language arts. Publicity accorded to any particular point of view does not imply endorsement by the Executive Committee, the Board of Directors, or the membership at large, except in announcements of policy, where such endorsement is clearly specified.

**Library of Congress Cataloging-in-Publication Data**

Teachers thinking, teachers knowing : reflections on literacy and
　　language education / edited by Timothy Shanahan.
　　　　p.　cm.
　　Papers originally presented at a conference held in Feb. 1992 and
sponsored by the National Conference on Research in English and the
Assembly on Research of the National Council of Teachers of English.
　　Includes bibliographical references and indexes.
　　ISBN 0-8141-5013-6 : $18.95
　　1. Language arts—Congresses.　2. English teachers—Training of—
Congresses.　3. English language—Study and teaching—Congresses.
I. Shanahan, Timothy.　II. National Conference on Research in
English.　III. National Council of Teachers of English.　Assembly on
Research.
LB1576.T3755　1994
728'.0071—dc20　　　　　　　　　　　　　　　　94-29237
　　　　　　　　　　　　　　　　　　　　　　　　　　　CIP

# Contents

# Introduction: First, Some Preliminaries Concerning Teacher Thinking

What you hold in your hands is a book. It isn't just one of those edited collections of pieces that have little reason for congregating on the same street corner, so to speak. This collection was an outgrowth of the "Teacher Thinking, Teacher Knowing in Language and Literacy" conference sponsored by the National Conference on Research in English and the Assembly on Research of the National Council of Teachers of English in February 1992. Nevertheless, it was conceived of as a book from its very beginning.

Often with edited volumes the authors either all say the same types of things in the same ways, or the chapters are so discordant that they seem like random treatments from disparate planets. This collection, though including a variety of seemingly discrepant voices, suffers from neither of these problems. The papers presented at the conference were commissioned intentionally to reveal a variety of methods, backgrounds, approaches, and perspectives. University- and school-based scholars presented papers. Teachers, professors, and school administrators had their say. Critical theorists, cognitive psychologists, progressive educators, and others were included. The emphasis shifted among elementary, middle, secondary, and college; it also shifted around issues of preservice and inservice education. The conference was so diverse that more than one speaker upon being invited exclaimed, "Are you sure you want to include my work? I don't agree with . . ."

In putting this book together, too, I sought diversity of approaches and beliefs not to create argument or division, but to bring to bear as broad an intelligence as possible on the issues of teaching. Although the chapters here reflect a range of opinions, the authors are very similar in some important regards. They are unified by their integrity, the seriousness with which they approach issues of teaching, and their high level of accomplishment in fostering teaching as an intellectual pursuit.

Despite its incredible breadth, and the quite different approaches taken and voices heard, the conference came together as a unity, as small conferences tend to do. About one hundred people braved Chicago in winter to take part in the proceedings, and in a manner of speaking we needed each other. But conferences are not books, and what it takes to make them come together is not the same. After several of the conference presentations we were able to break up into discussion groups, so a lot of provocative ideas were posed that aren't usually included in a book. Similarly, we broke bread and worried about flight plans together, and amplified ideas by asking questions and telling each other what we believed to be important. We even had informal topical discussion groups that operated, more or less, throughout the conference, and commentators who were charged with the responsibility of trying to help us make sense of the proceedings.

I invited the discussion coordinators and commentators to allow us to include their voices in this volume as well. Although there is no way to entirely capture the sidebar conversations and off-the-cuff wisdom of our colleagues, these participants tried to make sense of what was going on throughout the weekend. Sometimes these follow-up pieces provide insightful visions of the ideas explored in the papers, and at other times they allow for a sense of the reactions and extensions that came from the discussions. These follow-up pieces together do a masterful job of helping to bind these essays into a real book, because they express the themes of the entire collection.

When I first began to plan this conference with Lee Odell, Richard Beach, and Jerry Harste, I talked to many friends about what we were trying to do. I vividly remember telling a practicing elementary school teacher about our topic, teacher thinking. Her quick response was, "It sounds like a short conference." Similar bad jokes popped up from a number of quarters, as did a certain amount of defensiveness. One respected colleague mused as to whether it was condescending to talk about "teachers' thinking," in quotation marks, so to speak. She wondered how it would go over if the collection were about doctors' thinking or lawyers' thinking. I've done a bit of checking, and, indeed, there are well-respected scholars who look at the thought processes and learning of many other professionals, with neither apology nor insult (see for instance Coombs, May, and Small 1986; Gottfredson and Gottfredson 1988; Hawkins 1983).

Like every important profession—in which member judgment and decision making are hallmarks of the job—ours has two critical reasons for wishing to understand the knowledge and thinking of its members. First, it is essential for us to understand the thinking of teachers if we are to participate in the development and growth of our newer colleagues, rather than casting them forth with some ill-conceived degree that represents little in the way of true professional knowledge or accomplishment. Second, it is important that we come to understand how teachers think, and what they know, if teachers as professionals are to gain maximum power over their own thinking.

So why the defensiveness? In the past, teacher development has too often been seized upon as the province of the university professor—working in a sort of "How can I operate on teachers more effectively?" mode. The imbalance of power between school and university, teacher and professor, is palpable, as well as unnerving and potentially destructive. This collection was assembled from a somewhat different vantage point: Within this text it is recognized that teacher growth can be facilitated by universities, but that there are important avenues for such growth within the teaching community itself. Preservice issues are addressed, but so are developmental issues that extend well beyond the years during which most teachers are involved with their universities. Chapters were written by university professors who study teacher development and by classroom teachers and administrators who are immersed in the same issues. As we look at teachers throughout this volume—their (our) development, thought processes, knowledge, and inquiries—with a variety of lenses, please keep in mind that our effort is not to look down upon teachers. Our lenses were aimed neither up nor down, but straight ahead, colleague to colleague (and often at ourselves in a mirror). Not surprisingly, a number of the chapters deal with issues of power and authority.

This volume reflects an incredible ferment of ideas about teacher development. The authors present, and argue for, the use of different ways of accomplishing growth through teaching. The approaches put forth include the study of cases, autobiography, reflection, cultural ethnography, lore, and research, among many others. And while the techniques, practices, and examples are persuasive, I found the rich views of teaching articulated here to be even more compelling. By the end of the book, I felt that I had a much better idea of what a good teacher is—and how I might become a better one.

Be prepared to hear about the dignity of the teacher as an individual, the need for true community, the potential benefits of teacher inquiry, and the benefits of careful attention to the contexts and conditions of teaching. These are ideas that we in education hear a lot about these days, of course. What moves the discussions in this book from the purely rhetorical to something deeper and more meaningful is that these authors do not flinch from the complexity of these topics, and they make them come alive with the methods they use. This is a book, because as you take the journey from cover to cover, you will come to understand those four themes more profoundly.

—Timothy Shanahan
University of Illinois at Chicago

## References

Coombs, R. H., D. S. May, and G. W. Small, eds. 1986. *Inside Doctoring: Stages and Outcomes in the Professional Development of Physicians.* New York: Praeger.

Gottfredson, M. R., and D. M. Gottfredson. 1988. *Decision Making in Criminal Justice: Toward the Rational Exercise of Discretion.* New York: Plenum Press.

Hawkins, K. O. 1983. "Thinking about Legal Decision Making." *Issues in Criminal and Legal Psychology* 5:7–24.

# I Teachers Knowing: Toward an Understanding of How Teachers of the English Language Arts Learn and Develop

# 1 Knowing, Believing, and the Teaching of English

Pamela L. Grossman
University of Washington

Lee S. Shulman
Stanford University

*What do good teachers know and how do they construct their insights about literacy, interpretation, and craft? Pamela Grossman and Lee Shulman reflect on the scope of English education, and consider the nature of knowledge in English. They then carefully explore the development of teacher knowledge in English language arts instruction. On the basis of their analysis, they propose a professional education focused on the interpretation of "cases of teaching."*

In the halls of Congress and in the conference rooms of statehouses, knowledge has become politically significant. Even as the Cold War becomes a memory, the new economic crusades are boldly proclaimed. America has lost her economic primacy because she has lost her children's minds. Our educational standards have slipped, leaving us vulnerable to defeat on all fronts— economic, political, even moral. We must immediately pursue new campaigns of the mind and of the spirit, setting the highest standards for our students' intellectual achievements. We must become deeply concerned with the knowledge and skills our students develop and with systems of education and assessment designed to foster those accomplishments. The battles will be fought on fields named English, Mathematics, History, Geography, and Science. The generals are political leaders, the foot soldiers are students, and— apparently—the oft-ignored combat officers are the nation's teachers.

When serious educational problems become grist for political mills, polemic and hyperbole typically characterize the resulting discourse. But, as John Dewey recognized in his preface to *Experience and Education* ([1938] 1963), theoretical or ideological controversies typically underlie salient social conflicts. The concerns over what U.S. students ought to know and be able to do are more than convenient topics for political mischief. They are enduring

3

questions for each subject-matter domain of the school curriculum. On rare occasions the leaders of a curriculum area achieve a modicum of consensus regarding its content and scope. Even so, the question of what teachers should understand if they wish to teach a domain responsibly is no simple challenge. In the field of English teaching, where canons are under question and "consensus" is more frequently misspelled than accomplished, the problem of teacher knowledge is daunting.

How can we think about teacher knowledge in English? What are the grounds on which competing claims for needed teacher knowledge can be supported or dismissed? What are the implications of such positions for views of teacher preparation that include the liberal arts component of undergraduate education, as well as coursework in pedagogy? What kinds of research in learning, teaching, and teacher development can be fruitfully pursued in conjunction with these questions?

## The Diffuse Nature of English as a Subject Area

In order to study issues related to teacher knowledge in English, we first have to pin down the very subject called English—hardly an easy task! As Applebee remarked in his history of the teaching of English:

> Whether the model for the educational process has been growth in language, the four basic skills (reading, writing, listening, speaking) or the three basic disciplines (language, literature, and composition) some aspects of what teachers considered to be important have been lost.... Inevitably, the edges of the subject have blurred and wavered, creating for the teacher of English a perpetual crisis of identity. (Applebee 1974, 245–46)

Another author calls English "the least subject-like of subjects, the least susceptible to definition" (Rosen 1981, 5). Barnes, Barnes, and Clarke (1984) detail the alternative "versions" of English found in British classrooms, and in his account of the English Coalition Conference held at Wye, tellingly entitled *What Is English?* Peter Elbow comments, "This book is trying to paint a picture of a profession that cannot define what it is" (1990, v).

This crisis of identity and persistent ambiguity regarding the subject affect researchers in English education as well. Few of us attempt to look at the field as a whole. Instead, we choose to concentrate on the areas of writing, or literature, or language, with some attempts to interrelate perhaps two of these areas. Or perhaps we focus on the basic skills of language arts—reading, writing, listening, or speaking. Studies of teacher knowledge in English have often simplified the problem space of English by choosing to study teacher knowledge in one of these areas. One early study of teacher knowledge, for example, investigated preservice teachers' knowledge of literary criticism

(Madsen 1968). In our studies of teacher knowledge in the "Knowledge Growth in Teaching" research, we looked primarily at knowledge of literature, with some attention to knowledge of writing (Shulman and Grossman 1987). Researchers at the Center for Research on Teacher Education at Michigan State University have chosen to focus on teachers' knowledge of writing (Comeaux and Gomez 1990, 1991; Gomez 1988). Yet teachers of English do not have the luxury of simplifying their problem space in teaching—they must teach all of these curricular areas. The areas of language, literature, and writing are not as detachable in practice as we sometimes represent them to be in research. So the multifaceted and diffuse nature of English as a subject area poses dilemmas for research on teacher knowledge.

The very multiplicity inherent in English as a subject matter, however, is precisely what makes teacher knowledge such an important issue to grasp. As Grossman argues in a paper on English as a context for secondary school teaching:

> As an inherently ambiguous subject, which is less hierarchically organized than is math and encompasses a variety of subdomains, English may offer teachers greater freedom within the confines of the classroom. As it would be difficult, if not impossible, for teachers to cover all of the territory encompassed by the subject of English, teachers may necessarily select the purposes and areas they plan to emphasize in their classrooms. The inherent complexity of the subject, with its separate domains and subcomponents, may also offer teachers greater autonomy in developing curriculum. (Grossman 1993, 7)

This point regarding the potential for individual autonomy embedded within the very nature of English as a subject matter reflects analyses of role confusion and complexity in other domains; Coser (1975), for example, argues that the multiplicity of expectations facing an individual creates the possibility for individual choice.

The potential for individual autonomy within the subject matter of English places greater demands on teachers' understanding of the subject. In order to make informed curricular decisions, in order to decide to exploit one aspect of the "curriculum potential" of English rather than another (Ben-Peretz 1975), teachers rely on their own understandings and beliefs about the nature of the discipline.[1] Even in districts that prescribe a certain set of texts to be read, English teachers still exercise considerable choice about additional texts to include, and about ways to approach the prescribed texts. The adoption of whole language programs in a number of schools across the country also poses important questions about elementary teachers' knowledge of literature and language. Although part of the allure of whole language programs has been the greater autonomy given to teachers to shape curricula to meet the particular needs and backgrounds of students in developing literacy, such programs also place greater demands on individual teachers' knowledge of texts, literature, and language (Florio-Ruane, Mosenthal, Denyer, Harris and Kirscher 1990; Wells 1990). Again, the inclusive nature of whole language approaches, in which literature, writing, and other aspects of the language arts are combined, requires teachers to make decisions about which particular aspects of language arts to emphasize at particular times. What guides teachers' thinking and decision making in these contexts? Teachers' knowledge and understanding of literature and other language arts provides a potential source for pedagogical reasoning.[2]

## The Nature of "Knowledge" in English

The second problem in research on teacher knowledge is unpacking what constitutes knowledge in English. Much of the research in teachers' knowledge from the 1960s originated in the areas of science and math; many of the early studies, in fact, were done in the context of large-scale curriculum development, such as the School Mathematics Study Group (SMSG) work at Stanford. Current studies of teacher knowledge also have concentrated on the areas of science and math; for example, in the second volume of *Advances in Research on Teaching* (Brophy 1991), which is dedicated to the topic of teachers' subject-matter knowledge in relationship to teaching practice, six of the nine chapters address science or math, while only two chapters discuss English. In part, the research on teacher knowledge has been dominated by what Bruner (1986) has termed "paradigmatic ways of knowing." This focus on paradigmatic ways of knowing has implications for the nature of both research questions and methods. For example, in the areas of science and math, researchers often compare teachers' knowledge of a particular topic in science or math to disciplinary knowledge of that same topic, demonstrating how teachers' knowledge differs from that of experts in the field (see Ball 1990; Hashweh 1987). This may be a less appropriate research model for those of us who want to study teacher knowledge in areas that are characterized more by narrative ways of knowing, again using Bruner's distinction, or, perhaps more important, in areas characterized by considerable internal conflict concerning what can and should be known. If English represents a set of competing schools of thought regarding the very nature of reading and writing, what does it mean to know English well enough to teach it?

Part of the difficulty in studying teachers' theoretical knowledge of literature, for example, is that there are multiple theories against which to look at teachers' knowledge. And yet, understanding teachers' theoretical stances toward literature may be critical to understanding their approaches to teaching. As Elbow (1990) and Scholes (1985) remind us, any act of teaching is implicitly theoretical; "teaching and theory are always implicated in one another" (Scholes 1985, 102). In teaching a text, teachers act upon assumptions about the nature of text, the nature of literature, what it means to read a text, how one marshals evidence to support a particular reading of a text, and the very nature of evidence itself. What implications for teacher knowledge follow from this theory-laden view of teaching? That we implicitly adopt a theoretical stance when we teach does not necessarily mean that we are explicit about our assumptions or about the limitations inherent in any single critical theory. If we see the teaching of literature as teaching students a single critical stance to adopt toward text, then the tacitness of that theoretical stance may not be a problem. Students will learn through apprenticeship, by observing and participating in a particular way of reading text. But if, as the English Coalition Conference report suggests, we want teachers to engage in "the process of inviting and affirming multiple readings instead of a right reading and then explicitly reflecting on where those readings come from and where they go. . . " (Elbow 1990, 52–53), what then must teachers know and believe?

First of all, we might argue that teachers themselves must be fully literate, in Wells's definition of the term.

> This, then, is the empowerment that comes from engaging with texts epistemically: as a reader or writer (and particularly as a writer), by conducting the transaction between the representation on the page and the representation in the head, one can make advances in one's intellectual, moral, or affective understanding to an extent that would otherwise be difficult or impossible to achieve. To be fully literate, therefore, is to have both the ability and the disposition to engage with texts epistemically when the occasion demands. (Wells 1990, 374)

In part, this form of literacy may be a legacy of a liberal education, as people who are liberally educated develop a capability to engage in multiple interpretations of whatever texts they read—whether in literature, history, or science. The liberating feature of liberal education is the recognition that all sources of knowledge, all texts, are human constructions rooted in particular times and places. That some texts manage to transcend the particularities of their times and places, that *King Lear*, for example, can be read by contemporary Japanese readers, is testimony to a certain greatness in the text. Nevertheless, no text loses all vestiges of its genesis. Therefore, we have multiple readings of texts precisely because of the situated character of knowledge and its creation. All knowledge can thus be seen as text in context. Bevington (1990), for example, describes the many new alternative readings of Shakespeare—feminist, historicist, deconstructionist—and how each sheds a new light on an old text. For us, the history of alternative interpretations becomes the beginnings of a pedagogical repertoire, a set of alternative readings that can be used to transform the teaching of particular texts to diverse readers in different contexts.

The particular pedagogical value of multiple interpretations lies in the diversity of student readers. If reading is indeed a transaction between a text and a reader in a particular context, then teachers must believe that there are multiple readings possible of any given text—that the meaning they have constructed from a particular text is not the only possible meaning that *could* be constructed. This belief is central to teachers' ability to enable students to make their own meanings from texts. To prepare teachers who can identify and encourage multiple readings of texts may mean to prepare them not within a single theoretical community, but within multiple communities, and thus make them aware of the competing assumptions regarding the reading of text. It also means reengaging prospective teachers, elementary and secondary alike, in reading and talking about many different kinds of texts (Florio-Ruane et al. 1990).

Teachers must also have explicit knowledge about their own theoretical stances, or predominant orientations toward literature, in order to help others see the assumptions guiding a particular reading of a text. Polanyi's discussion (1962) of tacit knowledge helps us understand that we don't necessarily need explicit knowledge in order to perform a familiar skill, such as riding a bicycle, playing an instrument, or reading a text; we can rely on our tacit knowledge. But if our goal is to encourage multiple readings and to help others gain conscious control over different interpretive stances, to become critical consumers of texts and of theories, then teachers will need more explicit knowledge of their implicit theoretical orientations, as well as the ability to talk about the invisible aspects of interpretive processes.[3]

In order to support this vision of an English classroom, teachers will also need to know how to recognize the kernel of an interpretation lying beneath students' partial, incomplete, and sometimes floundering utterances. Students' tentative interpretations are themselves texts that require explication. It is not always apparent from where an interpretation is coming or where it's headed. Teachers must draw on their knowledge of their students and those students' backgrounds, their knowledge of the texts, and their knowledge of common and uncommon readings of central texts, as well as their knowledge of multiple critical theories, to help them to interpret students' readings.

In the area of writing, we must be concerned with the relationship between procedural and declarative knowledge. Teachers may possess declarative knowledge about writing, for example, about the different forms writing can take, but they possess procedural knowledge of their own writing, also. What is the relationship between knowing about writing and knowing how to write? Even more interesting, and potentially troublesome for researchers, is the tacit nature of much of our knowledge about language. For teachers who grew up speaking standard or mainstream English, the process of internalizing the rules was not a self-conscious one; in detecting and remediating errors, they may rely on what "sounds right." Yet how does this tacit knowledge of language play out in teaching? How do teachers respond to students who bring to class different experiences with language and different dialects? What is the relationship between the tacit knowledge of experienced language users and the more explicit knowledge needed to construct answers to student questions about language?

Yet another issue facing researchers who do research about teachers' knowledge concerns the distinction between knowledge of generic processes involved in language arts and English, such as processes involved in writing or processes involved in constructing meaning from text, and knowledge of particular content, such as specific literary texts or particular kinds of writing. As researchers, what do we focus on? Do we study teachers' knowledge of the different processes involved in writing in the abstract, or do we study that knowledge in the context of teaching about particular kinds of writing?

Now that we've explored the difficulties of studying teacher knowledge in English, we have to admit that the difficulties have not deterred us from trying to study it anyhow, researchers being a notably quixotic and unrealistic group. Let us tell you about some of the ways we have tried to study teachers' knowledge in English and some of what we've found.

## Knowledge Growth in Teaching Research

The intent of the "Knowledge Growth in Teaching" studies was to follow the growth and use of subject-matter knowledge among preservice teachers during their year of preparation and their first year of teaching. In these studies, we were particularly interested in both how teachers drew upon their knowledge of subject matter acquired during their undergraduate preparation and how they constructed new understandings of subject matter through the process of learning to teach.

There is a widely held misconception that our view of teacher knowledge is a static one, a view that teachers come to their instructional tasks with a fixed "knowledge base" that undergirds their work. This foundational view of teacher knowledge is misleading, as it appears to communicate that the knowledge for teaching exists somehow outside the teacher, derived from research and other authoritative sources, and is then applied to the challenges of teaching. The view we espouse is quite the opposite of a static one, although we suspect that our metaphor of a *knowledge base* unfortunately lends itself to just that misrepresentation. We did not see ourselves eliciting static knowledge from the minds of teachers, but rather observing the growth and construction of knowledge over time. We assumed that in the process of reading or teaching a text, teachers will develop new understandings of the text prompted by student readings, as well as through their own reengagement with it.[4]

In "Knowledge and Teaching," Shulman (1987) presents a model of "pedagogical reasoning and action" to portray how knowledge contributes to, as well as results from, the intellectual activities of teaching. In this model, teaching is seen as an alternating and simultaneous interaction of teacher understanding, transformation, action, evaluation and reflection, and progressive development of new understandings. The model of pedagogical reasoning is fundamentally a conception of how teachers continue to learn from their experiences in classrooms. The mechanism for both thought and learning is some form of reflection. During the processes of curriculum analysis and planning (comprehension and transformation), the teacher engages in reflection *for* action. The teacher rehearses and anticipates what might go on in the minds of the students and how different representations might relate both to the potential of the texts and the constructions of the readers. During active instruction, the teacher engages in reflection *in* action, processing experience, weighing alternatives, and shifting grounds as the teaching and learning unfold. After the active teaching, the teacher reviews and evaluates, playing back the experiences, examining pieces of student work, now reflecting *on* both action and thought. The way in which these processes, often tacit, accompany all the processes of pedagogical thinking and action remains elusive. But as pedagogical reasoning is one of the most important places where teacher knowledge develops, it is well worth our research interest and efforts.

In these studies, we used a variety of methods to investigate teachers' knowledge. Our measures of teachers' knowledge of English included self-reports of areas of greater and lesser understanding in English; transcripts of undergraduate and graduate coursework; transcript-guided interviews, in which participants talked about what they had learned from different courses; and a variety of tasks related to literature and writing, such as thinking aloud about a short story or poem, or responding to a sample of student writing. These think-aloud tasks perhaps come closest to drawing upon teachers' implicit theoretical stances toward literature or writing, but the responses themselves are not always easy texts to understand. Finally, we used observation cycles in which we observed teachers teaching a unit in order to get a sense of the relationship between knowledge and teaching practice.[5]

We recognize that this work poses significant methodological tangles, including the level of inference required to infer knowledge of literature or theoretical stance from readings of particular texts, the vagaries of self-report data, and the insufficiencies of "objective" data such as number of courses taken in a subject. Taken individually, each method is insufficient (see L. S. Shulman 1988 for a discussion of a union of insufficiencies in teacher assessment). We found that the particular responses to questions given by participants were less important than the thinking that lay behind the responses. For example, in Grossman's study (1990), she used Randall Jarrell's "Death of the Ball Turret Gunner" as a text in a think-aloud task. Following discussions in which participants constructed their own understandings of the poem, they were asked to think about teaching it to high school students. As part of the interviews, participants were given copies of textbooks in which the poem was used.[6] Both Lance and Vanessa, the teachers with the most and the least subject-matter knowledge in the study, responded negatively to the textbook question, "What is the meaning of this poem?" (from Brooks and Warren, *Understanding Poetry*), but they objected on different grounds. Lance objected on disciplinary grounds:

> Because you can't capture in prose what poetry does. I mean it's always this illusion that the poem meant, is saying, this thing and that . . . you could just say it. But you can't just say it. And so it promotes this kind of bad way of thinking about poetry, which isn't a good idea, I think. (Interview, 10 February 1987)

Jake, another teacher who possessed a strong background in literature, objected to the question on similar grounds: "I would never ask questions like that. I would say, 'Discuss the poem, or discuss the meaning or meanings of the poem.' I don't like these questions because they're reductive" (Grossman 1993, 33). Vanessa also objected, but for different reasons:

> I don't like these [questions] as well, because they're too specific. . . . I like to give my kids questions that they can't copy and that they can each have their own answer to and support them, and that way they'll have to and they will get more excited about what they're doing if they have to support what they're doing. This kind of stuff is good to help them start understanding a poem. (Interview, 3 February 1987)

While all three teachers objected to the textbook treatment of the poem, Jake and Lance objected on disciplinary grounds, while Vanessa seemed to object on pedagogical ones. From these texts, it is easier to infer something about Jake's and Lance's understanding and beliefs about poetry than it is to infer Vanessa's; rather, we get a sense of Vanessa's beliefs about the *teaching* of poetry.

Using classroom observations as a source of data poses similar difficulties in interpreting teachers' knowledge. For example, classroom observations of the teaching of science have demonstrated that beginning science teachers are less likely to ask open-ended questions about topics about which they are relatively less knowledgeable (Carlsen 1988). Yet using teachers' use of open-ended questions during classroom discussions as an indicator of their knowledge of literature may be problematic. One interpretation of these open-ended questions may be that they reflect an underlying knowledge of the underdetermination of literary meaning and the potential for multiple interpretations of a text. On the other hand, teachers' use of relatively narrow questions and reliance on the "initiation-response-evaluation" discourse structure described by Mehan (1987) may reflect their own experiences in school-based discussions of literature as much as their understanding of literature per se (Florio-Ruane et al. 1990).

What did we conclude from our studies, given all of the necessary caveats and cautions? First of all, we concluded that subject-matter knowledge matters. What teachers knew about their subjects, particularly what they knew and believed about how knowledge is constructed in a specific discipline, affected how they planned for instruction, how they selected texts and organized curricula, and how they interacted with students in the classroom (see Shulman and Grossman 1987 for a full description of the findings of the "Knowledge Growth in Teaching" project). In English, we focused particularly on how teachers' orientations toward literature, their theoretical stances, to use Elbow's term, affected what they believed about the goals of teaching literature, as well as how they planned for instruction and conducted classroom discussions (Grossman 1991).

We also concluded that subject-matter knowledge alone is not sufficient for teachers. Knowing English is not the same as knowing how to teach English to a diverse set of learners in particular contexts (see Clift 1991; Vendler 1988 for additional discussion of this issue). Teachers need to go beyond their own understanding of content to understand something about the purposes for teaching English or language arts at particular grade levels, the different underlying philosophies about teaching literature, language, and writing, and students' understandings and potential misunderstandings of that content. When the beginning teachers without teacher education in Grossman's study (1990) tried to teach what they knew about Shakespeare to high school students, they discovered the limitations of untransformed disciplinary knowledge, as Lance comments about his teaching of *Romeo and Juliet* to ninth graders:

> It was really hard for me to adjust my expectations in the sense that I was always interested in pushing ideas to the extreme, like proving the most obscure theses and showing little nuances in the language that no one had even seen and why that works. And these kids, of course I know that now, wanted nothing to do with that. That was just totally irrelevant to them. (Grossman 1990, 107)

Through the process of teaching, and, we would hope, through professional preparation, teachers engage in constructing their understanding of what it means to teach English. We see this construction of pedagogical content knowledge, as we've termed it, as a central task facing beginning secondary school teachers. Teacher education can help provide the frameworks for thinking about the teaching of English, and for helping students reexamine their own experiences as learners in English classrooms (Florio-Ruane et al. 1990). Teacher education can also help prospective teachers learn how to interpret students' difficulties in interpreting literature or in writing essays, as well as introducing prospective teachers to new ways of thinking about the teaching of writing (Comeaux and Gomez 1991). The data from Grossman's study (1990) suggest that teachers do not necessarily construct new conceptions of the teaching of writing, for example, from experience alone, even when experience teaches them that their current approach isn't working.

Yet pedagogical content knowledge is inextricably linked to other knowledge necessary for teaching. While new teachers can imagine wonderful discussions about literature that take into account multiple perspectives, they must also understand something about managing group dynamics in order to make that vision possible in a classroom setting (see, e. g., Clift 1991). The different domains of teacher knowledge are inevitably interactive and interdependent.

We have also learned that context matters in teachers' knowledge, that is, that teachers' knowledge both shapes and is shaped by the contexts in which they work. In a study of science teachers' pedagogical content knowledge, for example, Brickhouse and Bodner (1992) describe a beginning teacher caught between his convictions regarding science instruction and the constraints inherent in the context in which he is teaching. In a study of junior high school English teachers, Zancanella (1991) describes the effects of institutional constraints on how teachers teach literature. And in a study comparing English and math teachers in three different secondary schools, Stodolsky and Grossman have found that teachers' conceptions of their subject matter affect their responses to changes in the student context of their schools; at the same time, the contexts in which teachers teach begin to shape their conceptions of what it means to teach their subject matter (Stodolsky and Grossman 1992). Teacher knowledge, like all knowledge, is situated in the contexts of its use. We must begin to pay more attention to the contexts in which teachers work and to the complex relationships among content and context.

## Implications for Professional Education: The Uses of Cases

Studying teacher knowledge, its construction as well as its interplay with instruction, can help teacher educators understand more clearly the relationship between professional knowledge and professional education. As Feiman-Nemser (1983) observed, the teacher education curriculum provides a number of distinct opportunities for different kinds of learning to occur. A number of studies have indicated the importance of subject-specific methods courses in developing pedagogical content knowledge in English (Comeaux and Gomez 1990; 1991; Florio-Ruane et al. 1990; Grossman 1990; Grossman and Richert 1988; Ritchie and Wilson 1993). In all instances, these courses must find some way of addressing prospective teachers' past experiences as learners in English classes and their subsequent experiences as student teachers in English classrooms. Prospective teachers' own prior experiences as learners, and their apprenticeships of observation (Lortie 1975), may have inculcated ways of thinking about English teaching that do not support the vision of English advocated in teacher education coursework (Ritchie and Wilson, in press). In this sense, teacher education must adopt a form of teaching for conceptual change in order to have an effect. Teacher educators must also be aware of what prospective teachers are learning from their field experiences, and how those experiences mediate the lessons of teacher education coursework. Creating school-university partnerships, in which teachers and professors collaborate on the preparation of future teachers, provides an opportunity to diminish the potential dissonance between what prospective teachers hear at the university and what they experience in the schools (Athanases, Caret, Canales, and Meyer 1992).

The contextual and interdependent aspects of teacher knowledge help explain our interest in the uses of case methods in teacher education. As researchers concerned with knowledge acquisition in complex and ill-structured domains have argued (Spiro, Coulson, Feltovich, and Anderson 1988), teachers and doctors, among many others who work in such domains, must draw upon and integrate multiple knowledge domains under conditions of uncertainty and novelty. Classroom events rarely unfold the same way twice. To prepare teachers to deal with the complexity of the classroom, Lee Shulman and others have argued for the use of multiple cases of classroom teaching during teacher education. Cases of teaching, as opposed to prescriptive proclamations of best practice, can attempt to represent the messy world of actual practice, in which often neither the problem nor the solution is clear. To prepare prospective teachers for the widely diverse settings in which they will teach, proponents of case methods argue that it is better to engage them in discussions of ten cases of the teaching of *Hamlet* in a host of different contexts than to offer them the one best way. Cases also offer the opportunity for integration of knowledge, as the analyses of cases will usually draw upon issues related not only to the teaching of content but to issues of classroom management, school context, student diversity, the ethics of teaching, and many other areas.

In addition to reading cases of other peoples' teaching, prospective teachers can be encouraged to write cases of their own teaching as well (LaBoskey

1992; Richert 1992). Casting experience into narrative form provides a vehicle for reflection, an opportunity to select and analyze a particular episode of one's teaching. Learning to craft cases from classroom teaching can help prospective teachers learn from their own experiences. For English teachers in particular, writing cases can reengage them as writers, as they explore writing in a new and potentially unfamiliar genre.

Cases permit learners to explore a wider variety of settings and circumstances in the teaching of English than can ever be experienced directly. Some may worry that advocates of case methods want to supplant field experiences with cases, but we would never advocate cases as a replacement for direct experience in the field. Instead, we argue for a balance between the intensity of a few vivid experiences in the field and the vicarious exploration of a wide range of circumstances through cases. As the psychometricians used to observe about testing, we are always searching for a balance between "fidelity and band width;" while field experiences possess undeniable fidelity, cases provide greater band width. Field experiences are often difficult to share, as prospective teachers are encountering quite different circumstances in their separate classrooms and schools. When individuals report to a group on their own field experiences, no one else in the group has experienced those same circumstances. When all have studied the same well-crafted case, on the other hand, there is a parity of expertise in the group, which serves as an invitation for all to participate in the discussion. Moreover, when we shift to case writing as the mode of instruction, field experience is highlighted and illuminated. Far from replacing experience, the use of case writing enriches experience and makes it available for further conversation and group reflection.

Teaching with a variety of case methods, including both reading common texts and writing one's own texts, also reflects a particular perspective on teachers' knowledge. The knowledge and practical understanding teachers act upon daily in classrooms is unlikely to be composed of principles derived from research, not even the precepts of dedicated teacher educators. Rather, teachers' knowledge is composed largely of a repertoire of cases, of what happened in particular classes with specific kids. A curriculum built around the use of cases can provide both the beginnings of a case knowledge for prospective teachers and ways of constructing meaning from cases, initiating beginning teachers into explicitly pedagogical reasoning. Finally, helping prospective English teachers understand the multiple ways in which the teaching of common texts can unfold, helping them construct reflective and critical interpretations of these cases, and encouraging them to author their own cases of teaching has the additional benefit of modeling the kind of full and thoughtful literacy we want them to promote among their own future students.

**Future Research on Teachers' Knowledge and Thinking in English**

While a number of teacher educators have begun to experiment with the use
of case methods during teacher education (J. H. Shulman 1992), we know
very little about what prospective teachers actually learn from case methods.
One area ripe for future research lies in answering the many unanswered
questions about teaching and learning with cases (Grossman 1993). What
makes particular cases pedagogically powerful? What do prospective teachers
remember about cases once they are in the classroom? How do they draw
upon cases as precedents for practice in the process of pedagogical reasoning
and action, if they draw upon them at all? While there is a sparse literature on
learning from cases in the area of teacher education, we recognize that teaching with cases is but an instance of the larger phenomenon of teaching with
narrative texts. The questions we raise about how and what teachers learn
from both reading and writing cases of teaching are related to more general
issues about how and what people learn from narrative.

In addressing these questions, the community of researchers in English
education has the obvious advantage of having studied the processes of
understanding different kinds of texts (e.g. Langer 1989) or of what makes
certain texts "difficult" (e.g. Purves 1991), and of having studied what students learn through writing (e.g. Marshall 1987). As teacher educators grapple
with questions related to teaching and learning with cases, they would be wise
to consult with colleagues in English education.

**Case Studies of Teaching Common Texts**

Another area for future research in the area of English education lies in
documenting exemplary cases of the teaching of English in a wide variety of
contexts. One of the most fascinating strategies for observing how individual
knowledge and skill can be applied to exploit the potential inherent in a given
situation is to provide a number of practitioners with the opportunity to try
their hand at the "same" problem. Thus, in duplicate bridge we give all
competitors the same deal of the cards. In chess, we collect and publish
casebooks of great players employing the "same" gambits or defenses. In our
earlier work on medical diagnosis ("Medical Problem Solving" [Elstein, Shulman and Sprafka 1978]), we trained actors and actresses to present the "same"
clinical cases to several dozen experienced internists.

We propose a large set of studies in which researchers carefully examine
and analyze the ways in which both new and experienced English teachers

instruct students in the same texts, be they short stories, plays, novels, poems, or other works. Let us study a number of teachers at work with *As I Lay Dying* or *To Kill a Mockingbird*, or see how *Of Mice and Men, Beloved, Black Boy*, or *1984* plays out in different classrooms under the tutelage of diverse teachers and the constructive interpretations of diverse learners.

We and our colleagues have studied a number of novice teachers teaching Gina Berriault's short story "The Stone Boy" or the poem "The Death of the Ball Turret Gunner." Grossman (19902) has analyzed parallel pedagogies of *Hamlet*; Gudmundsdottir (1989) has done the same with *The Adventures of Huckleberry Finn* and U.S. history. Wilson and Wineburg (1988) have examined the teaching of the American Revolution by several exemplary secondary school teachers. The National Center for the Learning and Teaching of Literature has also begun to assemble a set of case studies of the teaching of experienced English teachers (e.g., Burke 1990; Forman-Pemberton 1989; Hansbury-Zuendt 1991). As we examine teaching under those circumstances, we come to appreciate the extent to which teaching is truly constructivist, an activity of continuing transformation of subject matter by both teacher and students. We come to understand why classroom management and organization prepare the ground for the substantive pedagogy to follow, but do not define it.

We therefore propose that extensive, analytic casebooks of English teaching be developed that focus on multiple teachings of the same or closely parallel works. The multiplicity and the parallel structures will forestall unwarranted temptations to convert described cases into prescribed orthodoxies. Cases will be analyzed, contrasted, and interpreted through commentaries and other glosses. Those who worry about inadvertent canonization, through treating the texts we study as the texts we must teach, need not be concerned. First, some texts are taught so widely that it would be irresponsible to ignore them (e.g., *Romeo and Juliet, Julius Caesar, To Kill a Mockingbird, Death of a Salesman*). Multiple case studies of the teaching of less-familiar texts may also provide support and encouragement for teachers to teach alternative texts as well.

In what sense is this research? We believe that the "knowledge base" of teaching must be composed, in large measure, of carefully collected and analyzed cases of teaching and learning. These cases provide contextualized instances of English teaching that can be compared with one another, analyzed for their distinctive features, and reviewed to understand the strategic and moral lessons of their stories. Principles can be derived from the analysis of these accounts (as they can from experiments and other more traditional forms of investigation) and tested against other accounts.

## Conclusion

We believe that discussions about teacher knowledge and belief are central to the discourse on teaching and teacher education in English. The interplay between knowledge and teaching is an intricate one, as, we believe, the process of teaching provides the impetus for the constant revision and renewal of what one knows and believes. Knowledge begets teaching, which in turn begets new knowledge.

Considerations of teachers' knowledge and the contexts that support its growth and renewal are particularly critical during periods of reform. The calls for educational reform are likely to continue. Standards will be stipulated, challenged, elaborated, and revised. In English, the debates may become more strident and the frameworks less coherent. The tensions between depth and coverage will be exacerbated. The classroom teacher will increasingly serve as practical broker and interpreter of the curriculum, struggling to construct pedagogical bridges between the school programs of a single state or district and the diverse sensibilities of children who are products of dozens of cultures. In the face of political imperatives and daily ambiguities, our nation's teachers will need ever greater knowledge and understanding, a scholarship of disciplines and students, a competence of communication, and a wisdom of practice.

At the heart of teachers' capacity to cope will be their developed pedagogical understandings, knowledge, and skills, and their dispositions and commitments regarding children, their subject matter, and the social conditions that surround both. Few teachers can flourish without the help of a supportive organization and a cadre of fellow teachers committed to similar values and initiatives. Nonetheless, no organization can overcome fundamental deficits of content and pedagogy in the preparation of its teachers. Central to reform in English education is the capacity of teachers to teach students the reading, interpretation, and writing of texts. When conversations about the attainment of new standards are pursued in statehouses and federal offices, we need to convince policy makers that such efforts represent empty rhetoric unless we can learn to educate the next generation of teachers adequately and support them appropriately in their work.

## Notes

1. We have always been sympathetic to Miriam Ben-Peretz's conception of "curriculum potential" in which any curricular text—including a detailed math or biology textbook and associated workbooks and materials, or a basal reading

series—is seen as the starting point for pedagogical thinking, not a finished product to be transmitted from teacher to student.

2. A recent study of elementary school teachers' perspectives regarding the role of literature in language arts, conducted under the auspices of the National Center for the Learning and Teaching of Literature (Walmsley and Walp 1989) concluded that "many elementary teachers had neither an instructional philosophy for the teaching of literature, nor a well-developed practical plan for making literature a part of their elementary curriculum" (from Center Update newsletter).

3. Wells (1990) also refers to the problems of tacit knowledge in apprenticeship models of literacy development. Observing overt behaviors of literate people is unlikely to provide learners with the knowledge they need. "Indeed, since these literate practices are, as we have just seen, essentially a matter of engaging with a particular text in a manner appropriate to one's goals on a particular occasion, it is difficult to see how such essential *mental* activities could be acquired by simply observing an expert's overt behavior. Equally, it is of little value to guide the novice's action if he or she has no understanding of the significance of the action to the overall goal of the activity. What this means, therefore, is that in the case of such cultural practices as those associated with literacy, talk in and about the activity can no longer remain an optional aspect of the collaboration . . . but must be seen as both central and essential" (Wells 1990, 380).

4. At times, the research itself became the opportunity for construction of new knowledge of content; through the nature of our interactions with preservice teachers, we collaborated in the construction of new understandings. The nature of the tasks may have prompted new insights, rather than eliciting prior knowledge. Any efforts to study knowledge will need to take this aspect into account.

5. Grossman's work on pedagogical knowledge in English (1993), Gudmundsdottir's work on pedagogical content knowledge in English and social studies (1989), and Clift's work on knowledge development in an English teacher all use similar methods (Clift, in press).

6. The poem was chosen, in part, because it appears in a number of secondary school poetry textbooks, including *Understanding Poetry*, edited by Brooks and Warren, *Ways to Poetry*, edited by Clayes and Gerrietts, and *Sound and Sense*, edited by Perrine. The poem also appeared in a textbook on American literature used by local school districts.

## References

Applebee, A. N. 1974. *Tradition and Reform in the Teaching of English: A History.* Urbana, Ill.: NCTE.

Athanases, S. Z., E. Caret, J. Canales, and T. Meyer. 1992. "Four against 'the Two-Worlds Pitfall': University-Schools Collaboration in Teacher Education." *English Education* 24, no. 1:34–51.

Ball, D. L. 1990. "Prospective Elementary and Secondary Teachers' Understanding of Division." *Journal of Research in Mathematics Education* 21:132–44.

Barnes, D., D. Barnes, and S. Clarke. 1984. *Versions of English*. London: Heinemann.

Ben-Peretz, M. 1975. "The Concept of Curriculum Potential." *Curriculum Theory Network* 5:151–59.

Bevington, D. 1990. "Reconstructing Shakespeare." *University of Chicago Magazine* (Spring): 21–25.

Brickhouse, N., and G. M. Bodner. 1992. "The Beginning Science Teacher: Classroom Narratives of Convictions and Constraints." *Journal of Research in Science Teaching* 29:471–85.

Brophy, J., ed. 1991. *Teachers' Knowledge of Their Subject Matter as It Relates to Their Teaching Practice.* Vol. 2 of *Advances in Research on Teaching.* Greenwich, Conn.: JAI Press.

Bruner, J. S. 1986. *Actual Minds, Possible Worlds.* Cambridge: Harvard University Press.

Burke, S. 1990. *Will Blake: Teaching and Learning Huckleberry Finn.* Report Series 2.12. Albany: National Center for the Learning and Teaching of Literature, State University of New York.

Carlsen, W. S. 1988. The Effects of Science Teacher Subject-Matter Knowledge on Teacher Questioning and Classroom Discourse. Ph.D. diss., Stanford University.

Clift, R. T. 1991. "Learning to Teach English—Maybe: A Study of Knowledge Development." *Journal of Teacher Education* 42, no. 5 (Nov.-Dec.): 357–72.

Comeaux, M. A., and M. L. Gomez. 1990. Why Sarah Doesn't Teach Like Sandra: Exploring the Development of Prospective Teachers' Knowledge, Beliefs, and Dispositions about Teaching Writing. Paper presented at the annual meeting of the American Educational Research Association, April, Boston.

————. 1991. Explicating the Text of Teacher Education: An Examination of the Role of the Special Methods Course in Teacher Preparation. Paper presented at the annual meeting of the American Educational Research Association, April, Chicago.

Coser, R. "The Complexity of Roles as the Seedbed of Individual Autonomy." In *The Idea of Social Structure,* edited by L. Coser, 237–64. New York: Harcourt Brace Jovanovich. Cited in L. S. Shulman 1983.

Dewey, John. [1938] 1963. *Experience and Education.* New York: Macmillan.

Elbow, P. 1990. *What Is English?* New York: MLA; Urbana, Ill.: NCTE.

Elstein, A., L. S. Shulman, and S. Sprafka. 1978. *Medical Problem Solving: The Analysis of Clinical Reasoning.* Cambridge: Harvard University Press.

Feiman-Nemser, S. 1983. "Learning to Teach." In *Handbook of Teaching and Policy,* edited by L. Shulman and G. Sykes, 150–70. New York: Longman.

Florio-Ruane, S., J. Mosenthal, J. Denyer, D. Harris, and B. Kirscher. 1990. Constructing Knowledge in Classroom Interaction: A Problem in Learning to Teach about Text. Paper presented at the annual meeting of the American Educational Research Association, April, Boston.

Forman-Pemberton, C. 1989. *Being There with Kevin Tucker.* Report Series 2.5. Albany: National Center for the Learning and Teaching of Literature, State University of New York.

Gomez, M. L. 1988. Prospective Teachers' Beliefs about Good Writing: What Do They Bring with Them to Teacher Education? Paper presented at the annual meeting of the American Educational Research Association, New Orleans.

Grossman, P. L. 1990. *The Making of a Teacher: Teacher Knowledge and Teacher Education.* New York: Teachers College Press.

————. 1991. "What Are We Talking about Anyhow? Subject Matter Knowledge for Secondary English Teachers." In *Teachers' Knowledge of Their Subject Matter as It Relates to Their Teaching Practice,* edited by J. Brophy, 245–64. Vol. 2 of *Advances in Research on Teaching.* Greenwich, Conn.: JAI Press.

————. 1993. *English as Context: English in Context.* Technical Report S93-2. Stanford: Center for Research on the Context of Secondary School Teaching.

Grossman, P. L., and A. E. Richert. 1988. "Unacknowledged Knowledge Growth: A Re-examination of the Effects of Teacher Education." *Teaching and Teacher Education* 4, no. 1:53–62.

Gudmundsdottir, S. 1989. Knowledge Use among Experienced Teachers: Four Case Studies of High School Teaching. Ph.D. diss., Stanford University.

Hansbury-Zuendt, T. 1991. *Voices Making Meaning: Reading the Texts with Tony Carrera.* Report Series 2.14. Albany: National Center for the Learning and Teaching of Literature, State University of New York.

Hashweh, M. Z. 1987. "Effects of Subject-Matter Knowledge in the Teaching of Biology and Physics." *Teaching and Teacher Education* 3, no. 2:109–20.

LaBoskey, V. K. 1992. "Case Investigations: Preservice Teacher Research as an Aid to Reflection." In *Case Methods in Teacher Education,* edited by J. H. Shulman, 175–93. New York: Teachers College Press.

Langer, J. A. 1989. *The Process of Understanding Literature.* Technical report 2.1. Albany: National Center for the Learning and Teaching of Literature, State University of New York.

Lortie, D. 1975. *Schoolteacher: A Sociological Study.* Chicago: University of Chicago Press.

Madsen, A. L. 1968. *Responses of Prospective English Teachers to a Test of Theories of Literary Criticism.* Urbana, Ill.: Statewide Curriculum Study Center in the Preparation of Secondary School English Teachers.

Marshall, J. D. 1987. "The Effects of Writing on Students' Understanding of Literary Texts." *Research in the Teaching of English* 21:64–91.

Mehan, H. 1987. "Language and Power in the Organizational Process." *Discourse Processes* 10:291–301.

Polanyi, M. 1962. *Personal Knowledge: Towards a Post-Critical Philosophy.* Chicago: University of Chicago Press.

Protherough, R. 1989. *Students of English.* London: Routledge.

Purves, A. C., ed. 1991. *The Idea of Difficulty in Literature.* Albany: State University of New York Press.

Richert, A. E. 1992. "Writing Cases: A Vehicle for Inquiry into the Teaching Process." In *Case Methods in Teacher Education,* edited by J. H. Shulman, 155–74. New York: Teachers College Press.

Ritchie, J. S., and D. E. Wilson. 1993. "Dual Apprenticeships: Subverting and Supporting Critical Teaching." *English Education* 25, no. 2 (May): 67–83.

Rosen, H. 1981. *Neither Bleak House nor Liberty Hall.* London: University of London Institute of Education. Cited in Protherough 1989.

Scholes, R. E. 1985. *Textual Power: Literary Theory and the Teaching of English.* New Haven: Yale University Press.

Shulman, J. H., ed. 1992. *Case Methods in Teacher Education.* New York: Teachers College Press.

Shulman, L. S. 1983. "Autonomy and Obligation: The Remote Control of Teaching." In *Handbook of Teaching and Policy,* edited by L. S. Shulman and G. Sykes, 484–504. New York: Longman Press.

———. 1987. "Knowledge and Teaching: Foundations of the New Reform." *Harvard Educational Review* 57:1–20.

———. 1988. "A Union of Insufficiencies: Strategies for Teacher Assessment in a Period of Educational Reform." *Educational Leadership* (November): 36–41.

Shulman, L. S., and P. L. Grossman. 1987. Final Report to the Spencer Foundation. Technical Report of the Knowledge Growth in a Profession Research Project. Stanford: School of Education, Stanford University.

Spiro, R. J., R. L. Coulson, P. J. Feltovich, and D. K. Anderson. 1988. "Cognitive Flexibility Theory: Advanced Knowledge Acquisition in Ill-Structured Domains." Technical Report No. 441. Urbana, Ill: Center for the Study of Reading.

Vendler, H. 1988. "What We Have Loved." In *Teaching Literature: What Is Needed Now,* edited by J. Engell and D. Perkins, 13–28. Cambridge: Harvard University Press.

Walmsley, S., and T. Walp. 1989. *Teaching Literature in Elementary School.* Report Series 1.3. Albany: National Center for the Learning and Teaching of Literature, State University of New York.

Wells, G. 1990. "Talk about Text: Where Literacy Is Learned and Taught." *Curriculum Inquiry* 20:369–405.

Wilson, S. M., and S. S. Wineburg. 1988. "Peering at History through Different Lenses: The Role of Disciplinary Perspectives in Teaching History." *Teachers College Record* 89:525–39.

Zancanella, D. 1991. "Teachers Reading/Readers Teaching: Five Teachers' Personal Approaches to Literature and Their Teaching of Literature." *Research in the Teaching of English* 25, no. 1:5–32.

# 2 Producing and Assessing Knowledge: Beginning to Understand Teachers' Knowledge through the Work of Four Theorists

Anthony Petrosky
University of Pittsburgh

*In this challenging essay, Anthony Petrosky considers the construction and assessment of teacher knowledge. To assist teachers in the development of knowledge, it is first necessary to have an understanding of what knowledge is. From an examination of the philosophical foundations of knowledge, Petrosky concludes it to be a form of discourse. He goes on to show how the National Board for Professional Teaching Standards is using this conception to evaluate and make sense of teacher knowledge in the English language arts.*

---

To make explicit what is usually allowed to remain implicit; to state that which, because of professional consensus, is ordinarily not stated or questioned; to begin again rather than to take up writing dutifully at a designated point and in a way ordained by tradition; above all, to write in and as an act of discovery rather than out of respectful obedience to established "truth"—these add up to the production of knowledge. . . .

—Edward Said, *Beginnings: Intention and Method*

Said is here concerned with a writer's production of knowledge. He offers the possibility of thinking about knowledge outside of essentialist "truth"-oriented models—those models that seek to identify what is held to be true or "known" in a particular subject or field—and proposes the language of discovery and production as metaphors for knowledge. Said offers an approach to thinking about knowledge in which knowledge is that which is created or produced by individuals in articulated acts, such as writing; this is quite different from essentialist notions of knowledge as that which can be identified categorically as instances of truth in subjects or fields that are assumed

The research for this project was supported in part by the National Board for Professional Teaching Standards under a contract with the Assessment Development Laboratory at the University of Pittsburgh. The opinions expressed, however, are solely those of the author.

to be historically linear, progressive, and additive accumulations of concepts, truths, and information.

## The Construction of Knowledge

For Said, knowledge is produced by individuals from that which is not, from that which exists, as one might say, within them, or, as Michel Foucault, in his *Archaeology of Knowledge* (1972) might say, within the possibilities of their language, their discourse. When thought of this way, knowledge is not a collection of discrete truths; knowledge is, rather, what people produce in and with discourse in response to problems. "Discourses," in Foucault's sense of the term, are "practices that systematically form the objects of which they speak" (49); they are not, as common language refers to them, "groups of signs . . . signifying elements referring to contents or representations" (49). "Of course," Foucault says, "discourses are composed of signs; but what they do is more than use these signs to designate things" (49). "Thus conceived," as Foucault asserts, "discourse is not the majestically unfolding manifestation of a thinking, knowing, speaking subject, but, on the contrary, a totality, in which the dispersion of the subject and his discontinuity with himself may be determined" (55). Discourse, in this sense, is exterior to the subject, but at the same time encompasses him or her in a subject position, in a position, that is, created in and with discourse. Discourse, then, according to Foucault in another statement that further abuses definitions, "can be defined as the group of statements that belong to a single system of formation," and we are able therefore "to speak of clinical discourse, economic discourse, the discourse of natural history, psychiatric discourse" (107); and, I would add, educational discourse.

The rules of formation, the discursive structures and practices, that operate in discourse, "operate not only in the mind or consciousness of individuals, but in discourse itself; they operate therefore, according to a sort of uniform anonymity, on all individuals who undertake to speak in a discursive field" (63). These rules of formation, as Foucault calls them, are not "universally valid for every domain; one always describes them in particular discursive fields . . . the most one can do is to make a systematic comparison, from one region to another, of the rules of formation of concepts" (63).

## Knowledge as Discourse

Foucault, then, is interested in describing and analyzing discourses and their rules of formation; he is interested also in the desires and powers—the formative elements of discourse—that privilege particular discursive structures and practices over others. For our purposes of imagining how teachers create themselves as teachers, and as thinkers about teaching and learning, in and with the discourse of English education, Foucault offers a way for us to describe and analyze the production of knowledge in this discourse. We can describe and analyze, as he does for the discourse of natural history, the rules of formation operating in our particular kind of educational discourse—the discourse of English teaching. And in doing so, we can take the position that knowledge, as an object of discourse, is produced by individuals who are themselves objects of discourse. Teachers, in other words, create knowledge with language and within a particular educational discourse in response to the various kinds of open-ended problems they solve, and they are also created as teachers and thinkers by the language they use within that particular educational discourse. The key moves, then, in describing and analyzing an individual's creation, or production, of knowledge have to do with (1) defining the discourse, the discursive structures and practices, in which the individual locates himself or herself, and (2) developing the terms, the language, to describe and analyze the individual's knowledge production as discourse.

Foucault's is an unusual way to think about knowledge in a culture accustomed to imagining people as containers into which knowledge or information is poured and then measured in various ways. It is a way of thinking about knowledge that locates knowing in discourse, in language, with all of its controls and desires, rather than in the identification or recognition of given truths; rather than, that is, in the metaphor represented by thinking of knowledge as peas in a can—the more knowledge one has, the fuller he or she is.

Traditionally, an essentialist position presents knowledge as "knowledge about" and "knowledge how to do" something—knowledge about a subject, in other words, and knowledge of how to do things within that subject. I can know about the books that are appropriate for middle school students, for example, and I can know how to analyze those books to judge whether they are appropriate for those students. The measure of my knowledge of the appropriate books would be, according to this essentialist thinking, the comparative match of my list of books to a true or right list, and the measure of my analysis of the books' appropriateness a comparative match to true or right methods and, of course, to subsequently correct conclusions. Assessments created in the spirit of essentialist notions attempt to find out what people know by asking them to reproduce or recognize truths or appropriate information. This kind of thinking values assessment tasks that lead to true or right answers rather than "ill-structured" (Simon 1973) tasks that lead to performances for which there are no single right answers or algorithms for arriving at answers.

**The Primacy of Ill-Structured Tasks**

Ill-structured tasks pose problems for which there are most likely many approaches and a range of possible solutions. Unlike problems for which there are single or even multiple correct answers, or algorithms for arriving at correct answers, ill-structured tasks can accommodate contextual variations and differences in individuals' solutions. Ill-structured tasks can serve, in other words, as occasions for individuals to create knowledge and to reflect on what they have created in a recursive process that privileges creation and interpretation with language in a particular discourse as central to the understanding of individual performances. In teaching, individuals represent their constructions of such things as knowledge, pedagogy, and sensitivity to students through their performances. In writing and speaking about their teaching, individuals create and communicate their interpretation of the situation from which, and about which, they write or speak. The understanding of an individual's teaching performance is in turn also an act of interpretation.

If one begins, then, with the assumption that only ill-structured tasks, tasks that serve as occasions for individuals to create and interpret knowledge, can capture teaching, and teachers' thinking about teaching and learning, then assessments must be quite different from traditional essentialist exercises that ask individuals for correct or right answers to problems governed, as Foucault might say, by the will to truth (219). By thinking of assessments of teaching and teachers' reflections on their teaching from the perspective that imagines knowledge as creation, or production, and from the perspective that locates opportunities for the creation of knowledge in ill-structured problems, we can imagine assessment tasks as opportunities for individuals to create knowledge in a recursive process that involves them in teaching, in reflections on teaching, and in critical reflections on professional issues, rather than as opportunities for them to reproduce information about teaching, the subjects they teach, or aspects of their profession in a discourse governed by the will to truth.

One doesn't need to belabor the issue to see that the will to truth has had its own history in our discipline. It permeates our notions of what it means to be knowledgeable and, therefore, our notions of what it means to assess knowledge. But, in a larger sense that acknowledges the desires of educational discourse, it also permeates our language. When, for example, we use the language of "appropriateness," whether in conjunction with canonical or moral or interest-based decisions, to choose books for students, the will to truth—the will to choose the right or appropriate books—results in restrictive, exclusionary thinking. This will to truth is, as Foucault writes, "reliant upon institutional support and distribution" and "tends to exercise a sort of pressure, a power of constraint on other forms of discourse" (219). Institutionalized as "appropriateness," for example, the will to truth makes it difficult, if not impossible, for us to imagine decisions about books for students, to continue with that example, in ways other than those created by the language of appropriateness. Why, for instance, if the desire is to get students to read, don't we encourage them to read detective or romance novels in school? By all accounts, these interest students. Why, too, do almost all students in America, according to a recent survey by Arthur Applebee (1990), read the same canonical books? The responses to these questions are all located, I would argue, in that discourse space defined by the will to truth in the language of appropriateness. And even though this example is nowhere near extreme, we can see, I think, the restrictiveness of the language of appropriateness at work in the discourse of English teaching, as Foucault might say, in this historical era.

The language of truth works in our discipline, as in others, to exclude possibilities, so that it is difficult for us to imagine knowledge as that which is produced in and with discourse rather than that which is identified or recognized as true or acceptable. And, therefore, it is equally difficult for us to imagine assessments of knowledge as opportunities for individuals to create knowledge in a recursive process that locates the problems to be solved in the space of ill-structured tasks in a particular discourse.

What happens, though, if we represent knowledge as that which is created by discourse, by discursive structures, in what we call disciplines? What, then, is the discourse of teaching English to young adolescents? What are the fields of this discourse? What are the terms of their formations, their discontinuities, their paradoxes and contradictions? And how might one "play," in the Derridian (1970) senses of play as that which we do on words and that which we do with or against rules in a game in order to move, to change positions, within fields of discourse as we create or produce knowledge? And what happens if we build an assessment system based on the notion that knowledge is created in and with language, a system that is not concerned with correct or incorrect responses but rather is based on offering individuals opportunities to create knowledge, to represent their creations, and to reflect on those creations?

## Knowledge of Teaching

To consider these questions, particularly the question of assessment, I would like to turn to the terms offered by Lee Shulman's work on the knowledge of teaching (Shulman 1987); but to do this, I would like to rethink the nature and purpose of Shulman's work, and his categories for analyzing knowledge of teaching, so that his categories of knowledge might be thought of as discursive structures, as language formations, that is, rather than as valid and discrete categories of behaviors. And in doing so, in thinking of them as discursive structures, we can allow them to be discontinuous formations, like all discursive structures, to be paradoxical and contradictory as well as coherent and continuous, to be fragmented throughout discourse rather than totalized as complete representations of one discourse. By thinking of Shulman's categories of knowledge as discursive structures and practices, rather than as categories of behaviors, we can use them outside the will to truth to describe a discourse—knowledge of teaching English—rather than to codify behaviors.

But, as Foucault cautions, discursive structures and practices must not be confused with "the expressive operation by which an individual formulates an idea, a desire, an image" (117); they are, instead, the bodies of "anonymous, historical rules, always determined in the time and place that have defined a given period, and for a given . . . area" (117). Discursive structures and practices are embodied in education, then, as functions of discourse in time, in history, and they are not only embodied in education but deployed in other fields in slight or major transformations that make them particular to those fields. Discursive structures and practices can be used to describe and analyze events within and across particular discourse fields without the totalizing effects of categorizing behavior—effects which work like doctrine, or the will to truth, to restrict and exclude formations not consistent with the categorizations. And since these historical rules, these structures and practices, are discursive, are objects of discourse, they are like discourse: coherent and formulaic yet paradoxical, discontinuous, and contradictory.

Shulman defines the knowledge for teaching as "a codified and codifiable aggregation of knowledge, skill, understanding, and technology, of ethics and disposition, [and] of collective responsibility." He proposes a theoretical model that identifies categories of knowledge as follows:

- *content knowledge;*
- *general pedagogical knowledge,* with special reference to those broad principles and strategies of classroom management and organization that appear to transcend subject matter;
- *curriculum knowledge,* with particular grasp of the materials and programs that serve as "tools of the trade" for teachers;
- *pedagogical content knowledge,* that special amalgam of content and pedagogy that is uniquely the province of teachers, their own special form of professional understanding;
- *knowledge of learners and their characteristics;*

- *knowledge of educational contexts,* ranging from the workings of the group or classroom and the governance and financing of school districts to the character of communities and cultures; and

- *knowledge of educational ends, purposes, and values,* and their philosophical and historical grounds.

By naming these categories, by making them visible—or at least making a representation of them visible—Shulman gives us a way to enable exchanges and communication on the discourse of teaching. By thinking of these categories as discursive structures and practices, then, we locate them in history, in the history of discourse on teaching. By thinking of these categories as discursive structures and practices, we can forestall, too, the already heated essentialist debates on the rightness or the discreteness of the categories (and the whole enterprise of categorization for the sake of exclusion) and make Shulman's thinking available to a larger field of play wherein his terms for teaching knowledge can be deployed as terms in a conversation about knowledge in educational discourse, instead of as slots in a box or categories with "real" truth values. If we can live with this rethinking, then, we no longer have to deal with his terms as "valid" categories. We can use them, instead, to represent structures that are free to disobey their own exclusionary rules and controls, that imply and transgress each other, in order to enable our exchanges and communication about teaching knowledge—and they can be used to account for coherence and continuity as well as contradiction and paradox in teaching knowledge.

When we approach knowledge as discourse, as the workings of discursive structures and practices in discourse, then we can allow the possibility for people, in their productions of knowledge "within the same discursive practice, to speak of different objects, to have contrary opinions, and to make contradictory choices" (Foucault 200) and still understand their various productions as knowledge of English teaching. When we take this approach, we are concerned, then, not with what individuals know, but with how they play or think in the discourse of their discipline.

Shulman's terms, to reiterate my argument, and to say finally why I want to enter them into this conversation, give us a way to represent discursive practices and structures for teaching and a way to think about, to describe and analyze, performances within the discourse of teaching knowledge without our having to pretend that they are or can be discrete or true categories. If we don't have to pretend this, then we can allow for the unallowable—discontinuity, contradiction, and paradox—in the production of knowledge. This method (if I might call it that) is, I think, much more useful for our description and analysis of teaching English knowledge than the categorization and codification of behaviors as objectively "this" rather than "that." It is more useful, too, I think, for its implications for how we might express and communicate our descriptive analyses of teaching English knowledge. Foucault's methods lead us to "readings" or interpretations of discursive events—events that can represent an individual's knowledge—rather than to the categorization and aggregation of codified behaviors as if they were objective or true, as we are accustomed to doing in essentialist analyses. Even though Shulman's work grows out of this essentialist tradition, I would like to argue that if we revise the conditions of his representation of knowledge, it then becomes available to us in a conversation about teaching and its assessment that allows us to imagine these as acts of interpretation, as creations or constructions, within a particular discourse rather than as sets of codifiable behaviors that can be categorized and aggregated to portray teaching and thinking about teaching.

**Assessing Teacher Knowledge**

For our work with the Assessment Development Lab (ADL) to create a national board certification process for Early Adolescence (students 11–14 years old) English Language Arts (EA/ELA) teachers, we designed an assessment whose philosophical foundation is more akin to Foucault's poststructuralist thinking about knowledge than to essentialist notions. We designed assessment tasks, as I said earlier, as opportunities for individuals to create knowledge in a recursive process involving them in teaching, in reflections on teaching, and in critical reflections on professional issues. Our assessment consists of three interlocking components—a School Site Portfolio, a Content Knowledge Examination, and Assessment Center Activities—purposely designed to represent multiple ways of creating knowledge and representing it to others. The School Site Portfolio, for example, asks candidates to produce videotapes of their teaching and their thinking about that teaching in reflective essays. It also asks for examples of students' written work and, again, the candidate's thinking about that work. The Content Knowledge Examination asks candidates to respond to tasks in writing, and the Assessment Center Activities give candidates opportunities to work in a group with other teachers, to view and critique videotapes of teaching, and to participate in on-site interviews. Our overall purpose in creating the various assessment components was to represent critical or key ways of knowing for English teachers and to give them multiple opportunities to present their creation of knowledge: in videotapes, in essays, in group discussions, in interviews, and in simulations.

Before going on to describe the thinking that created these assessment procedures, thinking that took a reimagining of Shulman's work in Foucault's and Simon's terms as a point of departure, it would be helpful for me to present a more detailed overview of the assessment components so that one can see how our exercises present candidates with ill-structured problems for which they create knowledge within the discursive structures and practices of English teaching. To begin with, the School Site Portfolio includes some background information, a partnership description relating to candidates' professional activities, and their performance on three exercises. For this component, candidates will have approximately eight months to prepare videotapes of their teaching as well as written commentary and notes related to their teaching. The portfolio includes the following exercises:

> *The Post-Reading Interpretive Discussion* asks candidates to videotape a session during which they have engaged students in discussions of literature to help them build interpretations and develop their discussion skills. Candidates are also asked to write a reflective commentary addressing specific aspects of the discussion.

> *The Student Learning Exercise* asks candidates to illustrate the kinds of writing and thinking that they encounter in their classrooms. During a three-month period, candidates are asked to collect and submit selected pieces of writing from two different students. They are also asked to submit artifacts of their instruction related to the students' writing that will help clarify the nature of their instruction. Candidates then write a commentary about each student, in which they analyze the student's development and comment on how their instruction might have influenced that development.

> *The Planning and Teaching Exercise* asks candidates to document how their teaching is evolving over time and the kinds of decisions they make as they plan and adapt teaching. To document their teaching, candidates submit three artifacts: a daily statement of proposed goals for three weeks of instruction, a daily chronicle of activities occurring in their classroom during those three weeks, and a videotape of their teaching. To document the decisions they make, candidates are asked to submit three written commentaries: one composed at the outset of the three weeks, explaining why and how their goals were decided upon; one written about the class session that they videotaped; and a third composed at the end of the three weeks, in which they evaluate their teaching.

For the Content Knowledge Examination we designed five prototypes of essay questions for a paper-and-pencil examination of "content knowledge." The examination asks candidates to play within the broad English teaching domains—composition, language study, literature, reading, and responding—on topics formulated in terms of the discursive structures described in Shulman's work: knowledge of content, pedagogical content, curriculum, and learners. The five types of prompts set the terms of candidates' play, and they have been designed to work within and across the broad English teaching domains, so that the particular tasks can be changed and varied by moving them in and out of the domains.

Here are prototypes of the Content Knowledge Examination prompts:

1. Candidates are given one article to read, and asked to write an essay in which they first summarize the article's key points and then evaluate them, offering support from other scholarship and classroom experience.

2. Candidates are given a topic and a series of questions or statements to prompt their thinking, and asked to write an essay in which they explain their understanding of the topic, supporting their views with scholarship and classroom experience.

3. Candidates are given artifacts that they would encounter in their classrooms (e.g., literature selections, examples of students' writings, and so on), and asked to write an essay in which they analyze the artifacts by using given sets of broadly defined criteria.

4. Candidates are asked to read two or three different views on a topic. The views are presented in the form of case vignettes and brief essays. Once they have read the views, they are asked to write an essay in which they explain the views, and take a position in relation to the views, supporting what they say with scholarship and classroom experience.

5. Candidates are asked to write an essay in which they define and explain the professional debate surrounding a given current, controversial, critical issue in the field.

As you can see, a number of these exercises present candidates with journal articles, topics, and series of questions to initiate their thinking and writing. The materials for these exercises are drawn from the broad domains of English teaching—composition, language study, literature, reading, and responding. We decided to choose these materials for our field tests to represent paradigmatic shifts in the discourse of the broad domains, because it seemed to us that the field's formulations of what teaching English means have been greatly affected by paradigmatic shifts in discourse in the past twenty-five years. One such shift, for example, has been in the discourse on writing from a number of different quarters; another relates to changes in the discourse of reading and responding to literature. Paradigmatic shifts in the thinking and discourse in broad fields interested us because they appear to be major historical markers or moments in the profession that accomplished teachers would be familiar with and involved in. It seemed to us that those candidates who were familiar with the thinking and discourse shifts in the field would be able to move or play in the language of these shifts from the perspectives offered by classroom experience and scholarship. Whether this is the case remains to be seen.

For the Assessment Center Exercises, the work asked of candidates is mostly oral performances recorded during interviews conducted by "trained" educators, although we are experimenting with versions of two exercises that ask candidates to write responses rather than to be interviewed. For some of the exercises, written commentaries are included as part of the performance. Unlike the School Site Portfolio, for which candidates draw heavily from their daily teaching, the Assessment Center Exercises ask all candidates to respond to the same situations. We have developed four Assessment Center Exercises:

> *The Cooperative Group Discussion* asks candidates to participate in a group discussion with three other candidates in order to reach a consensus on a particular topic for which they have had time to prepare in advance. Candidates are then interviewed individually to answer a set of questions about the exercise and their performance on it.

> *The Instructional Analysis* asks candidates to analyze a written account of an instructional episode, to observe a videotape of that episode, and to formulate their recommendations. We are experimenting with both an oral (interview) version and a written (essay) version of this exercise.

> *The Instructional Planning Exercise* presents candidates with a particular topic of instruction and possible materials for that topic, and gives them a certain period of time to plan a segment of instruction dealing with different aspects of the topic. Candidates are then interviewed individually to answer a set of questions on the exercise.

> *The Response to Student Writing* asks candidates to respond to various aspects of a set of student papers. Candidates are given time to prepare and then interviewed individually on their responses to the papers. We are also experimenting with both oral and written versions of this exercise.

In the design of these components and exercises, we took as a point of departure a rethinking of Shulman's work in Foucault's and Simon's terms. We did this by considering how knowledge is represented in English teaching, and what it might mean to assess a person's knowledge of English teaching, particularly if we think about knowledge as creation or production within and with discourse. We focused initially on the structures that Shulman's terms describe—knowledge of content, pedagogical content, curriculum, and learners—because of their interactions for and mutual implications with each other in discourse on teaching. We hoped that we could explain individuals' creations of knowledge in Shulman's terms, but we ended up revising them to be more particular to English teaching. His terms didn't work for us, finally, because they weren't grounded in English teaching or in the standards set by the EA/ELA Standards Committee. And although it seemed that it would have been possible to map the EA/ELA standards and our "dimensions" onto his terms, we decided to reimagine the discursive structures and practices from the discourse of English teaching available to us rather than adding another layer to our thinking. Even though we worked from examples of English teaching and from the work of English teachers thinking about teaching, especially from the work of the EA/ELA Standards Committee, to reformulate the discursive structures and practices originally available to us through Shulman's terms, traces of his work are still apparent in the structures that we identified.

From our work with the EA/ELA Standards and from our work with English teachers' performances, we identified, then, six discursive structures, which we called "dimensions," to create our exercises and to use as lenses for interpreting and evaluating candidates' performances on our exercises: learner-centeredness, cultural awareness, content knowledge, integrated curriculum, coherent pedagogy, and professional concerns. These "dimensions" have the puzzling property of being apparently generic as categories, the way Shulman's terms seem, but specific to English teaching when they are more closely defined by the traits they represent. The generic property of these terms seems to be one of the dangers or paradoxes of attempting to isolate subject-matter structures that are, in fact, closely interactive and hinged to each other in complex ways. I should be clear, also, that when I say "in Shulman's terms," or "in terms of the English teaching 'dimensions,'" that I am speaking of structures in language. This means that every use of a term, any term, like "content knowledge," for instance, or "coherent pedagogy," is subject to re-creations and transformations, because terms exist in language, and all uses of them are bound to particular desires and purposes. The terms exist, in other words, like the creations of knowledge themselves, always already subject to what we might call "readings" or interpretations. And whether these "dimensions" will hold up as discursive structures that allow judges to interpret/evaluate candidates' performances on our exercises, of course, remains to be seen. For a more detailed definition of these structures or "dimensions," see the table on pages 36–37.

We used these "dimensions," then, for our work with the ADL, but we didn't think of them as valid, discrete categories any more than we thought of Shulman's terms that way. We used them to help us describe the discourses of English teaching, and as heuristics to locate potential fields of discourse on which candidates might be asked to perform. We wanted, in other words, to design our exercises purposely to capture candidates' performances in terms of the "dimensions," and we wanted, also, to use them in turn to describe and interpret those performances. We wanted our judges to be able to write descriptive analyses—what we are currently calling interpretive summaries— of individuals' creations of knowledge in terms of these "dimensions." To this end, our judges, working in pairs, write multiple-paragraph interpretive summaries of candidates' performances in order to make their reasoning explicit and to document their interpretations and their productions of knowledge as they collect and use evidence to interpret/evaluate a candidate's performance along the "dimensions" (along, that is, the English teaching discursive structures for a particular task). In writing these interpretive summaries, the judges, 75 percent of whom were accomplished English/language arts teachers of early adolescents, worked from their extensive study of the exercises and candidates' responses to them, performance anchors in the form of exemplary interpretive summaries of a range of performances, and descriptive information on the exemplary performances, including such things as videotapes, reflective essays, and other artifacts collected for the exercises.

It should be clear by now that we built an expert judging system that relies heavily on the expertise, experience, and training of the judges. It should also be clear that the act of judging, as it is expressed and substantiated through interpretive summaries, is also a production of knowledge, not a process to codify candidates' behaviors. In order to develop stability across judges, we worked with NCTE's advisory committee to the ADL to establish criteria for selecting judges from exemplary writing, literature, and literacy projects around the country that volunteered to participate. We agreed that at least 75 percent of the judges should be exemplary teachers while up to 25 percent could be persons who hold English/language arts administrative or university positions; the judges' philosophical views on teaching and learning should fit those presented in the Early Adolescent English/Language Arts Standards that have been developed for the National Board for Professional Teaching Standards; the judges should be recommended by their project directors in conjunction with NCTE's ADL advisory committee; when possible, judges should complete the exercises that they are judging; judges participate in training where they study, discuss, write interpretive essays on, and judge a range of responses to the exercises that they will be judging; and any judges with philosophical or performance differences that cannot be resolved with the judging group are eliminated from the pool.

Our field test results should give us an indication of whether our "dimensions" hold up as ways to prompt, analyze, interpret, and evaluate candidates' performances; whether the interpretive summaries actually capture the discursive structures and practices defined by the "dimensions"; and whether our paired expert judging added to the judging process.

## Dimensions for Evaluating Teaching Performance

| Learner-Centeredness | Cultural Awareness | Content Knowledge |
|---|---|---|
| Understands:<br>• Patterns of cognitive, social, emotional, and physical growth and development typical of young adolescents<br>• What to expect when young adolescents engage in literacy tasks (e.g., interpreting, composing)<br>• Themes, texts, and activities of potential interest to students and/or relating to their experiences<br>• The learning and literacy patterns of individual students | Understands:<br>• Learning and literacy patterns related to various cultural groups<br>• Issues of culture as they apply to curricular materials, literature, and non-print media<br>• The impact of cultural differences on ways of understanding and authority in the classroom | Understands:<br>• Theories of reading and interpretation of texts, including their instructional implications<br>• Theories of composing and their instructional implications<br>• Theories of language structure, use, and evolution and their instructional implications<br>• Conventions of spoken and written text<br>• Strategies for composing and interpreting |
| • Treats students equitably and respects students' thinking and language use<br>• Designs instruction that attends to the literacy development of students<br>• Differentiates instruction to help individual students develop as composers and interpreters of language<br>• Investigates the reasons for student language performance | • Provides opportunities for students to identify and reflect on the cultural view(s) represented in literary and other texts<br>• Asks students to become critically aware of variations in the ways individuals and groups use language, as well as the contexts for those variations<br>• Teaches reading and writing strategies that allow students to understand the influence of their own cultural perspectives on how they understand and use language | • Uses a variety of strategies to interpret texts<br>• Writes prose acceptable for professional situations<br>• Evaluates professional readings in light of theories and their instructional implications<br>• Designs instruction that reflects knowledge of theories, conventions, and strategies<br>• Analyzes student performances in light of knowledge of theories, conventions, and strategies |
| • Analyzes design and adaptation of instruction in light of literacy development of students<br>• Explains student performance in light of early adolescence and individual student development | • Explains how own instruction promotes students' sensitivity to cultural diversity<br>• Uses knowledge of cultural differences in learning and literacy development to understand student performance in the classroom<br>• Reflects on own patterns of learning and literacy and the impact of these factors on the learning of students | • Explains relationships between theory and practice<br>• Debates professional issues related to instruction in ELA |

## in the English Language Arts (ELA)

| Integrated Curriculum | Coherent Pedagogy | Professional Roles and Concerns |
| --- | --- | --- |
| Understands:<br>• Possible connections within the content of ELA<br>• Possible connections between ELA and other content areas<br>• Instructional strategies that help students understand connections within ELA and across content areas | Understands:<br>• Ways of supporting students' intellectual growth (e.g., scaffolding, zone of proximal development)<br>• Concepts of instructional design that support student growth in composing and interpreting (e.g., sequencing, elements of instruction—motivation, engagement, evaluation)<br>• Repertoire of ELA instructional strategies<br>• Repertoire of classroom management techniques | Understands:<br>• The role of professional organizations and resources<br>• The role of community groups interested in improving the learning opportunities for children<br>• Available community resources<br>• Community events and needs |
| • Organizes instruction around issue, theme, concept, and/or genre<br>• Asks students to apply concepts or information learned in other subject areas to what they are learning in ELA | • Creates classroom environment to support students' literacy learning: management of routines for movement and talk, emotional climate<br>• Moves students to more sophisticated levels of composing and interpreting; scaffolds learning; connects elements of instruction<br>• Shifts instructional strategies, calling on a range of ELA practices | • Can assess the components of another teacher's teaching<br>• Can make realistic recommendations for instructional improvement to another teacher<br>• Participates in curriculum and staff development projects within the school<br>• Participates in professional groups and maintains an active professional development profile<br>• Makes use of community resources to augment school-based resources<br>• Is an active participant in community affairs |
| • Explains how instruction is integrated<br>• Makes explicit how, where, and why connections are being made<br>• Traces integration across a series of instances | • Explains own role in student growth in composing and interpreting<br>• Explains how instructional sequences support student growth in composing and interpreting<br>• Explains logical connections among elements of own instruction<br>• Critiques teaching in light of effective ELA instructional practice | • Explains how recommendations for instructional improvement are adjusted to respond to different levels of professional development<br>• Explains how recommendations contribute to an integrated curriculum and a more coherent pattern of instruction in the classroom<br>• Explains how professional participation has contributed to own growth and development<br>• Explains how use of community resources or own contributions in the community have influenced living and learning environments for students |

## References

Applebee, A. N. 1990. *A Study of Book-Length Works Taught in High School English Courses.* Technical Report. Albany: National Center for the Learning and Teaching of Literature, State University of New York.

Derrida, J. 1970. "Discussions." In *The Language of Criticism and the Science of Man: The Structuralist Controversy,* edited by R. Macksey and E. Donato. Baltimore: Johns Hopkins University Press.

Foucault, M. 1972. *The Archaeology of Knowledge* and *The Discourse on Language.* Translated by A. M. Sheridan Smith. New York: Pantheon Books. Originally published in Great Britain by Tavistock Publications, Ltd. Originally published in France under the title *L'Archeologie du Savoir* by Editions Gallimard, 1969.

Said, E. W. 1985. *Beginnings: Intention and Method.* New York: Columbia University Press.

Simon, H. S. 1973. "The Structure of Ill-Structured Problems." *Artificial Intelligence* 4:181–202.

Shulman, L. S. 1987. "Knowledge and Teaching: Foundations of the New Reform." *Harvard Educational Review* 57:1–220.

# 3 Teacher as Learner: Working in a Community of Teachers

Judy Buchanan
School District of Philadelphia, Philadelphia Writing Project

*For Judy Buchanan, an urban elementary school teacher, a teacher's own questions are the heart of the growth and development process. In this intelligent account of the maturation of her ideas about race, culture, and teaching, Buchanan shows how she worked with the Philadelphia Teachers' Learning Cooperative. That community of teachers provided her with the opportunity to share her inquiry with others, and to benefit from their reflections, insights, and questions. Significantly, the questions that she pursued emphasize the needs of her students.*

## Beginnings

Recently my five-and-a-half-year-old daughter said to me, "When you get older and you remember what you used to do, you feel kind of dumb." Being older, but feeling much the same way, I wondered about my beginnings as a teacher. While I knew that my beginning years of teaching, as a young white woman new to the area, were shaped and supported by experienced teachers asking questions, offering advice, and talking about their students, my recollections of specific details from my early years of teaching were largely blurred by the passage of time. I had been an elementary classroom teacher in Philadelphia for seventeen years and I still had deep questions about teaching and learning.

Through my membership in the Philadelphia Teachers' Learning Cooperative (PTLC), a teacher collective in Philadelphia, I had access to the accumulated notes of the group, kept weekly since 1978, and thus a way to search out some of the questions I had asked as a beginner, and later as a more experienced teacher. Through studying my questions I hoped to find some of the ways I had come to know about my own practice as a teacher and understand the needs of my students. I initially thought of this research with some nice charts in mind, with the years at the top and the questions neatly lined up underneath, available for analysis and interpretation. Using these notes, I could find out about my beginnings as a teacher and the things I "used to do."

39

What I found, however, as I read the notes, were interesting clusters of questions, and I wondered about how my questions developed, as well as what they actually were. I found myself drawn to these clusters, both to their content and to the overlapping edges. How did my questions emerge in the context of the teachers' group? Which questions were universal for teachers? Which were a result of being an elementary school teacher in Philadelphia since 1974? Which questions were a reflection of my race, gender, and class? Thus, this task proved both more exciting and more daunting than I had imagined; the notes not only disclosed a rich history of some of those things I "used to do," but also presented a complete historical record of urban teaching since 1978.

This chapter is the first in what I hope will be a series of articles in which members of the Philadelphia Teachers' Learning Cooperative use the notes of our collective study of children, schools, and educational issues to explore, analyze, and interrogate our own histories as teachers in the last thirty years of this century. Members of this group have already written about their work (PTLC 1984; Guerin 1985; Buchanan 1993; Kanevsky 1993; Strieb 1985) and they continue to share the way the group is conducted with interested educators in many parts of the country.

The purpose of this chapter is to offer a description of one group of teachers and our work together and a description of my own questions in that group. While I have benefited greatly from reading the detailed narratives of other teachers, I plan to offer a much less detailed account of my own classroom. Some aspects of my classroom practices will be explored, but it is the questions I am highlighting here, not the practices themselves. While the analysis of my questions will be my own, I hope to provide the reader with a glimpse into the collective work of a teachers' group. The rhetoric of educational reform talks about groups of teachers working together over time, but much published work about teachers' knowledge and practice is about individuals. While this work is important, it is also necessary to describe what happens when groups of teachers work together to unpack the complex issues of daily teaching within the larger social and political issues of their lives.

In trying to create a full picture of one teacher's questions and knowledge within the social context of both a teacher community and the larger academic community, I see many tensions which need to be revealed and examined. Within the elementary classroom, for example, there is tension between the needs of an individual student and the needs of the group. Within the PTLC community there is tension between individual questions and the need for collective action. Within the larger community of teacher-researchers, there is tension between what teachers know in their daily practice as teachers and in how to raise questions, analyze, and interpret this knowledge through teacher inquiry. Finally, there is tension in talking about teachers as "they" in these times (Allen et al. 1992), while we try to sort out how to reform the institutions of American education. Teachers can be displayed, in both the literature and the popular press, as both saviors and the ones from whom the students must be saved; partners in the educational reform movement, while at the same time needing to be reformed, retrained, or researched themselves. It is hard work to imagine creating a dialogue across all of these boundaries and to find the voice with which to raise and discuss these issues.

## Setting the Context: The Philadelphia Teachers' Learning Cooperative

Let me begin by framing the context of the Philadelphia Teachers' Learning Cooperative and my own life as an elementary classroom teacher. This group began in 1978 as a way for interested teachers to continue meeting together after the closing of the last local teacher center. Its roots date back to teachers working together in Follow-Through programs throughout Philadelphia and to a now longstanding relationship with Patricia Carini, founder of the Prospect Center and Archive of Children's Work in North Bennington, Vermont. PTLC was constituted as a freestanding group of teachers, not affiliated with any university and open to all teachers in the Philadelphia area. The group was formed as a teacher collective to support inquiry about practice. While the group does "systematic, intentional inquiry into practice" (Lytle and Cochran-Smith 1990), it does not define itself as a "teacher research" group and its roots are not directly related to the world of the university.

Some members have remained since the beginning of the group; new members also join each year and others leave. At various times, teachers in independent schools in the Philadelphia area have been active members of the group. Currently there are elementary teachers from Philadelphia and suburban public schools and the Pennsylvania School for the Deaf, as well as a director of a publicly funded day-care center. Attendance varies at weekly meetings, but usually there are about fifteen teachers present.

The group meets every Thursday afternoon during the school year from 4:15 to 6:30 p.m. to discuss educational issues, using structured oral inquiry processes to guide the talk. Occasionally the group invites outside speakers, but it views its members as the primary sources of support and knowledge for one another. In an article describing the group, PTLC members wrote:

> From the beginning we agreed that the group would be a cooperative and that all responsibilities would be shared. We use formats which have been developed through our continuing work with Patricia Carini and the Prospect Center and Archive of Children's Work. Two and a half hours of talk each week: not informal teachers' lounge chat, but formal discussions. Though each year one person volunteers to chair planning meetings and to take charge of keeping our notes in order, each week's meeting has a different chairperson, presenter, and note taker. (PTLC 1984, 732)

## Formats and Structures

The weekly sessions use inquiry processes called "Documentary Processes" (Prospect Center 1986) as the way to organize the talk and reflection every Thursday afternoon. The formats themselves, including the Descriptive Review of a Child and the Descriptive Review of Children's Work, have evolved and changed as communities of teachers have used them over time, but their basic structure has remained the same.

The Documentary Processes are structured ways of conducting oral inquiry with a group. Each person has an opportunity to contribute to the dialogue, to raise questions, and, where appropriate, to make recommendations to the presenter. The collected threads of the conversation are summarized by the chairperson, with opportunity for members of the group to add to the summary. Detailed notes of each session are kept and the entire process is open to critique at the end of each meeting. This provides an opportunity to discuss pieces of the process which may not have worked (e.g., it is harder to describe a piece of student writing that has already been edited than a first draft). This aspect of the process also gives new members the opportunity to state when things are unclear or confusing for them.

The work of PTLC is based on a phenomenological approach to understanding children as thinkers and learners. Carini states:

> From my point of view . . . all children are active learners for the reason that they have common capacities: the power of expressiveness, the capability to make things happen, the inclination to wonder and to question, the desire to narrate, the ability to give order and meaning, the impulse to value. This is where learning and development do start. It is where teaching—and inquiry—should start. (Himley 1991, 25)

It was with these assumptions about children as learners that PTLC was founded and it is within this theoretical framework that my inquiry as a teacher began.

For the purposes of this chapter, I will explain the format of one of the structured oral inquiry processes, the Descriptive Review, in order to describe in some detail the theoretical framework with which PTLC approaches questions and to reveal the ways of knowing that the review itself makes possible. (A more detailed description of the assumptions about the Descriptive Review process can be found in Kanevsky, 1993.) It is this process itself, which requires note taking, that has allowed me the opportunity to look at my own questions over time.

In preparing for a review, the teacher writes a focusing question about the child and then prepares a presentation using the following headings: Physical Presence and Gesture, Disposition, Relationships with Children and Adults,

Activities and Interests, and Formal Learning. The focusing question arises from a concern, question, or uncertainty that the teacher has in working with the student. The gathering of the descriptive information often provides a new insight for the teacher that may have eluded him or her before this careful observation and documentation. However, the "primary purpose of the Descriptive Review of a Child is to bring together varied perspectives, in a collaborative process. . . . The perspectives through which the child is described are multiple, to insure a balanced portrayal of the person, that neither over-emphasizes some current 'problem' nor minimizes an ongoing difficulty" (Prospect Center 1986).

The fullness of the description varies depending on the focusing question asked by the teacher and the clarity with which the teacher is able to see the particular child. When the description is very full, the questions are used to clarify and sharpen what has already been described; when it is more difficult for the teacher to give a rich description (the child is relatively new to the classroom or is "hard to see"), the questions from the group help to bring out more descriptive information from the teacher's perspective before the group moves to recommendations. The purpose of doing a Descriptive Review is to offer a guide to the teacher in provisioning the classroom and in adapting practices to further educate the child. Recommendations are given to the teacher which "draw upon the child's strengths, interests, and power to make and do things" (Prospect Center 1986).

It was through using these descriptive processes with PTLC that I learned to teach and to inquire about my teaching, and learned to facilitate discussions, to find common patterns and threads in what we were saying, and to see new perspectives on concerns facing many classroom teachers. It was also through having this extended time to talk and reflect that I began to generate knowledge about my practice as a third- and fourth-grade classroom teacher. That knowledge, in turn, helped me to see ways to work collectively with other teachers to try to bring about change in schools. When PTLC sets up its schedule every eight weeks, it does so within many nested layers of context. Both individual concerns and larger educational issues are included in the planning. The eight-week planning cycles are a way of planning a thematic unit around an idea, a way to look at an issue from various levels: the individual student, the classroom, the system, and the wider community. Planning meetings often begin with the same questions that an individual teacher might ask: What are the burning issues for this year? What do we need to make time for?

Several years' schedules illustrate the connection between planning for individual teachers and the surrounding context of the larger community. In 1984, for example, the Philadelphia school district had recently adopted a standardized curriculum and a strict student-promotion policy in an attempt to achieve equity throughout the district's schools. That year PTLC focused its investigation on assessment, evaluation, resistance, and retention as large issues. Reflections on "assessment" and "evaluation" were followed in later sessions with a discussion on current trends in evaluation, with Edward Chittenden of the Educational Testing Service as a guest, and with a descriptive review of a seven-year-old boy who had been retained the previous year. The final thematic session of the year was devoted to a reflection on "standards" as we focused on what we as teachers affirmed and resisted in education. We were working to understand the fit between the structures and standards imposed on us and our own views of the purposes of education and the function of standards in schooling.

The schedule for 1991–92 provides another example and reflects changes in the Philadelphia school district as well as our evolving understanding of the processes of institutional change. It includes structured oral inquiry discussions on change and on dialogue with parents, as well as a review of a particular site's questions about school-based management. There was also a descriptive review of a first grader, and discussions of math problems from everyday experiences and of how children gather information outside of school. Not every session brings about dramatic insights or huge changes in a teacher's way of thinking about classrooms and students, or produces recommendations for policy changes at the local level. However, each one does offer the possibility of changes in perspective on both the classroom context as created by the teacher and the view of the students which the teacher holds. In addition to the ongoing learning that occurs weekly and over the year, this way of looking has opened the door for a variety of teacher-initiated projects, including grant proposals and work with other groups interested in educational reform.

The final meeting of each school year is devoted to a summary of the year, looking back to view how our questions, issues, and ideas have been woven together. At various times tensions and questions have surfaced as the group worked to remain focused on classroom issues, but also sought dialogue with the larger education community. A discussion of these issues over the last fourteen years is beyond the scope of this chapter; in the future I hope that many members of PTLC will examine both their own questions and the content and context of these fourteen years of meetings.

Questions about language, literacy, and assessment account for many of the questions teachers ask. However, there are also other strands which are a significant part of the work: for example, describing artwork, reflecting on science discussions, and focusing on living things in the classroom including silkworms, hatching eggs, and the life cycles of butterflies. These interests of teachers currently seem to be on the outer edges of any discussion of educational reform and teacher knowledge, and it is here where university- and classroom-based teachers may live parallel lives. Knowing about the life cycle of a Monarch butterfly from a book and using live caterpillars in the classroom are quite different ways of knowing. This kind of knowing by teachers is sometimes either dismissed or displayed like the folkways of other cultures. Within PTLC, however, listening to recommendations from other teachers and hearing detailed descriptions of individual classrooms has allowed all of us to learn from one another over time about such varied things as Monarch butterflies and children's literature. The sharing has also allowed the collected knowledge of one generation of teachers to be passed to the next generation.

**Investigating My Own Questions**

During the decade from 1979–89, I presented thirteen sessions at PTLC meetings and listened to and participated in about three hundred. Three clusters of my own questions emerged as I studied the notes of the group. As I studied the data, I came to see the clusters of questions as lenses that clarified my expanding vision of my role as a classroom teacher.

The first lens I used was one of looking at individual students within the classroom community; the second lens involved broadening my vision to include what students bring to school from their cultures and experiences; and the third lens was made up of the first two and added the dimension of a longer view over time. These lenses are not neatly lined up on the chart I had originally envisioned, but rather are overlapping circles with many areas of intersection.

*Looking at Individual Students: Boys and School*

During my first year in PTLC I listened carefully to many weekly sessions and took notes. I presented my first descriptive review in the spring of 1979 and two more in the winter of 1980. All were about fourth-grade boys. Two students were African American and one was white. However, while race and gender were stated as a part of the description of the student, I was not focused in 1980 as much on my role as a white teacher with a diverse student population as I was on gender. A large question I had was how to see the world and the world of school from a ten-year-old male's point of view. While the focusing questions were different in each case, they were linked by a concern for helping my students "make it" in school. Many boys were succeeding in my classroom; these particular students were ones I needed to see more clearly.

Paul seemed lonely; when he tried to enter into groups of students engaged in classroom games and activities he usually ended up disrupting things, rather than becoming a part of the activity. I wondered, "How can I support

Paul in developing relationships with other students in the classroom? Can I help him find productive ways to work with other students?" His parents thought he was immature and wondered if he should repeat fourth grade. I wanted to look closely at what was happening in the classroom before I made any recommendation.

Using the descriptive review process within the group helped me to unpack the social and academic dimensions of learning. As I described Paul to the group, I realized that his academic learning was proceeding apace; the recommendations helped me to find ways to support his social relationships in the classroom community and to describe to his parents his strengths as a student, while recognizing their concerns for his overall development. The recommendations contained specific ways to work with Paul within the boundaries of the classroom, including, for example, setting up opportunities for Paul to connect with other students through projects based on shared interests, such as playing math strategy games and writing comic strips.

I offered my second descriptive review in 1980, presenting Warren, a fourth grader who had repeated second grade. The focusing question I asked was: "How can I support and encourage Warren in his academic work? Even though he has made gains, he still has to struggle." The process helped me to see Warren's strengths as a reader and writer, his somewhat dry wit, and his vulnerability when he saw others progressing at a faster rate. His diligence, combined with his sense of humor and his love of sports, suggested ways to support his learning in the classroom. Recommendations ranged from writing topics, such as creating a book of limericks and writing his own television commercials, to suggestions for interaction within the school community through tutoring a younger child in something Warren knew well, as well as ways to tie his interest in sports to the struggle he had with some math concepts.

The recommendations were about ways I could provision my classroom to support Warren; they were suggested ways of linking Warren's strengths as a learner to the world of academics. Although sometimes it is hard to get in touch with a student's strengths, since they are not always visible on the surface, when a teacher attempts to view the whole child first and then looks for ways to build on that child's strengths he or she can help the child reach full potential. Those words are empty, however, without both a theoretical framework and a way to enact classroom practices which meet students' needs. Teachers are not always aware of the theoretical frameworks and assumptions they use to enact their practices. Using the documentary processes helps put meaning into the words teachers often use, and helps to make explicit the underlying beliefs and knowledge they hold.

During the same two years, I described a third boy, Anthony, who was often disruptive in the classroom, easily frustrated, and visibly unhappy. My question was related to sense of self: "How can I help Anthony express positive feelings about himself?" He was a student who had suffered great personal tragedy; his mother had died when he was quite young and his father was ill. I was looking for other perspectives to help me teach Anthony. He had a need to feel successful, but attainment of that feeling seemed to be very difficult. The group's recommendations during our discussion included ways to support Anthony in the classroom, ways to nurture the good feelings he did have, and ways to provide him with a safety net for some of the difficult times. Specific ideas included giving him lots of opportunities to be first: first to choose an activity at choice time; first to be captain of the football team at recess; first to help with the cooking projects which he seemed particularly to enjoy.

By fourth grade, we often expect students to have a well-developed sense of fairness, to be able to handle things like taking turns and not always getting one's first choice. Anthony needed support to meet the expectations of the school and classroom, while at the same time having his special needs for nurturing and recognition met. These ideas may sound like platitudes, but it is the particular way that simple practices are enacted in daily classroom life which can often change how students view school and sometimes themselves. The students' lives are a part of the descriptive process, but the recommendations focus on what a teacher can do in the classroom. Anthony's father was struggling to keep his family together in very difficult circumstances. He supported Anthony as much as he could, but some of the extra support needed to come from other sources. While I could not change the conditions of Anthony's life, I could find ways to support his growth in the classroom. I found the knowledge of the group invaluable in situations like these.

In education we are far from having unpacked all of the issues of gender and schooling. There has been a great deal of discussion of early schooling and the role of gender differences: What is the relationship between gender and school success in elementary school? Do boys need more male role models in the early grades? Are schools meeting the needs of African American males? Is there a "math gap" between boys and girls in elementary school? In looking closely at these three boys I was able to take a focused look at a small area of this complex territory. The reviews offered a way to look closely at different aspects of Paul's, Warren's, and Anthony's intellectual and social development, and they provided me with some new ways to think about these specific students, my classroom practice, and broad issues of gender and schooling.

I am not implying here that everything was always smooth sailing with the girls in my classroom. However, gender differences provided me with my first lens for looking at myself as a teacher and the classroom environment I was trying to create. The opportunity to ask specific questions about my students provided me with a variety of perspectives to think anew about difficult issues in their daily lives. Over time, participating in such reviews generates knowledge about practice that has implications beyond one teacher's classroom. Through using these processes the group's knowledge is deepened by trying collectively to understand the relationships among the classroom context, the teacher's questions, and the individual student.

### The World Outside the Classroom: What Students Bring to School

From 1975 to 1983 my classroom was located in a four-story elementary school with twelve hundred students. Beginning in 1976, many Southeast Asian refugee families had settled in the West Philadelphia neighborhood surrounding the school. With little notice, the school population ballooned over the course of two years to include four hundred children from Vietnam, Laos, Cambodia, and Thailand. The school was given little support from the district, and the teachers were given little support from the school administration in incorporating students who spoke other languages into their classrooms. In these early years, the ESOL programs were not large enough to meet the mushrooming needs of the schools, and many teachers and students were left to fend for themselves. Racial tension increased at the school as it took in this diverse population of students and had few new resources for them. My questions about boys and schooling shifted to questions about teaching students who come from other cultures. They represented a shift in what was most pressing for me to examine in my teaching. Gender issues did not disappear, but moved aside as I explored issues of cultural diversity.

Within PTLC we described some of our new students' work, since several teachers worked in schools with changing populations. We used one of the documentary processes, a reflective conversation on the word "memory," to begin our careful looking at several pieces of artwork. Thinking deeply about a word, such as "memory," can open up a discussion in a powerful way. What would it be like to produce artwork in one culture with memories of another? What perspectives might the word itself evoke from the group?

Through drawing and craftwork many of the students had been able to move into their classroom communities; children appreciate fine artwork done by fellow students, and their classmates often found the drawings of the Southeast Asian students to be quite striking. Teachers found them striking too, for several reasons. Some were scenes of war, pastoral images of rice fields with bombs dropping from airplanes onto the people below. Others were drawings of animals and flowers marked by a different aesthetic than was commonly seen in the drawings of American children.

Over these years there were many struggles and painful times as I tried to balance the needs of my students, deal with issues of diversity in the school as a whole, and learn how to teach when I did not speak the language of all of the children in my classroom.

In 1981 I described two Hmong students from the mountains of Laos. One ten-year-old girl, Mia, had had a very difficult time adjusting to the classroom. Other Hmong students had done so with greater ease, and so her obvious unhappiness was very painful to watch. She often ran out of the classroom, refused to walk through the halls with the rest of the students, and had difficulty socially, even with other students with whom she could communicate. I felt particularly frustrated because I couldn't find out what was wrong by simply asking. As I prepared a descriptive review at the end of the first six months she was in my room, I had an insight. Perhaps Mia was not running away from the classroom, but running *to* something. In carefully describing her actions and activities, I noticed that often her forays into the hallways ended with her staring into another classroom; perhaps she was trying to make sense of this huge place called school. Our class only used the first floor and the basement. This building may have been the largest structure she had ever been in; its tall ceilings and wide hallways were a bit forbidding even to me, and I wondered how it must feel to be new in this country and in this building. I had spent a lot of time trying to make the children feel comfortable, but through Mia I learned to look more closely at what it might mean to be "other" to mainstream American culture. In trying to see the world through Mia's eyes, I could "make the familiar strange" and see the school building itself as a forbidding structure and Mia's behavior as one way to try to create a world for herself that made sense.

My question was more straightforward for another new student: "What further steps could be taken to support Yaitong in his learning to read?" Despite the many hurdles to be overcome, other Hmong students had learned to read. The differences within the groups of students from other cultures in my classroom seemed as wide as differences across cultures. Learning to read was critical for future success in school, and I felt inadequate as a teacher when some Southeast Asian students seemed to be making very little progress.

In addition to the descriptive review, I made a tape of Yaitong reading aloud from a familiar and an unfamiliar text after a discussion of reading at a planning meeting. Some members of PTLC were participating in the ETS Collaborative Research Project on Reading (Bussis et al., 1985) and suggested that we listen to a child read as we followed along with the text. After describing Yaitong and his strengths as a learner, we listened to his reading aloud. He could read simple texts, but without comfort or fluency. The group's recommendations encouraged me to move away from the books I was using, which used a sight word approach ("I can see the tiger in the zoo"), to texts which included a more natural flow of language. Many ideas from first-grade teachers were particularly helpful.

The careful looking and listening to a student's reading helped me to provision for him in the classroom, and materials were shared with me that I did not always have access to as a fourth-grade teacher. The group's recommendations invited me to raise questions about the materials I had gathered, and supported my search for new resources which would aid the literacy development of my students. With all that we know about language and literacy learning today, these suggestions may seem obvious. However, for a fourth-grade teacher a decade ago they were not so transparent. It has taken years for me to build up a classroom with rich resources and many kinds of materials and texts. Access to materials may again seem like a very basic idea, but it is essential if teachers are to develop as professionals with their own resources to draw upon and share with others.

## Looking over Time as a Way of Knowing

On a sabbatical at the University of Pennsylvania for the 1986–87 school year, as the first Philadelphia Writing Project scholar, I read about issues of schooling, language, and literacy. When I returned to my classroom the following year, I began a yearlong inquiry project about one of my students and his writing. On the second day of school, Anwar, a fourth grader, asked a question during math class. I had written an assignment on the board after a math lesson using the abbreviation for "page" and Anwar had said: "There's just one thing. What exactly does *p.* mean?" The question surprised me. Had I forgotten what most fourth graders knew after being away from the classroom for a year? Why didn't anyone else speak up? Anwar was able to complete the math assignment without difficulty. His question intrigued me, though, and it led me to focus more on Anwar and his work.

Through Anwar I returned to the questions I had been exploring throughout my history in PTLC: gender, race, and my practice as a teacher. This time I began my work with questions about my practice, specifically questions about language and literacy development. I explored Anwar's growth as a writer, coupled with my reflections on the content and structures that supported students' language and literacy development in my classroom. In some ways Anwar represented aspects of all of the questions I had been asking over time: he was an African American boy who had struggled with learning to read and had repeated an early grade in school. What were his questions? In what ways could I help him succeed in school? Were there further changes I needed to make in my practice in order for him to be successful?

In addition to my colleagues in PTLC, I was now a member of another community of teachers, the Philadelphia Writing Project. I shared Anwar's work with other teachers through institutes and staff development meetings, and found their questions about my practice and Anwar's writing to be illuminating. Through careful listening to Anwar's voice, teachers heard his strong determination to succeed and his careful asking for guidance when he didn't understand something. The questions in PTLC were about my relationships with my students and my classroom program in the context of my question about a particular child; here the questions were about my practice in setting up opportunities for reading and writing in the classroom—everything from how I graded Anwar, to how I got him to write in so many different genres, to observations about his perseverance and his voice. Teachers entered into looking at Anwar's work from many different perspectives and with varied approaches to literacy learning. Across these boundaries, what was most powerful was being able to see Anwar's growth over time, a perspective often lacking in our fragmented teaching lives (Buchanan, in press).

## Conclusion

My questions as a teacher-learner are very much the same as when I entered teaching, but I see schools and my students through new eyes. Each year the classroom community offers up a rich new mixture of children's voices, some that I can hear right away and others that I have to struggle to sort out. This year I do not have my own classroom and I am spending time with other teachers in their classrooms, listening to their questions and trying to hear their voices. They are Philadelphia Writing Project teachers who are members of the Urban Sites Writing Network of the National Writing Project, a culturally and racially diverse group of experienced urban teachers who are asking questions and conducting their own teacher-inquiry projects. The Philadelphia Teachers' Learning Cooperative continues to grow and change as an organization. The school district of Philadelphia is in a new phase of growth and struggle with school reform, shared decision making, and school-based management. How we view teachers' knowledge and teachers' learning in these times will contribute to the success or failure of these reforms.

I have only described and examined a small part of PTLC. The notes of the group reveal many concerns and questions that span the group's history, particularly issues of assessment and evaluation. The focus of this chapter has been on my questions; however, the notes also document a complex history of speaking out on important issues in education and working to understand them at many levels—classroom, local, state, and national. Creating a dialogue with school administrators, parents, and others in the wider education community has been a part of the group's work over the past fourteen years. PTLC has also engaged in ongoing discussions of creating an archive of teachers' and students' work to preserve the diverse voices of teachers and students in the Philadelphia region. While I cannot develop either of these ideas in this chapter, it is important for the reader to know that the collective work of teachers can generate both knowledge and possibilities for others in the education community.

By reflecting on what I "used to do," I see new ways of thinking about the same questions I asked in 1979. Learning to teach is not a linear process. Rarely is it possible to have an idea or create a structure that can remain fixed and unchanged over time. Teaching is a deeply contextualized profession, in which experiences both shape the learner and must be continuously reexamined and interrogated. I know much more now than when I began formally investigating my practice, but I am still asking some of the same questions about individual students. How to help a student become a part of a classroom community or to support a struggling beginning reader are still questions that I have to ask about students I teach or students I observe in other teachers' classrooms. It is having the opportunity to keep asking these questions that has contributed to my growth as a teacher, and it is the support of communities of teachers that makes asking these questions possible.

## References

Allen, J., J. Buchanan, C. Edelsky, and G. Norton. 1992. Teachers as "They" at NRC: An Invitation to Enter the Dialogue on the Ethics of Collaborative and Non-collaborative Classroom Research. Paper presented at the National Reading Conference, December, San Antonio.

Buchanan, J. 1993. "Listening to the Voices." In *Inside/Outside: Teachers, Research, and Knowledge,* edited by M. Cochran-Smith and S. L. Lytle. New York: Teachers College Press.

Bussis, A., E. Chittenden, M. Amarel, and E. Klausner. 1985. *Inquiry into Meaning: An Investigation of Learning to Read.* Hillsdale, N.J.: Lawrence Erlbaum.

Guerin, K. 1985. "'Bounced-Around' Teachers and Leftover Children." *Education and Urban Society* 17, no. 3:284–91.

Himley, M. 1991. *Shared Territory: Understanding Children's Writing as Works.* New York: Oxford University Press.

Kanevsky, R. 1993. "Descriptive Review of a Child: A Way of Knowing about Teaching and Learning." In *Inside/Outside: Teachers. Research, and Knowledge,* edited by M. Cochran-Smith and S. L. Lytle. New York: Teachers College Press.

Lytle, S. L., and M. Cochran-Smith. 1990. "Learning from Teacher Research: A Working Typology." *Teachers College Record* 92, no. 1:83–103.

Philadelphia Teachers' Learning Cooperative. 1984. "On Becoming Teacher Experts: Buying Time." *Language Arts* 61, no. 7:731–36.

*Prospect Center Documentary Processes.* 1986. North Bennington, Vt.: Prospect Center.

Strieb, L. 1985. *A (Philadelphia) Teacher's Journal.* Grand Forks: North Dakota Study Group on Evaluation.

# 4 Is There a Problem with Knowing Thyself? Toward a Poststructuralist View of Teacher Identity

Deborah P. Britzman
York University

*In this critical analysis of the development of one student teacher, Deborah Britzman sensitively explores the role of identity in teacher development. This essay considers what it means to become a teacher, and how the "self" of the teacher becomes defined in that process. The process of teacher development is explored within a political context as well.*

---

As to those for whom to work hard, to begin and begin again, to attempt and be mistaken, to go back and rework everything from top to bottom, and still find reason to hesitate from one step to the next—as to those, in short, for whom to work in the midst of uncertainty and apprehension is tantamount to failure, all I can say is that clearly we are not from the same planet.

—Michel Foucault, *The Use of Pleasure*

I was aware of the fact that identity is an invention from the very beginning, long before I understood any of this theoretically.

—Stuart Hall, "Minimal Selves"

I once saw a coffee mug on a teacher's desk that tried to represent teachers. It read, TEACHERS ARE PEOPLE TOO! I'm not sure whom this emphatic statement addressed and whether such a cultural appeal could remedy the stereotypical images that seem to steer the teacher's identity in such odd directions. Could this slogan signify vulnerability and fallibility, the uncertainty that plagues even teachers? Was it a warning to all involved that teachers are affected by their work, the feelings of others, and the power struggles engendered by being in front of a class? Was it an attempt to disengage one's "real self" from the myriad rules and procedures teachers are expected to enforce?

This essay is a revision of my article "The Terrible Problem of Knowing Thyself: Toward a Poststructural Account of Teacher Identity," *Journal of Curriculum Theorizing* 9, no. 3 (Spring 1990): 23–46.

Could such a sign separate the pedagogue from the pedagogy? Perhaps the attempt was to reproduce a generic notion of humanity, ushering in the blankness of sameness and emptying out the dissonance of difference. Why didn't the mug declare that TEACHERS ARE FEMINISTS, TOO! or, TEACHERS ARE ANTI-RACIST, TOO! As it stands, the mug seemed to neutralize the scary question of identity to the dreary, predictable essentialism that beneath the skin we are all the same. Still, in my reading, at least three kinds of concepts uncomfortably collide: the messy meanings of identity, of experience, and of knowledge. How are selves produced and reproduced through social interactions and daily negotiations, and within particular contexts that are already overburdened with the meanings of others?

There is a problem when the teacher's identity is taken for granted, when it is approached in some literal way, as an outcome of pedagogical skills, as an aftermath of being there in the classroom, or as a function of experience. Part of this problem concerns the separation of teacher thinking from teacher identity, as if the knowledge the teacher possesses does not also fashion the self. Another part of this problem concerns the a priori view of identity embedded in the normative discourse of teacher education. There, the glorification of firsthand experience nonproblematically scripts teacher identity as synonymous with teacher's role and function (Britzman 1991; Nespor and Barylske 1991; Smith and Zantiotis 1989). These simplistic orientations dismiss the most unsettling moment in learning to teach: the realization that the teacher's role and the teacher's identity are not synonymous. The newly arrived teacher learns early on that whereas role can be assigned, the taking up of an identity is a constant and tricky social negotiation. One must consent to signification. Indeed, the significant, albeit hidden, work of learning to teach concerns negotiating with conflicting cultural representations of and desires for what a teacher is and does. One must ferret out how multiple interpretations of the meanings of social experience and classroom life structure one's thoughts about identity. This involves scrutiny into how we come to know ourselves when we are trying to become teachers. What orientation to knowledge might structure this kind of look?

Utilizing the poststructuralist opposition between what Linda Brodkey calls "the possibility and impossibility of a unified self in language and discourse" (1987, 138), this paper argues that the problem of identity is a problem of language, and thus a problem of fabrication. I explore the occasion of how one newly arrived student teacher thought about her struggle to negotiate and invent her teaching identity. This is the work of carving out one's own territory within preestablished borders, of desiring to be different while negotiating institutional mandates for conformity, and of constructing one's teaching voice from the stuff of past, that is, student experience. The struggle to borrow, to negotiate, to claim ownership, and to take up that which seems already completed suggests the contradictions within which teacher identity is constructed and deconstructed. Suggested as well is the problem of how normative discourses about the teacher's identity can collapse identity into a literal problem of acquiring a role. That is, we may well know that these two constructs are different, but the pressure to act as if they are not constitutes one of the most vulnerable moments in learning to teach. The circumstance of student teaching, then, provides the contextual arena wherein the student teacher, as part student, part teacher, has the delicate work of educating others while being educated, and of attempting unification in an already contradictory role.

Drawn from a larger ethnographic study of learning to teach (Britzman 1991), this paper critically analyzes some dissonant moments in the narrated life of one white, working-class student teacher in secondary English education, fictitiously named Jamie Owl. Hers was the painful dilemma of hating school, loving literature, and wanting to become a teacher. Within this dilemma, Jamie attempted to construct and negotiate both her identity as a teacher and the knowledge that might effectuate being recognized. My focus is on what happens to a student teacher when practice does not lead to competence, when the student teacher becomes more uncertain the longer she teaches, when those who surround her lack patience with her hesitations, and when lived experience is fraught with ambiguity, ambivalence, contradiction, and creepy detours. How does the student teacher explain such dissonance to herself?

My purpose, however, is neither to propose the "worst-case scenario"—although I do look at the underside of learning to teach—nor to offer advice as to how one can avoid being mistaken. Instead, I want to explore the vulnerabilities of teacher thinking, the contradictory discourses one individual uncomfortably borrowed as an interpretive frame through which to view the conditions of teaching and her own histories in education. In this way, I want to raise some thorny questions about what it is that structures identity. My concern, then, is not just with how identities think but with how to think about identity. As Keya Ganguly asserts, "It is important to underscore the ways in which identities are fabrications—that is, both invented and constructed—because doing so is a necessary step in accounting for the centrality of representation in the constitution of the real" (1992, 30). This paper, then, is meant to suggest one way to think about how teachers construct "the real" of teaching and learning. The first part introduces poststructuralist perspectives on identity and what these perspectives offer in terms of understanding the slippery relationships among knowledge, experience, and the construction of the self.[1] Drawing upon this theory, I then analytically re-present four of Jamie Owl's reflections about her struggle to invent her identity as a teacher. I conclude with a discussion of the politics of identity in teacher education and with what politics have to do with how we might think about teacher thinking.

## Poststructural Orientations to the Language of Identity

The notion of a unitary self, of a singular, cohesive, and essential identity, is currently being "deconstructed" by poststructuralist theorists (Alcoff 1988; Ellis 1989; hooks 1989; Weedon 1987). Under challenge is the idea that individuals have an authentic core or pure essence that has somehow been repressed by society. Rather than appeal to a timeless or transcendent human nature and hence to a discourse of universality, poststructuralist thought traces "the constitution of the subject within a historical framework" (Foucault 1980, 117). It does so by addressing how, for instance, such identity markers as race, sex, gender, and class are unevenly and uncomfortably lived within specific histories, and how, for instance, the discourses individuals borrow to represent themselves are already overburdened with the representations of others. Poststructuralist orientations to identity attend to both the specificities of identity and the acknowledgment that everyone does not get the same message from the same phenomenon (Britzman, Santiago-Valles, Jimenez-Munoz, and Lamach 1991; McCarthy 1990).

There is a concern with how subjectivities become configured as an effect of history and how they are then "produced at the intersection of meaning with experience" (de Lauretis 1986, 8). In poststructuralist versions, meaning is unruly. Despite our best authorial intentions, language cannot deliver what it promises: unmediated access to "the real." Nor is reality, in any sense, understood as objectively "out there" or simply apprehended through language. This is not, however, to assert that "the real" does not exist. Rather, the real must be continually imagined and articulated. In this way, language—or more specifically, discourse—becomes the site of struggle, a place where the real is constructed, truth is produced, and power is effectuated.[2] Poststructuralist theories are concerned with the inherited and constructed meanings that position and regulate how social life is narrated and lived. The object of study, then, is with the politics and poetics of narration and with what relations of power have to do with inscriptions of the self.

Disputed in poststructuralist thought, for example, is the prevalent view that experience contains an inherent and essential meaning (Foucault 1980). The primary category of analysis is the discourse of experience rather than experience itself. Here, experience does not "tell" us who we are, what we see, or even how to act; we are the tellers of experience. And yet our potential to retell, set by the conditions of history and discourse—and hence by which narratives are made available and at what cost—is always transposed by our own history, the social markers we bear, and by an odd combination of our own deep commitments and normative notions of what constitutes truth, power, authority, and knowledge. Foucault's definition of experience suggests these constraints in that it accounts for "the correlation between fields of knowledge, types of normativity, and forms of subjectivity in a particular culture" (1985, 4). In this version, experience is a sort of regulating and necessary fiction. How one understands experience depends upon what it is that structures one's capacity to name something as experience in the first place. And in naming something as an experience, the "I" of that experience must also be constructed. A poststructuralist approach to identity, then, is concerned with tracing identity as subjected to the constraints of social structure and to the practices of discourse. As discursive boundaries shift, so, too, do identities and the lived experiences that name them. Listen to Stuart Hall describe how he understands the identity of his family:

> If you've lived, as I've lived, in Jamaica, in a lower-middle class family that was trying to be a middle class Jamaican family trying to be an upper-middle class Jamaican family trying to be an English Victorian family. . . . I mean the notion of displacement as a place of "identity" is a concept you learn to live with, long before you are able to spell it. Living with, living through difference. (1987, 45)

Or listen to Joan Nestle, a participant in the sit-in demonstrations of the Civil Rights movement, recall her identities there:

> I wore a double mask in these early sixties years, in those white restaurants [of the South]. My first deception was to the enemy: the pose of a nice white person who could be let in and would sit down and eat in quiet tones, ignoring the battle for human dignity that was happening outside the windows. The second was to my friends: the pose of straightness, the invisibility of my queerness. They did not know that when the police entered, with their sneers and itchy fingers, I was meeting old antagonists. Perhaps their uniforms were a different color, but in the Lesbian bars of my other world I had met these forces of the state. I never told my comrades that I was different because a secret seemed a little thing in such a time in history. (1987, 52–53)

Stuart Hall and Joan Nestle speak of their identities in relation to appearances, the fictions others create to make sense of their own, and the splits, or the crises of representation, engendered by difference. Each of these writers bears, although in a very different way, the contradictory meanings of race, of sex, of gender, of class, and of generation, and of what it might mean to be subordinated within an appearance that might suggest something different. For Stuart Hall, the meanings of race—of what it means to be black in Jamaica versus what it means to be black in Britain—can be neither equivalent nor stable. For Joan Nestle, being white in a Southern civil rights restaurant sit-in is not the same as being white in a Northern lesbian bar. Lurking within these differences, then, are not pure essences, or what each individual really is.

Rather, these shifting identities collide with and are displaced by the fictions of their history. In each retelling, these identities may collude with or confound the imaginary communities that are mobilized and dismissed. They are an effect of particular and unstable interpretive practices, meanings, and historical structures. These kinds of displacements represent what Homi Bhabha terms, "the repeated negations of identity" (1987, 5).

There is a continual slippage of identities as they are reinflected with the accents of others, which one may not choose but must, nevertheless, confront (Mariani 1991). Our identities, overdetermined by history, place, and sociality, are lived and imagined through the discourses or knowledge we employ to make sense of who we are, who we are not, and who we can become. While a part of this struggle entails the conscious and unconscious borrowing and discarding of socially received and produced definitions of things like normality, deviance, and the authentic, the fashioning of identity is not a matter of free-floating individuals merely deciding who they want to become or which real they want to construct. Rather, identity always signifies relationship to the other in specific historical contexts. Consequently, as Chris Weedon asserts, identity must be negotiated precisely because it is social:

> A poststructuralist position on subjectivity and consciousness relativizes
> the individual's sense of herself by making it an effect of discourse which
> is open to continuous redefinition which is constantly slipping. (1987,
> 106)

Constituting identity as a fiction—as an effect of representations—however, does not doom one's identity to the despair of aimlessness, though this, too, may become a condition. Nor does my focus on representation and fabrication suggest an equal-opportunity endeavor, that any representation is available for the taking or that all representations are equivalent. But the play of relativity is rooted in the push and pull of social meanings and the histories that form and transform them. As each of us struggles in the process of coming to know "the self" through "the other," we struggle not as autonomous beings who single-handedly perform singular fates or as free agents who merely choose the discourse of the day. Rather, the fabricated nature of identity suggests the vulnerability of social subjects who produce and are produced by culture, history, language, and the social positions inhabited. This orientation to identity refuses the singularity of the term, concentrating instead on how we come to take up positions, make alliances, perform practices, and weave the justifications for the things we do. In such a drama, we might better attend to how identity performs a set of shifting answers and questions to normative expectations (Butler 1991). These answers are not, however, fixed, closed, or even satisfactory. They hint at the tensions of our times and the contradictions of our places. In this way, identity is dialogic.

Gramsci suggests such dialogic tensions in his often quoted "warning" about knowing thyself.

> The starting point of critical elaboration is the consciousness of what one really is and is "knowing thyself" as a product of the historical process to date which has deposited in you an infinity of traces without leaving an inventory. (1976, 324)

Knowing thyself is not about transcending the negotiated order of things, or the social markers each of us bears. Instead, Gramsci intimates the ambiguously dialogical relations among structure, language, history, and consciousness. These relations produce the contradictory space for negotiating identities that have the potential for both contesting the order of things and legitimating existing designs. Gramsci simultaneously suggests that delicate discursivity between the exigencies of the critical and the constraints of the historical. The critical elaboration of the self, in Gramsci's terms, requires an awareness of one's historical context—in terms of the present and the past—and an acknowledgment of sedimentary meanings one may not intend but must nevertheless take into account. As Keya Ganguly puts it: "Everyday subjectivity is constructed out of a sediment of understandings about the ways in which the past permanently marks the present" (1992, 30). On the one hand, critical elaboration depends upon a persistent questioning of one's own deep investments in, resistances to, and desires for challenging the status quo. On the other hand, critical elaboration requires an awareness of how the present shapes one's understanding of the past. To engage in this kind of elaboration is to engage with others and to call into question the categories we use to construct what each of us takes to be "the norm."

## The Lived Experience of Social Meanings

Any discussion of identity must consider the meanings of social experience as a significant moment in its construction. This dialogue—between individual identity and social experience—becomes clearer when we consider the identity of "teacher." It is an identity that is at once familiar and strange, for we have all played roles opposite teachers for a significant part of our lives and this student experience seems to tell us what a teacher is and does. The identity of teacher, however, does not seem so transparent once one steps into the teacher's role; once there, role and identity are not synonymous. That is, role speaks to public function, whereas identity voices subjective investments and commitments. Role, or what one is supposed to do, and investments, or what one believes and thinks, are often at odds. The two are in dialogic relation and it is this tension that makes for the "lived experiences" and the social practices of teachers.

The category of experience is key to the dynamics of teacher education and the authorial process whereby one becomes a teacher. There, normative notions collapse the distinction between acquiring pedagogical skills and becoming a teacher typically by objectifying experience as a map. Everything is already organized and complete; all that is left to do is to viscerally follow preordained paths. Conventional wisdom such as "we learn by experience" or "experience is the best teacher" renders as legitimate not so much experience itself as a particularly normalizing discourse of experience. When experience is perceived as a map, experience seems to organize perception. Absent from this version is the social activity that confounds our meanings and that shapes and disturbs our views of the world. Poststructuralist thought takes up this absence, and, consequently, turns the above prescription on its head.

The work of Volosinov (1986) on language challenges the orthodoxy that experience contains an objective lesson. Volosinov argues that consciousness and experience have no independent reality outside of the cultural codes that deploy knowledge. "We do not," Volosinov argues, "see or feel an experience, we understand it. This means that in the process of introspection we engage our experience into a context made up of other signs we understand" (1986, 36). These signs are those of language. Volosinov explains:

> There is no such thing as experience outside of embodiment in signs. Consequently, the very notion of a fundamental, qualitative difference between the inner and outer element is invalid to begin with. . . . It is not experience that organizes expression, but the other way around—*expression organizes experience*. Expression is what first gives experience its form and specificity of direction. (1986, 85)

Volosinov's work contests the normative wisdom taken up by teacher education, that experience is instructive in and of itself. We are required to consider how we perceive the world through particular epistemological commitments, symbolic orders, and discursive communities, and how these meanings are organized as they organize and produce the linguistic positions we inhabit. Consequently, we are challenged to reflect upon the contradictory processes that structure experience as meaningful, irrelevant, or problematic.

For those learning to teach and for those already working in classrooms, the valorization of experience is particularly apparent during the teaching apprenticeship. Yet this valorization becomes an effect that precludes acknowledgment of the constraints of expression and of the process whereby history "deposits its traces." Silenced as well is the tenuousness of "lived experience." As James Donald explains:

> In a common-sense way we often take experience to mean simply what happens to us—the *lived experience*. . . . But that *lived* already implies the ambiguity of the term—it hints at a process whereby we attribute meaning to what happens to us. Our cultural identities are formed as the

experiences of our biographies accumulate: we *become experienced.* And that entails the conceptual ordering of what happens to us within consciousness. (1987, 59)

When the processes by which we come to know, or the conceptual orderings we employ, become taken for granted or are never known consciously, and instead are attributed to the nature of things, our capacity to theorize critically about the vulnerabilities and possibilities of our conditions and practices is diminished. We, in turn, are diminished as we take on blame for not conforming to what experience dictates. This blame places undue pressure and undue culpability upon the individual. The cycle of self-blame is evident particularly during the teaching apprenticeship; there, the normative expectation is to assimilate into a predetermined role. Absent in this valorization of experience is an interrogation into how the dynamics of social expression produce our understanding of experience in the first place. "A [poststructuralist] model in which people speak and act as subjects from within a discursive field that they did not set up," Kate Ellis argues, "allows people to look at the problem rather than themselves" (1989, 40). Such a view may also lend insight into how identities become lived as the site of struggle.

The work of Bakhtin (1988) offers insight into the discursivity of social expression, that is, how expression becomes the condition for one's struggle for voice, an intimate dynamic in the fabrication and elaboration of identity. In Bakhtin's terms, identity is not about fixity; it voices a range of contradictory and competing positions negotiated with others through language. Language, for Bakhtin, is neither a neutral medium shaped by individual desire or intent, nor bordered by objective meanings; it is the symbolic terrain upon which hegemony and consent are worked out. Using language is always a negotiation because words are slippery and elusive; they bear the capacity to assert another intention, another meaning, another word. When we work with language, we are speaking for others at the same time we attempt to speak for and individuate ourselves. As Bakhtin explains:

> All words have the "taste" of a profession, a genre, a tendency, a party, a particular work, a particular person, a generation, an age group, the day and hour. Each word tastes of the context in which it has lived its socially charged life; all words and forms are populated by intentions. (1988, 293)

In Bakhtin's terms, language is borrowed, and it is just this borrowing that makes language social. The struggle to borrow, to negotiate, to claim ownership over that which cannot be possessed, to take up that which seems already finished, constitutes what Bakhtin calls "the ideological becoming" of a person. His use of "becoming" suggests the incompleteness of identity. In this ideological process of becoming, two types of discourse clash, two forces push and pull in the process of coming to know. There is the centripetal force, or the tendency toward the norm which is embodied in authoritative discourse, and the centrifugal force, or the push against authority, the refusals, the breaks—the imaginative space that constitutes internally persuasive discourse.

Each form of discourse presupposes particular images of knowledge, history, power, and agency. Whereas authoritative discourse demands our allegiance and is embodied in "the word of the father, parent, teacher . . . " internally persuasive discourse is tentative, suggesting something about one's own subjectivity and something about the subjectivities and conditions one confronts. It may be helpful to imagine authoritative and internally persuasive discourse as rejoinders in an argument. Each becomes intelligible through the matrix of the other. It is the dialogical relation—between authoritative and internally persuasive discourse—that allows each discourse its fluidity, constraints, and possibilities. The struggle for voice begins within this dialogic relation.

To theorize about identity, then—and the thinking which seems to instantiate it—we must be concerned with how language inscribes experience as it positions the self. If we view identity as a struggle for voice and thought amidst voices and thoughts that are not our own, we can come to understand something about the difficulties of reaccentuating a role, such as teacher, that is already suggestive of a monolithic meaning. That is, we can begin to deconstruct the essentialist dualism that positions the identity of a teacher as either the generic human suggested by the teacher's coffee mug or the functionary of a normative discourse which collapses, rather than transforms, role and identity. Theories of poststructuralism that challenge the valorization of experience and the stasis of unitary meaning permit us to question how such meanings are socially produced and to become concerned with the extant power such productions engender. In the world of teacher education, where those learning to teach confront what appears to be an already completed role, decentering the unitary notions of the teacher while helping them move beyond the meanings that posit role as synonymous with identity can permit newly arrived student teachers the spaces to reflect upon the persons they are becoming and thus critically elaborate the traces of their own narratives.

The following section makes concrete these concepts of identity, experience, and language through the interpretation of four moments in the discourse of one student teacher, Jamie Owl. These instances of narration, taken from a larger ethnographic study (Britzman 1991), illustrate the clash of voices Jamie attempted to negotiate as she engaged in the terrible process of *inventing* rather than assuming an identity. Jamie Owl's telling is particularly painful, for her work is to construct an identity based upon not fitting into the traditional roles teachers are expected to take up. As it did for Joan Nestle and

Stuart Hall, displacement for Jamie becomes the place of identity and is uncomfortably lived. As we shall see, Jamie is involved in the messy process of rejecting normative versions of what it means to be a teacher while negotiating visions yet to come. Within this process, Jamie struggles to find a language that might voice the complications she lives. Two conflicting kinds of voices are relevant here: the centripetal, or authoritative, voice that defines what a teacher is and does in relation to the kind of authority and power teachers are expected to deploy; and the centrifugal, or internally persuasive, voice, that speaks to one's deep convictions, investments, and desires. These two voices are in constant tension, positioning multiple identities, but not enabling the practices that might move Jamie beyond the mistaken and debilitating construct of the stable, humanistic self.

## Four Moments of Identity

The magnified moments that follow were spoken in in-depth interviews of approximately two hours each held weekly during Jamie Owl's student teaching internship, from September to December 1983. Because of Jamie's unique circumstances—the perception, on the part of school administrators and her cooperating teacher, that Jamie's student teaching would best be played out without a researcher's classroom presence; the illness of her cooperating teacher, which literally left Jamie on her own; and, the teachers' union vote of work-to-rule which lasted for eight weeks—I was not able to observe Jamie's classroom teaching. Thus I learned of Jamie's struggles through her language. Our interviews focused on Jamie's stories, what she felt had happened during the week, particular incidents she found significant, and clarifications of previous interviews.

Throughout these interviews, my intent was to understand how Jamie understood her own process of learning to teach. This kind of intervention was not designed to aid Jamie in her pedagogical strategies, although throughout our time I did become a sounding board for her ideas, fears, frustrations, and deep investments. The very process of questioning provided a significant safe space for Jamie's reflections. However, two tensions must be admitted into this discussion. First, this type of ethnographic work concerns speaking for Jamie even as I read her words through the prism of poststructuralism. A related tension involves my theorizing about another's identity, presenting it as if it were frozen in time. This is the problem of the ethnographic present, a sense of time that often loses its qualities of contingency and context. The drama of Jamie Owl's student teaching as presented here, then, must be read as partial and as incomplete. What these represented moments suggest is my reinterpretation of aspects of the lived experiences of Jamie Owl.

Jamie entered secondary-school teacher education with deep ambivalence. On a practical level, given her undergraduate English major, taking education coursework seemed to provide a way to put her knowledge of literature to use. Moreover, as a young white working-class woman, Jamie had already experienced a series of factory jobs, and desired more meaningful work. Teaching seemed to offer that. Yet while Jamie believed that teachers' work could be meaningful, her past work as a student was not. Perhaps because of this lack in her own education Jamie felt she could make a difference in the lives of students, by being different from the authoritarian teachers inscribed in her own educational biography. She spoke of that biography as oppressive, and described herself as suffering from "class shock," a condition that caused her to believe that her white middle-class cohorts were better prepared, smarter, more entitled, and more attuned to the demands of schooling than she was. For much of her education, Jamie felt "dumb." Those few times in her school biography when Jamie felt competent were contrasted with memories of humiliation, subordination, and, by the time she reached adolescence, resistance to school authorities. And while her grades were good, Jamie believed she rarely "put her heart" into her work. Upon graduation from high school, she left for college because it was a way out of a small town. She attended a large state university and there became a "nontraditional student," dropping out twice before completing her English major and eventually entering the department of secondary education.

Early on in her student teaching, Jamie described her relationship to school:

> I haven't fully reconciled being a teacher [with] hating school. Partly I think I dislike my own school so much, because I dislike my education and what I see going on, that perhaps there's some way [to understand it]. One [way] is to understand how much of it was me and how much of it was the educational process I underwent that made me think as I thought about myself and the lack of skills I took with me to college. And partially because I feel things can be different. And they should be different and perhaps I can do it differently.

Jamie's view of her educational biography is ambivalent. First, she wonders if she is to blame for her experience or whether the experience was to blame. In one sense, this is a question of how expression organizes experience. If Jamie believes that experience has an inherent meaning, she has lost. If Jamie views the normative discourse of education as positioning her sense of self-blame, then she can transform this blame into a desire to change the system.

The above story unleashes a struggle between authoritative and internally persuasive discourse. The discourse of education, with its grades, regimentation, and pull toward conformity, partly conditioned Jamie's meanings about education and the role of teachers. Those who "cannot fit in" are blamed for their own fate, and thus identities—as opposed to the discourses on identities—become the problem. Jamie's internally persuasive discourse, her own push against authority, on the other hand, suggests that things could be different and that she could be different. Yet another ambivalence, rooted in Jamie's supposed dualism of hating school and wanting to teach, seems to dismiss difference as a "problem" solved by assimilation.

This second ambivalence is rooted in Jamie's tenuous relationship to school. She disliked it, yet returned to take on an identity that required her to identify with what she disliked. Such a circumstance triggers a crisis of identification, lived as a sort of psychic despair effected when one brushes identity against the grain and attempts to define oneself in terms of what one rejects. To make sense of being there, Jamie's work was to construct an identity contingent upon not belonging, an identity that could celebrate difference, not as a disruption but as a source of hope. This is reminiscent of Stuart Hall's notion of "displacement as a place of identity." In order to continue as a student teacher, Jamie had to learn to value her difference and to find sources of social validation. Her struggle required not only negotiation with the present and with her students, but also with the revision of how she understood her student past. The painful question—Can one become a teacher while hating school?—is about the struggle between tradition and change, negotiating one's own territory and enacting one's own intentions amid preestablished spaces already "overpopulated" by the intentions and practices of others. Within this precarious struggle, Jamie began to negotiate her identity as a teacher.

A month after Jamie began student teaching, she considered leaving. Jamie's own image was of "removing [herself] from the educational system." She sought escape because her attempts to negotiate her own space while learning to teach were constantly thwarted by institutional demands to cover the material, control her students, and assert the authority of the text, all functions in which Jamie had little investment. She was also alarmed at her students, who seemed to demand such traditional activity and would only recognize Jamie as a teacher when she enacted these forms of social control.

Jamie's cooperating teachers, aware of her deep doubts about whether education is possible in schools, suggested she hold such doubts about identity in abeyance and defer to what was required to get through. Once she had the teaching certificate, some argued, she could then do what she wanted and perhaps become "a real teacher." They asked her to accept the traditional powerlessness student teachers often experience when they attempt to be different yet are not quite sure how to do things differently. Jamie, however, would not forget her deep investments in making a difference and her desire not to be mistaken for an authoritarian teacher simply because she stood in front of a class. Most disconcerting was that while Jamie had no investments in maintaining the status quo, she found herself taking actions she philosophically disputed. This was contradictorily expressed as "learning what not to become." For example, in one incident, Jamie recalled her refusal to allow a student to use the bathroom. Simultaneously, she wondered why. In another class, Jamie started giving pop quizzes to police student homework while realizing that such disciplining efforts only positioned her as an authority figure. In both instances, Jamie found herself acting in ways that supported school authority despite her intentions to do otherwise. She was, then, becoming someone she did not want to learn to be.

After an arduous decision-making process, Jamie decided to continue as a student teacher. But in order to stay, she began to construct an alter-identity, one that attempted to allow for both her own private doubts about education and the imagined public vulnerabilities of learning to teach. Jamie negotiated a way to embrace the conditions of inexperience, vulnerability, and self-doubt, conditions unaccounted for in the normative view of teacher identity. As Jamie told it:

> I have finally decided when I enter the school building in the morning, I am not a teacher. I am a human being who's assuming a role that has been designated "teacher." And I carry out some of the functions of that teacher. But when things go against my grain, [and] I don't want to do it, I don't believe in it, or just don't know, then I can admit that. And that way I can save my own peace of mind and I can deal with the situations that arise. And O.K., I don't know everything, but I'm not a teacher any more. I'm a human being, which, in a lot of ways, was my own expectations of what a teacher should be when I walked in there.

Jamie knew the difference between a teacher's function and a teacher's identity. The problem was that those who surrounded her kept collapsing this difference and acting as if such dissonance was not an issue to be explored. Jamie needed their recognition in order to perform as a teacher, yet their recognition did not include an acknowledgment of how the self must negotiate teaching. Ironically, however, in asserting her humanity as an individual, Jamie's "internally persuasive" discourse dehumanizes both "teacher" and all that makes her an individual. While Jamie refused to allow instrumentalism to be the criterion for identity, and desired to assume an identity that had tolerance for not knowing, she emptied out the very signifiers that might help her understand the vulnerabilities of being uncertain and of being mistaken.

What, then, is Jamie asserting? What does the construct "human being" actually explain? What discourses of knowledge does this identity effect, and what does it dismiss? What kinds of practices are possible once vulnerability, ambiguity, and doubt are admitted? What kinds of power and authority are taken up and not admitted? What if Jamie had said, "I want to be a feminist teacher"? In other words, what if Jamie had committed herself to more than her imagined self? Such questions suppose a community and the willingness of others to engage in dialogue about the personal struggles of teachers. If this condition and these questions had become available to Jamie she might have been able to take creative action, because while rejecting the status quo is a precondition for social change, one must also be prepared to assert different visions and actions and to negotiate these practices with others. Instead, Jamie retreated into her "private" self, creating a particular separation that precluded the critical elaboration of what identity feels like in the context of teaching. In some ways, she became the generic person suggested on the slogan of the teacher's coffee mug. Her certainty now resided in an essentialist view of who she was rather than in her ability to act. Her delineation of role and identity enabled Jamie to suppress aspects of her experience that she did not understand. Yet while initially comforting, this strategy of disengagement was not helpful, because it shut out what should have been admitted: that teaching, like identity, is a problem of interpretation and social negotiation.

Because she was a "mere" human being, Jamie felt entitled to her doubts. In this version of self, doubts are a natural part of the human condition, not an effect of social structure, history, discourse, and relations of power. The problem is that if the sources of doubt can only be attributed to the self then social relations make no sense. In positioning herself outside of social roles and relations by stating, "I am not someone who fulfills the role," Jamie is attempting an impossible transcendence. Cleo Cherryholmes links this desire to transcend to an attempt at stabilization: "One way to stabilize meaning in a text or discourse is to appeal to a transcendent idea that rises above a text or discourse" (1988, 32). For Jamie, a "human being," and not a "teacher," could rise above the messiness of classroom life. Her definition of humanity was an imaginative attempt to harness that which cannot be stabilized. So while Jamie could reject repressive notions of the teacher's identity, this process of rejection—itself dependent upon escape or transcendence—did not lend insight into just exactly what or who she could become. Instead, she was trapped in the persistent uncertainty between presence and absence, being there but not being who one really is.

Jamie attempted to dismiss the image of the teacher as expert. But what images of identity and of knowledge did she embrace? In actuality, Jamie had imaginatively split herself in two. There was the "real" Jamie and the "teacher" Jamie. This division is reminiscent of the split between internally persuasive and authoritative discourses. The "real" Jamie—the one that is internally persuasive—transcended social roles, while the "teacher" or authoritative Jamie defined herself by involuntarily performing compulsory functions. This dualistic identity, while perhaps protecting the vulnerable construct of Jamie's internally persuasive values, was not an identity that could engender critical work. Rather, it was a protective strategy for coping with the terrible problem of identifying oneself as a teacher when what it means to be a teacher is not to know or be known as who one "really" is. For Jamie, then, being a teacher is a case of mistaken identity. By the middle of her student teaching, Jamie began to understand that the promise of transcendence would not help her define her work or her identity. Simply adopting a category did not illuminate the problem of action or provide access to the knowledge necessary to move beyond the self. However, in exploring her own sense of humanness, Jamie was beginning to question what this "essence" called "self" has to do with the work of teachers.

> I'm a human being who's undertaking the activity known as teaching and is at a loss as to what to make of it and what to call herself. Student teaching doesn't make it in any real sense of the word for me. Student teacher? Someone who is learning to teach? If I listen to Carl Rogers, I would say, no way. No one can teach another person, everyone must teach themselves. I have all these feelings and doubts about it and yet I'm still trying to figure out what it's all about.

Jamie was caught in the dilemma Linda Brodkey terms "the possibility and impossibility of a unified self in language and discourse" (1987, 138). Her practice was not resolving the conflict, and the normative discourse of progress through practice seemed to betray her efforts. So, too, did her humanistic discourse of the self. For if one believes, as Jamie did, that no one can teach anyone to teach and that one must learn this on one's own, how exactly does one learn? The problem is that Jamie's theory of the self and of learning shut out the social. She might carry out the teacher's duties but this activity, in and of itself, contained no insight into meaningful practice. How can "the self" be depended upon to learn if "the self" is not there? Beyond one's self, what are the sources of pedagogy? What place do others have in this process? How does one convince one's students that a teacher should be reinvented with each new class? These questions may be implied in Jamie's internally persuasive discourse. The problem was that Jamie barely had a language to describe herself to herself, let alone a language to describe herself as a burgeoning teacher. The available discourses were not satisfactory.

The title of student teacher is another odd contradiction. For Jamie, this doubling of identity—of educating others while being educated—does not guarantee that each activity is valued in tandem or that each position possesses equal power. The mistakes of a student, while performing in a role that requires a shell of certainty, are rarely tolerated. At the same time, "student teacher" also bestows no credibility upon its bearer: suggesting neither a real student nor a real teacher, "student teacher" may well be an oxymoron. How it is looked upon reflects the prevalence of dualistic notions of teaching and learning. This dualism positions the student teacher as little more than a person who lacks classroom experience. And in this version, teaching and learning can somehow be understood as transcending the messy problems of language, negotiation, and identity because it posits learning to teach as a problem of acquiring the "right experience," without actually articulating either what constitutes "the rightness" of practice, or how one fashions validity from experience.

Another level is also operating here: this is the level that Stuart Hall and Joan Nestle suggest when they decenter the notion of identity as unitary and acknowledge the multiple selves that shift with one's histories, contexts, and interpretive practices. In Jamie's case, what she was as a student teacher did not have the same level of complication that she knew as a person. In that context, such a level of complexity was not acknowledged by those who worked with her and hence the potential power of the role—the coupling of teaching and learning—was dissipated.

Throughout our interviews, Jamie continued to struggle with her own identity in learning to teach. In one of her last reflections, however, Jamie began to situate her own process of becoming in relationship to others: she began to explore how her present conditions were contingent upon past discourses.

> You're learning more of the things you don't want to do than the things you want to do because you are feeling your way out and don't know quite where your beliefs, philosophy, your whole personality in the classroom [stands], [so] you end up falling back on what's been done previously. The things you remember. And a lot of that just doesn't seem to work.
>
> I don't have a view of the master teacher. I have an idea of what a teacher should be like and then I rebel against it 'cause that's not right either. I don't know for myself what a teacher is. That was one question I started out with and one. question I haven't answered yet. And yet, in between, I've always—whether from inside or outside—gotten those crosscurrents of, gee, that is a good teacher, and gee, this isn't a good teacher, and I'm not doing this right and I'm not doing that right. I don't know if it's internal pressure or outside pressure.

Both good and bad teachers are a part of Jamie's subjectivity, part of the deep convictions, desires, beliefs, and investments that seemed to haunt her teaching internship. Pulled by the crosscurrents of internally persuasive and authoritative discourses, Jamie was attempting to unweave her understanding of teaching in order to imagine an identity that could embrace displacement as a place. In acknowledging these forces, Jamie was also becoming more engaged with her own ideological process of becoming, a process that requires dialogue with the past and the present, with other people, and with the contexts and histories that coalesce in our process of coming to know. This exploration began despite the institutions that claimed to be pedagogical, namely compulsory schooling and teacher education.

## The Politics of Identity in Teacher Education

These fragments of Jamie Owl's story resonate with the tensions of what it means to learn to teach and with the problems of taking up an identity as a teacher in contexts that refuse to account for complexity. Her stories can serve to remind us that neither pedagogy nor identity is an effect of experience. One's subjectivity intervenes, as a condition of engagement with the social world. The terms of identity are social, and, as Teresa de Lauretis argues, conditional.

> Identity is not the goal but rather the point of departure of the process of self-consciousness, a process by which one begins to know that and how the personal is political, that and how the subject is specifically and materially en-gendered in its social conditions and possibilities of existence. (1986, 9)

Such a tentative view of identity refuses the singularity of the term and serves as a reminder that identity, as a shifting set of questions and answers to conventions of representation, is never completed. Identity becomes a site of struggle in learning to teach when it is positioned as if it were already present and stable. This essentialist view is only capable of asserting identity as a noncontradictory and fixed essence. The problem is that while these narratives about identity push each of us toward a unitary self, the narratives of others subvert such formulations. Because identity is negotiated with others, within situational and historical constraints, and by particular orientations to knowledge, its invention and its construction are dependent upon contradictions that cannot be reconciled. In the case of a teacher's identity, it is our conceptual ordering of experience, rather than experience itself, that makes available the answers and the questions necessary for critical elaboration.

The field of teacher thinking has not yet explored thinking as a problem of conceptual orderings and hence as a problem of language. There still remains a rather celebratory view of teacher thinking that works to reduce thought to a problem of the correct action, capable of residing outside of relations of power. Without a theory of power, the field has no other choice but to valorize thoughts at the expense of bodies. Here, I am suggesting that the thinking of teachers cannot be understood without acknowledging that teachers are raced, classed, sexed, and gendered, and that these social markers organize teachers' thoughts in ways we are just beginning to imagine. The memories of Stuart Hall and Joan Nestle point to more complicated realities: that thinking cannot transcend the histories and social markers each of us bears. The question that needs to be explored in more complicated ways concerns how our views of language and of identity set the terms for imagining and constructing the imperatives of teacher thinking and the practices of pedagogy. As Roger Simon offers: "What is required is some attention to what one might call 'the social imaginary,' the way of naming, ordering and representing social and physical reality whose effects simultaneously enable and constrain a set of options for practical action in the world" (1992, 37).

Linda Alcoff suggests that any discussion of identity should include "the politics of identity":

> One's identity is taken (and defined) as a political point of departure, as a motivation for action, and as a delineator of one's politics. . . . one's identity [is] always a construction yet also a necessary point of departure. (1988, 432)

The politics of identity refers to questions of what it is that structures identity and how identity is narrated. Jamie Owl, for example, narrated her identity as a private affair despite the fact that the classroom context compelled her to take up a particular version of who she might become. In viewing herself as capable of transcendence, she shut out the conditions that caused her such misery and doubt in the first place. That is, in not linking identity to forms of sociality, to school structure, and to specific and competing histories, Jamie Owl could not make sense of what it was that structured and bothered her thinking about identity. Her return to the self actually produced the conditions for self-blame. Had she explored the politics of this maneuver, she might have been able to elaborate critically the terms of her identity in less constricting ways.

Linking identity to practices and to sociality may well allow us to rethink the visions we can have about what teachers can become and who we can become as teachers. Elizabeth Wilson put it this way: "Certainty never resided in who I was, but in the ability to act" (1989, 172). We might move beyond the repressive cultural myths that attempt to construct the teacher as already completed, as an omnipotent knower, and as the key actor in the drama of education. To do this means that teacher education must uncouple the imperatives of social control from the teacher's identity (Britzman 1986). Most significantly, if we can help future teachers theorize about the politics of identity—and this means becoming concerned with how normative discourses position identity as a private dilemma in their dismissal of the contradictory meanings of race, gender, sex, and class, and in their refusal to recognize the contexts that provoke constrictive versions of identity in the first place—then the newly arrived may be better able to critically elaborate their own thinking in the delicate process of becoming.

Within this process of theorizing about how we come to know ourselves when we are trying to become teachers, Bakhtin's work may be particularly helpful, because Bakhtin is concerned with words and their meanings, with the problem of language. A word such as *teacher* is already overpopulated with other contexts; its multiple meanings can never be isolated from the speaker, the listener, or the situation. At the same time, the word *teacher* always has the potential to assert an external character that excludes the person fulfilling the role. Allon White, in analyzing Bakhtin's recent popularity, discusses the issue of appropriation, of making the ideas of another one's own. White argues that all ideas must be "reinflected, imbued with a different profile by the dialogic struggle of contending parties" (1987/1988, 220). Contained within the word *teacher* are contending parties, inside and outside forces that we must take into account if we are not to dismiss the contradictory realities we bring to the profession of teaching and ultimately dismiss the potential complexity engendered when we take up the work of teacher. Those of us in teacher education need to engage in dialogue with student teachers about each of our ideological processes of becoming, in order to open spaces for a discourse that, while concerned with slippage and displacements, can move beyond the normative discourse of who a teacher is and can become, and on to the critical awareness of the constructedness of knowledge and how these images set the terms for and boundaries of identity.

The idea that schools produce knowledge and people is just beginning to take hold in teacher education. In terms of teacher identity, there is a concern for how pedagogy produces the subject-teacher. And advocates of reflexivity are no longer rare. Research methodology has evolved to enable students to study their own biographies and practices critically (see, for example, Grumet 1988; Haug 1987; Lather 1991; Miller 1990; Nelson 1986; Smyth 1987; Walkerdine 1990.) At the same time, the process of studying practices cannot conclude once practices are narrated. When practices become text, they must be read not as guarantees of essential truths, or as literal recipes for action, but as representations, as fabrications of particular discourses that produce as they implicate the voices of teachers and researchers in larger interests and investments. Unless the narrations of practice are read through theories of discourse—that is, as representing particular ideological interests, orientations, communities, and meanings, and as deploying relations of power—there remains the danger of viewing the teacher's practical knowledge as unencumbered by authoritative discourse and as unmediated by the relations of power and authority that work through every teaching and research practice. Cameron McCarthy and Michael Apple are quite clear on this point: "The production of educational theory and research is itself a site of ideological struggle" (1988, 30).

If we can extend these ideas to the murky world of identity, and provide spaces for student teachers to rethink how their constructions of the teacher make for lived experience and for what one might imagine as pedagogical practices, then I think students like Jamie Owl will be better able to elaborate critically the terrible problem of knowing thyself. This problem, when the political dissipates into the personal, requires more than affirming coffee cups if we are to understand the complex constructions of identity and to transform particularly constricting versions of it. It means, on the one hand, thinking about the cost of identities places like school seem to offer. And, on the other hand, it means admitting the social into the question of identity.

## Notes

1. I am using the term "poststructuralist" to refer to a set of theories about the work of language and about the constructedness of meaning. This theory begins with the recognition that meaning is produced and constructed in language. That is, language does not reflect preexisting meanings and cannot transcend history and social relations of power. Rather than being concerned with narration, or stories, poststructuralist theories go "behind" the narration to consider what it is that structures and dissolves particular meanings and at what cost. What cannot be said because of what is said is of interest. Part of the focus, then, is on the instabilities of meaning in discourse and with how discourses govern and produce meaning.
2. I am defining the term "discourse" as the particular language social groups use to interpret events and to make sense of the self and the other. A discourse becomes powerful when it is institutionally sanctioned and thus governs how something is said, as it makes present communities of agreement and disagreement. Forms of discourse intone particular orientations, values, and interests, and thus versions of how power, authority, and knowledge are represented. In English education, for example, the discourse of humanism, or the discourse of practical criticism, conditions how the self and novels are spoken about. The concept of discourse raises the question of what it is that structures representations.

## References

Alcoff, L. 1988. "Cultural Feminism versus Post-structuralism: The Identity Crisis in Feminist Theory." *Signs* 13:405–36.

Bakhtin, M. M. 1988. *The Dialogic Imagination: Four Essays.* Edited by M. Holquist. Translated by C. Emerson and M. Holquist. Austin: University of Texas Press.

Bhabha, H. 1987. "Interrogating Identity." In *Identity,* edited by L. Appignaesi, 5–11. London: Institute of Contemporary Art.

Britzman, D. P. 1986. "Cultural Myths in the Making of a Teacher: Biography and Social Structure in Teacher Education." *Harvard Educational Review* 56, no. 4:442–56.

———. 1991. *Practice Makes Practice: A Critical Study of Learning to Teach.* Albany: State University of New York Press.

Britzman, D., K. Santiago-Valles, G. Jimenez-Munoz, and L. Lamach. 1991. "Dusting Off the Erasures: Race, Gender, and Pedagogy." *Education and Society* 9, no. 2:88–99.

Brodkey, L. 1987. "Postmodern Pedagogy for Progressive Educators." Review of *Literacy: Reading the Word and the World,* by Paulo Freire and Donald Macedo. *Journal of Education* 169, no. 3:138–43.

Butler, J. 1991. "Imitation and Gender Insubordination." In *Inside/Out: Lesbian Theories, Gay Theories,* edited by D. Fuss, 13–31. New York: Routledge.

Cherryholmes, C. H. 1988. *Power and Criticism: Poststructural Investigations in Education.* New York: Teachers College Press.

de Lauretis, T., ed. 1986. *Feminist Studies, Critical Studies.* Bloomington: Indiana University Press.

Donald, J. 1987. "Language, Literacy, and Schooling." In *The State and Popular Culture,* edited by S. Hall, J. Donald, and P. Willis, 41–74. Milton Keynes: The Open University Press.

Ellis, K. 1989. "Stories without Endings: Deconstructive Theory and Political Practice." *Socialist Review* 19, no. 2:37–52.

Foucault, M. 1980. *Power/Knowledge: Selected Interviews and Other Writings, 1972–1977,* edited by C. Gordon. New York: Pantheon Books.

———. 1985. *The Use of Pleasure.* Vol. 2 of *The History of Sexuality.* Translated by R. Hurley. New York: Pantheon Books.

Ganguly, K. 1992. "Migrant Identities: Personal Memory and the Construction of Selfhood." *Cultural Studies* 6, no. 1:27–50.

Gramsci, A. 1971. *Selections from the Prison Notebooks.* Translated and edited by Q. Hoare and G. Nowell-Smith. New York: International Publishers.

Grumet, M. R. 1988. *Bitter Milk: Women and Teaching.* Amherst: University of Massachusetts Press.

Hall, S. 1987. "Minimal Selves." In *Identity,* edited by L. Appignaesi, 44–48. London: Institute for Contemporary Art.

Haug, F., ed. 1987. *Female Sexualization: A Collective Work of Memory.* Translated by E. Carter. London: Verso Books.

hooks, b. 1989. "The Politics of Radical Black Subjectivity." *Zeta Magazine* (April): 52–55.

Lather, P. 1991. *Getting Smart: Feminist Research and Pedagogy with/in the Postmodern.* New York: Routledge.

Mariani, P., ed. 1991. *Critical Fictions: The Politics of Imaginative Writing.* Seattle: Bay Press.

McCarthy, C. 1990. *Race and Curriculum: Social Inequality and the Theories and Politics of Difference in Contemporary Research on Schooling.* London: Falmer Press.

McCarthy, C., and M. Apple. 1988. "Race, Class, and Gender in American Educational Research: Toward a Nonsynchronous Parallelist Position." In *Class, Race, and Gender in American Education,* edited by L. Weis, 9–42. Albany: State University of New York Press.

Miller, J. L. 1990. *Creating Spaces and Finding Voices: Teachers Collaborating for Empowerment.* Albany: State University of New York Press.

Nelson, C., ed. 1986. *Theory in the Classroom.* Urbana: University of Illinois Press.

Nespor, J., and J. Barylske. 1991. "Narrative Discourse and Teacher Knowledge." *American Educational Research Journal* 28, no. 4:805–23.

Nestle, J. 1987. *Restricted Country.* Ithaca, N.Y.: Firebrand Books.

Simon, R. I. 1992. *Teaching against the Grain: Texts for a Pedagogy of Possibility.* New York: Bergin and Garvey.

Smith, R., and A. Zantiotis. 1989. "Practical Teacher Education and the Avant-Garde." In *Critical Pedagogy, the State, and Cultural Struggle,* edited by H. Giroux and P. McLaren, 105–24. Albany: State University of New York Press.

Smyth, W. J., ed. 1987. *Educating Teachers: Changing the Nature of Pedagogical Knowledge.* London: Falmer Press.

Volosinov, V. N. 1986. *Marxism and the Philosophy of Language.* Translated by L. Matejka and I. R. Titunik. Cambridge: Harvard University Press.

Walkerdine, V. 1990. *Schoolgirl Fictions.* London: Verso Books.

Weedon, C. 1987. *Feminist Practice and Poststructuralist Theory.* New York: Basil Blackwell.

White, A. 1987/1988. "The Struggle over Bakhtin: Fraternal Reply to Robert Young." *Cultural Critique* 8:217–41.

Wilson, E. 1988. *Hallucinations: Life in the Postmodern City.* London: Radius.

# 5 Cultural Differences as Resources: Ways of Understanding in the Classroom

Beverly J. Moss
The Ohio State University

*Teachers must learn how to think about the cultural differences that exist within a classroom. In this thoughtful essay, Beverly J. Moss explores the importance of understanding both the similarities and differences in our students. She demonstrates how the use of ethnographic methods of inquiry can be used both to explore the unknowns of a community and to reveal important differences that might not be immediately apparent. True cultural sensitivity seems unlikely without a grasp of the distinctions suggested here.*

## By Way of Introduction

For most of us, much of the work we do and the way we teach has to do with where we come from, who we are, what our assumptions are about people, how we view ourselves in light of these assumptions, how we want to be perceived, and what we want people to assume about us. Almost everything we do is shaped by how we see ourselves as different from or similar to other people. I am no different from most people in terms of what has influenced the work I do, the way I teach, and the way I look at teaching and research in my field, composition studies. What is different are the specifics of my experiences. Therefore, I begin with an introduction to who I am because who I am has a great deal to do with what I have to say about cultural diversity in the classroom.

While some people probably think that it's perfectly natural for me to discuss ways of understanding cultural diversity in the classroom, given my obvious memberships in two of the groups that mark one as diverse (African Americans and women), I questioned whether those memberships were enough to warrant my being invited to write on such an important topic. The answer, of course, is no, they aren't. So I spent a considerable amount of time wondering what my contribution to the conversation might be. After much self-reflection, I realized that the work I do and the way I teach, especially the way I teach writing, provides me with a perspective on cultural diversity in the classroom that allows me to contribute to this conversation.

So, by way of introduction, let me tell you a little bit about me, what I do in the academy and where I see myself. I need to feel that my research, my "scholarly pursuits," are connected with real people and real problems, and that the voice that emerges from my work is not that of the distanced Researcher (with the capital R), that my voice is heard mingled with the voices of the people whose lives become intertwined with mine in my roles as researcher and teacher. My place in the academy is linked indissolubly with my place outside the academy, with my roots as an African American woman from the South whose assumptions and values (which have their sources in these roots) are also the sources for how I see myself as a scholar-teacher. And it is in this role as scholar-teacher, or, more comfortably, teacher-researcher, that I offer my perspectives on cultural differences as resources in the classroom.

I do research in two sites: the community (outside of the academy) and the classroom (inside the academy). Specifically, through ethnographic methods, I examine literacy in the African American church, and I examine the role of ethnography in first-year writing courses, with basic writers and honors students.

Imagine three African American male preachers in the Chicago area preaching the Word to their predominantly African American congregations and preaching in the tradition of African American preachers; each preacher is well-educated, and each preaches at a mainline Protestant African American church: one at a Baptist church, one at a Pentecostal church, and one at a United Church of Christ (UCC). Now juxtapose that with twenty white eighteen- and nineteen-year-old honors students from small-town Ohio sitting in their very first college writing course with their very first African American teacher. What do these two "scenes" have in common, and what can they tell us about understanding cultural diversity and how to use it as a resource in the classroom?

## Diversity and the African American Church

I begin in the African American church, where most of my work on literacy is focused. I have done ethnographies of three African American churches, focusing on the African American sermon as a literacy event as well as examining other uses of literacy in that community. While many interesting findings emerged from this study, what was consistent throughout was a notion of similarities on the surface—being within the boundaries of the

African American preaching tradition—yet diversity beneath the surface, that unique voice of every minister and church.

What stood out was that these three ministers, ages fifty-five, forty-five, and thirty-five, and in three different denominations, worked hard to tap into an already established tradition. Therefore, there were important similarities. Music was a major part of each church's service and sermon. Each minister and congregation participated in a call-and-response pattern—a pattern in which the congregation carries on a dialogue with the minister throughout the sermon. Each preacher relied on shared information between him and his congregation to make points in the sermon. For example, the minister of one church regularly made references in his sermons to entertainers such as Teddy Pendergrass, James Cleveland, and David Peaceton, and local politicians such as Ed Vrdolyak, Ed Burke, and Harold Washington, without defining or explaining the references, because he assumed that he and his congregation shared common backgrounds and, therefore, common information. Each preacher placed himself within the center of the community of the people he served while still maintaining the "proper" distance in his sermons (i.e., using "we" to identify with the group, and "you" to distance himself from the group). By using examples from popular culture that parallel biblical points, or by using music with a secular sound but with sacred words, each preacher integrated the secular with the sacred.

Yet in spite of these similarities, each minister and church had a unique voice; within the tradition stood wonderfully rich examples of diversity. For example, the Pentecostal church and its preacher were far more conservative than the other two churches in the way the service was conducted and in the subject matter of the sermons; the congregation was a little quieter during service than those in the other churches; and there were two distinct populations in the church—an older, less educated, working-class group and a younger, highly educated (M.B.A.'s, Ph.D.'s, M.D.'s), upwardly mobile group. The Baptist preacher and his congregation were for the most part suburbanites from north of Chicago who were upwardly mobile, with a fairly large university student population; the preacher and the congregation were fairly liberal and very race-conscious; and anything could be talked about from the pulpit. The UCC preacher and his congregation represented the largest group in the study. This congregation was three times larger than the Baptist congregation and four times larger than the Pentecostal. While this congregation was probably the most diverse in terms of socioeconomic background, it was also the most prominent in terms of members' status—a school superintendent, professional recording artists, television personalities, noted scholars, and so on. This preacher and congregation were the most politically active of the three churches. Most of the sermons touched on political or social concerns of the day, especially as they dealt with African Americans. This church's theme was "We are unashamedly Black and unapologetically Christian." Also of interest in this church was the role of women—they were in positions of power within the church and were treated within the sermons as people of power and position.

I knew before going into these churches that there is such widespread diversity within the African American community that to expect sameness is illogical—that to speak of an African American "community" rather than "communities" is misleading. Yet here I was going into a community institution (one in which I had been raised) which demanded that certain expectations be met—that tradition be followed—or the ministers risked failure. What I found was that these expectations were met, and yet that these ministers and congregations were still able to hold on to what made each of them unique. Through their uniqueness, each was able to contribute something different to the tradition of African American churches. They had three different voices. I had to listen to these voices within the community to understand that the diversity that exists within the tradition is what keeps the tradition going.

So what does this have to do with a first-year composition class and with ways of understanding diversity in the classroom? My insights into the rich diversity of the African American church provided me with another perspective from which to think about my own classes, and the diversity within them, and how to get students to appreciate and learn from this diversity. This diversity operates on two levels: first, diversity within a seemingly homogeneous group, like my honors class and like most classes at OSU, and second, diversity within a heterogeneous group, which is what most people think of when they think of those who are culturally diverse or culturally different—people of color and so on.

## First-year Students Learning about Diversity through Ethnography

As I noted earlier, I recently taught an honors composition class. Students place into this course by achieving a certain score on the ACT or the SAT. Most often students who are in honors composition courses are also members of the honors college, and therefore live in the honors dorm or, if they're on a need-based scholarship, the scholarship dorm, which is housed in the football stadium. So not only were these students taking courses together, many of them were also living together. The population in my course, twenty white students from Ohio, was typical of first-year English honors courses. However, the content of the course was atypical, and it was the content that moved my students and me toward an understanding of diversity in the classroom.

I focused this course on small ethnographic projects. Students identify a community which they then study for the quarter. Granted, it's impossible to teach students how to do ethnographies and then have them do sophisticated ethnographies within a ten-week quarter; however, it is more than possible to teach them basic ethnographic principles and send them out into communities to collect data and write essays based on these observations. After having taught this kind of class twice, and collected data on the classes while they're doing the projects—conducting an ethnography on students conducting ethnographies—I've learned that such projects can be used as more than tools to teach people how to write and think critically. Something else happens. Once these students have immersed themselves in the communities they are studying (many times communities to which they are complete outsiders), they start to see the very same things I saw with my three churches: that is, the boundaries that distinguish the community—those things that people share that make them members of the community—and the diversity within it—those things that make each member unique and the community complex. The students, through the kinds of research and ways of thinking that they must engage in to be successful at this kind of project, begin to understand the multiple voices within a community. They start to understand that although there are characteristics that bind people together to make a community, there are also characteristics that mark people as different within that community and that break down stereotypes. This is not easy for students to grasp initially, nor for many teachers. Yet it's the starting point for many of my students in their reeducation about diversity. And I think it should be the starting point for most of us as we think about diversity in our classes.

How does this principle play itself out for the students in my classroom? Let me begin by providing some concrete examples. The principle played itself out interestingly for Ann, who studied Campus Crusade for Christ, particularly their Thursday general meetings known as Prime Time. This student, from a fundamentalist background herself, had just joined Crusade and thought it would be a good idea to study the organization. She went into the group and the study with major assumptions about the "community," most notably that all members were there for the same purpose, to share with others how they came to be Christians and to experience fellowship with people like themselves.

Once Ann started talking to people in the organization, observing the routines of the meetings, and immersing herself in the community, however, she had to reassess her assumptions. One of the first things she had to face was that not all those in the organization were there because they were Christians. Some were just curious about what went on in this group; some were searching for a student organization that would make them feel that they belonged; some were Christians but not the kind of Christian that she was and therefore could recognize. That was the second assumption Ann confronted—that maybe people worshipped differently, and had differing opinions on the relationship between secular and sacred.

This student found diversity within a group to which she belonged, Christians, and for which she had operated as if there were only one standard—that to which she had been introduced in her small, predominantly white church, in her small Ohio town. The irony, of course, is that she always complained about non-Christians stereotyping Christians as Bible-thumping, fire-and-brimstone types. She kept saying, "We're not like that." Yet she couldn't go further and say, "We're all different," because she didn't know that until she had to confront the differences. When we reached the tenth week, she was beginning to grasp an unspoken principle in Crusade, that Christians come in all sizes, shapes, colors, and styles of worship. This principle was not an easy one for Ann to come to terms with. It challenged an important set of values she'd grown up with. She spent the first six weeks of the course refusing to recognize any actions by other Crusaders that were contrary to her beliefs. When I asked for evidence for her claims from field notes, interviews, and artifacts from the community she was studying, then, I was pushing Ann to become a part of Crusade, to really interact with, and learn about, the members of the community. It was this close contact and interaction with other Crusaders that finally led Ann to think about the diversity within her group. She began to learn about diversity within a group in which diversity can be a particularly difficult issue.

A second example involves an eighteen-year-old, blonde, green-eyed Caucasian girl who became a participant-observer in the Asian American Association (AAA), a student group on campus. She could not conceal her identity in this group even if she had wanted to. A word about Beth's background: she is a self-described "Army brat." She's lived in Germany and several places in the United States. Despite these experiences, however, she's always lived within a fairly homogeneous group. Her father is an officer, so her family has always lived among predominantly white, middle-class families. When Beth arrived at OSU this past fall, she found that she had an Asian American roommate who was always going off to these AAA meetings. Beth became curious about why her roommate and her friends joined such an organization. So she decided to join the group.

In her first essay, Beth focused on why the organization seemed to be important to its members, people with shared experiences and common backgrounds getting together to socialize. Although at first when she talked about differences they were superficial differences such as hairstyles and clothing, in her next two papers Beth began to explore other aspects of the community—for example that the members, while all Asian American, were from different backgrounds (e.g., Korean, Chinese, Filipino) and were in the group for various reasons. One of the more interesting parts of the project was Beth's description of an ongoing discussion at the meetings about the purpose of the group. Some people thought AAA should be strictly social; some thought it should be politically active; some wanted to compromise and serve both purposes. Through this discussion, Beth became aware of the bonds that held this group together and the individual strands that signaled the diversity within the group. She also began to understand the various reasons the Asian American students belonged to this organization.

The final section of Beth's paper, however, was most telling for me as a teacher in assessing the value of this experience for her in her understanding of this issue of diversity:

> I think that every person who has never been the minority in a situation should make an effort to put themselves in a position to be one at least once. If all people would have such an experience, perhaps our society would be more tolerant. We are all familiar with the term "minority," but many of us are not at all acquainted with the realities of being the minority. Many of us live in a type of oblivion. I am glad that I no longer do. I wish that other people could escape theirs.

While Beth did not spend enough time in this community to really understand "the reality of being the minority," she had a taste of it. She was not welcomed with open arms by everyone in this group. She experienced looks of mistrust from many members, who did not approve of a white person joining their organization, and some people refused to speak to her. And although others befriended her, they never let her forget her obvious difference; hence her nickname, "imploded Twinkie"—white on the outside and yellow on the inside. Beth thought her experience important enough to change her in some small way. She was gaining a different perspective on cultural diversity.

These examples illustrate a process through which students learned about diversity in fairly homogeneous communities outside of the classroom, and it was what they learned from their communities that contributed to their understanding in our class. As they were doing their ethnographies outside the class, we were using the classroom as an example to illustrate points or deal with problems they were running into. This meant that we were asking the same kind of questions about ourselves as a group that they were asking in their communities. We were doing a classroom-based ethnography—the students in a less formal way (through discussions and in-class writing assignments) and me in a formal way (with field notes, a research assistant–participant observer, interviews, and so on).

One of our more interesting weekly exercises was having students describe different aspects of the class, sharing those descriptions with the entire group and then examining how the descriptions changed. By the end of the course, the students felt that our class had established a sense of community, that we shared common goals and characteristics, that there were many similarities. Yet, they came to understand how different they all really were from each other even though eighteen out of the twenty of them were from small rural towns in Ohio, they were all honors students, and seventeen of the twenty were women. The differences among them became points of discussion. For instance, the one student from Cincinnati, who was in the Navy ROTC, learned about Future Farmers of America from a young Appalachian woman from a rural town in southern Ohio who had been the first female president of FFA, a powerful organization, in her high school. His assumptions about Appalachians were both confirmed and contradicted as he got to know Emily, as her assumptions about students in the Navy ROTC program were confirmed and contradicted as she got to know Jason. The students learned that small-town life is similar from place to place, but that no one small town is like another and, therefore, that each student comes from a culturally different background. Again, they recognized the sameness/diversity continuum.

Of course, the students' most obvious struggle with diversity began on the first day of class, when I walked in the door, began to pass out the syllabus, and said "I'm Beverly Moss, and this is H110C." I don't think they knew what they were expecting, but it wasn't an African American teacher. While none of the students said anything directly about my race, it became clear during the first couple of weeks that it was an issue. If, during class discussion, I brought up any example that dealt with racism, the class became silent. We could talk about sexism with no trouble, but racial issues were touchy. When anyone finally garnered enough courage to speak about an issue dealing with African Americans, there was always the qualifier "Correct me if I'm wrong," or "I'm not sure, but," and there was the stumbling over "colored people," "Negroes," "black people," or "African Americans."

The students were overly self-conscious, and unsure of how to deal with me. Should they really treat me like all their other professors (once they were convinced that I was a professor and not a T.A.)? They were so focused on me as different from them that they seemed unable to get past that. However, as the quarter progressed and they got to know me, the differences began to balance out with the similarities. Yes, their teacher was an African American woman from the South with a Ph.D., something that was alien to all of them. They had no concept of what it was like to be discriminated against on the basis of one's race, but their teacher could tell them about it from personal experience. But their teacher also liked sports and could talk football, baseball, and basketball with the best of them, something she shared with a few people in class. Their teacher was a religious person, something she had in common with some of her students. Their teacher watched television, something she had in common with too many of her students. When they understood that my differences allowed me to bring something unique to the class, and that my similarities provided me with a starting point for sharing some of the uniqueness, they became less reserved. However, it was only through getting involved in discovering what made the class a community, and each person's role in that community, that they got to this understanding. What most, though not all, finally came to was that I could be both different from and similar to them, and that that was okay. They also learned that at least one African American didn't fit the stereotype that they had been introduced to in the popular media.

## Teachers Understanding Diversity

So far I've focused on students' understanding of diversity. But this topic also concerns teachers, so I want to address briefly how the principle of sameness and diversity played itself out for me, the teacher, in this class. I recognized that I had had an advantage over my students, because I had been expecting twenty white students. In my four years of teaching at Ohio State University, I've taught only one undergraduate course that had more than two students of color in it—Introduction to African American Literature (no surprise!). Yet, even though I knew what to expect, I was taken aback (as I usually am) by the sea of white faces staring at me when I walked into the class. And I grew a little weary from having to try so hard to get them to relax. However, as I was collecting data on this class and discussing them with my research assistant and other members of our research team, I started to see all the differences in the group. They became less homogeneous, less a sea of white faces and more a group of individuals with different voices. Some of these voices blended harmoniously and some were incompatible. But what I learned is that harmony is not a goal that I really desire. If it happens, that's fine. But I don't seek harmony because many times when voices blend together some voices are not heard; some voices are silenced, and an off-key voice (difference) is punished. This was really brought home to me with the Appalachian student, who didn't just march to the beat of a different drummer; she had a whole other marching band. She was truly one of a kind, and every time I tried to get her to become part of the group, she would become quiet and reserved. But when she was "on the margins" of the group—literally and figuratively—she would contribute to the class discussions in her unique way. During the course, I came to understand the struggle she was having as an Appalachian in central Ohio. Her accent stood out; her rural background stood out. She was identified as different. So instead of seeing her as being like every other Appalachian student and as vastly different from her other classmates, I began to see Emily as Emily, who had some unique contributions to make to the class. She seemed to appreciate being our expert on farming, but not being called on to give the Appalachian perspective on any given topic. She was allowed to be a member of the group and an individual at the same time.

Even though this group had many similarities, I could not think of a more diverse group of people that I had taught in a long time. As a teacher I sometimes find it difficult to remember that homogeneous groups aren't all that homogeneous, that there can be and usually is multiculturalism within an all-white class. And if we can deal with the diversity within a seemingly homogeneous group, then we may be ready to start thinking about a multicultural class in the more familiar sense (e.g., people of different ethnic backgrounds, religious backgrounds, or genders).

A truly multicultural class must pay attention to the sameness/difference continuum; yet that's exactly what's been missing from the debate on cultural diversity. Whenever I listen to the debate on diversity in our classrooms, I tend to hear or sense two strands of argument: one, that we should treat all students the same, and teach to that ideal student—in other words, don't recognize any differences; the other, that we should focus on our students' cultural differences. We get either this "common culture, common literacy" approach; or a multicultural literacy–multicultural classroom model, in which "only the differences count." What seems missing in both approaches is that sameness/diversity perspective. We're either focusing too much on how we're all the same—which usually translates into all of us being held up to one single standard held by a group in a power position—or we focus on how we're different. There never seems to be a sense that we need to do both. This polarization contributes very little toward a successful model for teaching culturally diverse student populations or for introducing diversity into seemingly homogeneous classes. Teachers have to rethink how we approach this issue. My way, as is evident in this paper, is to explore the differences as we explore the similarities. Yet the dominant way in American education is to deny the differences, mostly in an attempt to silence those who see themselves—or who are seen—as different, or to see only the differences—mostly to point out deficiencies.

This is not a new debate in American education. The language seems to have changed only a little, if at all. We seem always to be asking, "What are we going to do with *them?*" This discussion of how we deal with diversity in the American education system seems to reveal the contradictory nature of American society, a society that is driven toward homogeneity yet is supposed to be the land of the individual.

What pushes me to continue thinking about refining my "sameness/diversity model" in my teaching and my research is my own position in the academy as a teacher-researcher. I want my differences to be recognized and celebrated, and I want my similarities to be recognized and celebrated. It's the combination of the two that shapes my work in the classroom and in the community, that affects what I teach, how I teach, how I see myself in relation to others, and how I use diversity in the classroom.

I think that the next time I teach an undergraduate course I will begin with Langston Hughes's "Theme for English B." This poem captures the essence of the sameness/diversity model or "duality" in a way that I may never be able to.

Theme for English B
by Langston Hughes

The instructor said,

*Go home and write*
*a page tonight.*
*And let that page come out of you—*
*Then, it will be true.*

I wonder if it's that simple?
I am twenty-two, colored, born in Winston-Salem.
I went to school there, then Durham, then here
to this college on the hill above Harlem.
I am the only colored student in my class.
The steps from the hill lead down into Harlem,
through a park, then I cross St. Nicholas,
Eighth Avenue, Seventh, and I come to the Y,
the Harlem Branch Y, where I take the elevator
up to my room, sit down, and write this page:

It's not easy to know what is true for you or me
at twenty-two, my age. But I guess I'm what
I feel and see and hear, Harlem, I hear you:
hear you, hear me—we too—you, me, talk on this page.
(I hear New York, too.) Me—who?
Well, I like to eat, sleep, drink, and be in love.
I like to work, read, learn, and understand life.
I like a pipe for a Christmas present,
or records—Bessie, bop, or Bach.
I guess being colored doesn't make me *not* like
the same things other folks like who are other races.
So will my page be colored that I write?
Being me, it will not be white.
But it will be
a part of you, instructor.
You are white—
yet a part of me, as I am a part of you.
That's American.
Sometimes perhaps you don't want to be a part of me.
Nor do I often want to be a part of you.
But we are, that's true!

---

As I learn from you,
I guess you learn from me—
although you're older—and white—
and somewhat more free.

This is my page for English B.

# 6 Teacher Research: Seeing What We Are Doing

Glenda L. Bissex
Northeastern University

*Glenda L. Bissex challenges teachers to become active researchers. She shows, through wisely selected exemplars, how teachers develop understanding and insights into student learning and their own instructional practices by being researchers. According to Bissex, the inquiring teacher learns "with dignity."*

———————

This year Laura Pitts, one of the teacher-researchers I'm mentoring, is studying the effects on her students of a new global studies curriculum she's team-teaching. Recently she wrote me:

> You know, if it hadn't been for this case study project, I don't think I'd have appreciated the changes in Andrea nearly as much, nor would my other students have noticed the changes in themselves that my questioning has brought into focus. Would I have such a visible record that Andrea really has changed inside and out? Without my periodic questioning and faithful recording and analysis—which she's seen all along the way—would she write pages for me in response to the *big* inquiries, or forge a friendship with Fred [her team teacher] and me beyond the classroom? She never did before, according to her previous teachers and the support staff of our school.

An inquiring frame of mind, relatively simple research tools such as a double-entry notebook for recording events and reflecting on them, and audio- or videotapes of classroom events and of interviews with students enable teacher-researchers to see things that otherwise might not be evident. Dora Glinn, a special educator who studied a group of first graders she was co-teaching and co-researching with reading teacher John Goekler, reported that they wouldn't have listened to the children's conversations among themselves if they hadn't been doing research. They would probably have been concerned instead with keeping the kids quiet. As researchers, however, they had video-taped a number of activities in their classroom, and the more they reviewed one particular tape, the more they saw—for example, how the children were actually supporting one another's learning. Although these conversations were going on right under their noses, they could easily have heard them as only noise interfering with work. This kind of research requires a certain frame of mind, a readiness to hear and to see, a capacity for suspending, or being jolted out of, our usual interpretations of classroom events.

## Teacher Research: Looking and Seeing

When you start researching—looking again, which is often actually looking for the first time—there's no limit to the kinds of things you'll see. Some time ago, as I was responding to student papers, I caught myself doing something that doubtless I'd done for many years without thinking. I found I was responding differently to students whose papers were quite accomplished than to those whose language and thinking seemed unclear. To the more accomplished students, I responded as a reader and as a colleague; I talked mostly about their ideas, sharing my own thoughts on issues that obviously interested me, too. To the writers of the more troublesome papers, I responded as an instructor, helpfully describing how they might improve their organization and explanations. I wish I knew what triggered my recognition of that difference. Possibly it was some combination of internal readiness and an external prod such as reading other research. Anyway, I stopped my pencil in its tracks as I thought of how I must sound to Alyssa, who was just orienting herself to American academia, juxtaposed with how I might be heard by Maureen, an already accomplished writer and historical researcher. I'd been responding to the Maureens as thinkers, as persons with something interesting to say. In contrast, I realized, I'd been indirectly telling the Alyssas that they had nothing to say that I took seriously enough to converse about with them, and I realized how lifeless and demeaning those responses were. The snowball effect on the Alyssas of years of such responses, not only from me but surely from many other teachers as well, none of us taking their ideas and interests seriously, may have been devastating.

What if, instead of instructing them from behind my teacherly desk, I stepped out and sat with them, conversing? I decided to find out. One thing that happened was that responding to them became less tedious. Changing my role enabled me to see them differently, less negatively, as I looked for ideas, even incomplete ones, to discuss. What was in their papers, I discovered, was determined by the reader as well as by the text. As soon as I assumed an instructor's role in reading them, my vision and response narrowed. Unlearning this role has taken time, and still I catch myself in it. But having seen, I can never blind myself again, I can only keep catching myself and changing my responses into those that make me a better teacher and Alyssa a better learner.

Teacher research means seeing what has been in front of us all the time. It means seeing something we didn't expect to see, a sure sign of learning since what we expect is what we already know. Teacher research is not about what we can prove but about what we can learn—about what we can see in our classrooms that we have not seen before, that instructs and empowers us. Some people refer to this as action research. Indeed, our wonderings and questionings arise out of the actions in our classrooms. Our investigations are carried out in the midst of action, the teacher's and the students'. Through making visible what had been unclear or invisible, through extending our understanding, the research changes our actions.

The most difficult things to see are often those things closest to us, things so familiar that we overlook them, we are hardly aware of them, or we don't think to question them. Or things we don't see because we're blinded by what we "know," which means that our first step must be unlearning. "What happened in my classroom changed because suddenly I observed what was going on there," reports my colleague Nancie Atwell (1991):

> At the end of each quarter I conferred with individuals about their uses and views of writing, documenting and analyzing what they said, set goals with them for the next nine weeks, and set a grade on their progress toward the goals of the previous quarter. One November, during our first round of evaluation conferences, I made an occasion for students to articulate the themes of the opening months of writing workshop by asking, among other things, "What's the most important or useful thing you've learned as a writer in the first quarter?" . . . In mini-lessons that autumn I had stressed leads and conclusions, self-editing and proofreading, and a writer's need to be his or her own first critic. I assumed that my students would give me back what I had given them, so that I could begin to formalize a sequence of mini-lessons for the eighth grade. Instead, the twenty-three students in just one of my classes named almost forty different kinds of knowledge, from new conventions to new techniques to new habits. . . . I had to rethink my teaching again. (4–8)

What enabled Nancie to see—to get beyond her initial assumptions? Her systematic research practice of asking students about their learning, of recording their responses, and of reflecting on them. What she could not see with her eyes, she could see through her students' eyes once she had taken that bold step of asking them what they saw and of accepting what they reported seeing. Teacher-researcher Susan Hohman pointed out to me another way that getting beyond our own perspective by seeing through our students' eyes is valuable for researchers: "By conversing with our students, we can figure out the important questions, the ones that might not even occur to us when we look from our single perspective. That may be even more important than finding the answers. We probably have a pretty good idea of the answers to our preconceived questions already."

A student provided Pat Fox with a provocative question that changed the direction of her research. Pat was seeking to understand the variations in quality of writing she observed within individual seventh graders. "Some writing tasks you do better than others," she told her class. "What kinds of writing do you do best and worst?"

> Etai's response to my question created our first striking moment, a moment of tension, a moment of discovery, and a major turning point in our study. "Best and worst according to whose standards, yours or ours?"
>
> At the moment I turned to him and said, "Now that's a good question—is there a difference?" our fruitful collaboration began. Etai had reserved the right to value a piece of writing in a way other than the way in which the teacher valued it, and he was not alone. This point was made over and over again in the discussion that followed. My student writers had a strong sense of their own strengths and weaknesses as writers which was based on their own criteria for good and bad writing. (1988)

Fox's research pursued this new question of students' criteria for evaluating their own writing, revealing significant differences from teacher evaluations.

## New Questions, New Ways of Seeing

Questions we had not envisioned can arise as we listen to replays of classroom events, when we are relieved of the pressures of being participants and can become spectators. One of Lolly Ockerstrom's responsibilities was training new teachers of writing. As a teacher-researcher she wanted to explore what happened when first-year teaching assistants began to teach for the first time. Ten new teaching assistants volunteered to be her informants, and she set up a series of meetings with them, which she taped.

> There was no agenda for the meetings; I simply wanted to hear what first-year teaching assistants thought about as they began their teaching. . . . Through a free-form structure, I might learn about issues facing new teachers of writing that researchers in composition might have overlooked previously. As I reviewed the tapes of the meetings, [I noticed that] the voices that dominated were male voices. I told myself that it didn't matter, that the women in the group were a little more shy than the men in speaking out, and that as we continued to meet and get to know each other better, the women would speak, too. But I realized that I was ignoring the voice within myself that screamed a protest: Why did I hear male voices and not female voices speaking? Why were women not speaking? When they did, why did they allow themselves to be interrupted by male voices, and displaced in the conversation? What was going on in those group meetings that I didn't understand? . . . I knew that what isn't spoken is as important as what is spoken; I found myself listening to gaps and silences and in particular to the absence of women's voices as much as I listened to what was said and who said it. . . .

I had no idea I would study gender differences when I began this case study. But the nature of the verbal interactions between the men and women in the group struck me immediately, and the more I noticed men speaking and women not speaking, the more I realized that this was important to look at. As I focused on gender and language, I realized that I was looking at issues in my own teaching and learning—why I felt blocked from speaking out in groups, why I doubted my own authority, and, most important, how I could change self-defeating behavior into action that allowed me to speak when I need to speak. (1989)

Systematic records such as field notes, comments on student works, and tape recordings that we review and reflect on *with the intention of learning about our practice* can improve our vision. Ferguson McKay (1987) heard himself more clearly through tapes of his student conferences.

I've been using a tape recorder much more than I was before because I found that it makes me honest. You don't really understand what you've heard somebody say until you listen to it two or three times. What really helps is making a transcript. You've got to pay attention to what's on the tape. I listened to my tapes, copied them out, and wrote comments on them, either the day they were made or within a few days thereafter, but usually the day they were made. Then I went back and reexamined them and reinterpreted them later on while writing the paper. And the second interpretations were not the same as the first. The interpretations I made of the conference in the morning always caused me to see the conference totally differently from the way I'd seen it when I was meeting . . . [I had] had a whole series of ideas about what the effect of this or that procedure was which half the time weren't right. Seeing that is threatening and exciting at the same time. (153)

And what enables teacher-researchers to see things that are threatening? McKay describes his experience: "This kind of research makes you aware of yourself—because it gives you some internal support, some increased self-respect; it makes it easier to look at yourself. You're not so afraid, or threatened, by the revelations that come" (155).

## Developing Understanding and Insight

Neither I nor the teacher-researchers I've worked with are doing what Stephen North in *The Making of Knowledge in Composition* (1987) calls "practitioner inquiry"—accumulating practices that "work" in their classrooms. All teachers do this, but not all teachers are, formally or informally, researchers in their classrooms, looking again at what has happened there. In contrast to North's notion of practitioner "lore," the focus of teacher research is not essentially on what "works," on collecting practical strategies, but on gaining understandings and awareness. Teacher research is more interpretive than pragmatic. "The hermeneutics of practice" (Carson 1990, 173) aptly describes it. "Reflective practitioners" (Schon 1983) is a fitting phrase for teacher-researchers, whose understandings and awareness reshape, reform, their practice.

Writing this paper was for me an act of teacher research. I've examined again (re-searched) eight years of inquiries—conversations with my students, letters to and from them, drafts and final reports. I've reviewed comments these teachers made, in writing and in taped discussions, about how their research affected their teaching. I've looked again at my field notes and constantly revised teaching plans. Writing and rewriting this paper has taught me more about the kind of thinking and the kind of knowing that teacher research is.

I understand better now how I have invented and evolved my way of teaching teacher-researchers—why, for instance, naturalist Samuel Scudder's little autobiographical reflection (1992) on learning from his teacher, Louis Agassiz, to look and look and look again at the fish he was given to study is central to my case study course and is often recalled as most helpful by participants. As a teacher-researcher, I'm seeing what I do. You could say I'm uncovering the theory underlying my own practice. As a teacher, this aware-ness of the ground of my practice is the most valuable fruit of my researching, more valuable than building an overarching theory or model of teacher re-search—although I am, of course, tempted to lay my truths on other teacher-researchers.

After much researching to find what for me was the essence of teacher research and thus the title for this paper, I reread a discussion about their experiences among the first group of teacher-researchers I ever taught. There, right in front of me where it had been from the beginning, was what I had just discovered. Peggy Sheehan (1987, 159) had said it: "We examine ourselves more; we look at ourselves more while we're in the classroom as teachers and *see what we're doing* [my italics] and how we're interacting. I think that's a value, if nothing else."

For Anne Alpert (1991), who teaches at a magnet school, teacher research meant the shock of seeing for the first time the assumptions or theories on which she had been basing her practice as a writing teacher. As a final instance of teacher thinking and teacher knowing, I offer her complete essay on her inquiry, which allows us to follow the process of a teacher's reflective learning.

"Just Like Lightning!"

Anne Alpert

> Someone once told me, and I'm sure it was a teacher, that often it's more important to figure out the right questions than to come up with answers.

---

Reprinted by permission of Anne Alpert and the Connecticut Writing Project.

I have been struggling for a long time with the problem of motivating children in my fifth-grade class who produce very little writing. What was I failing to do for them that I seemed to be doing for the others?

I decided to concentrate on finding out what I was doing wrong. I began taping my conferences with the children I had labeled "reluctant writers," hoping that, by listening to my part in the conferences, I would find some answers. After hours and hours of taping and transcribing, however, I was no closer to any real insights than when I had started.

Ironically, a conference with one of my [other] students, . . . Tom, helped me to find some answers and pose some important questions. I had not taped my conferences with Tom because he was not one of those I had targeted as a reluctant writer. By March, when we had this conference, he had already published ten pieces. He is very cheerful about writing. He confers with friends often and loves to share his pieces with the class at whole-group share—not at all what you would call a "reluctant writer." Since I didn't tape the conference, this is approximately how it went.

*Anne:* What would you like me to help you with, Tom?

*Tom:* I'm publishing this piece.

*Anne:* How long have you been working on it?

*Tom:* Since Monday [two days].

*Anne:* Are you sure it's ready to be published?

*Tom:* Sure . . . I'm done.

*Anne:* Okay, let's hear it. [He reads the piece to me.]

*Tom:* Can I publish now?

*Anne:* Is there anything you want to add?

*Tom:* Nope . . . that's it.

*Anne:* What will you do next?

*Tom:* I'm going to write about going bowling with Rohan yesterday.

*Anne:* Tom, would you consider trying a different form of writing, like those poems I've been reading to you, or a fairy tale?

*Tom:* I like this.

*Anne:* I know . . . and you work hard at Writers' Workshop. You can mess around with different things, too.

*Tom:* Can I publish now?

*Anne:* It's your choice.

*Tom:* Okay . . . I'll publish.

I watched him saunter over to the computer to "publish" his piece and I realized that most of his conferences were like this. They were boring for both of us and I never felt satisfied that we had accomplished very much. After school, I decided to take out Tom's "Final Copy Folder" to see what he had published so far. All his pieces were personal narratives, and all about his best friend, Rohan. They were all about the same length and pretty much the same level of complexity. Tom certainly wasn't a risk-taker, and he had been resisting my suggestions for a long time. He had been turning out pieces, though . . . so why was I feeling so uneasy about him? After conferring with him all year long, I realized I really didn't know him as a writer.

I began to think about the three students I had been taping all these months. What did I really know about them as writers? Maybe instead of asking questions about their writing, I needed to ask them questions about themselves as writers. I decided to have individual conferences with each of them . . . very different conferences than I had been having. These are the conferences verbatim: the first is with Jesus, the second with Samantha, and the third with Ronnie. Jesus and Ronnie have published one piece each this year, and Samantha has published none. (This is March.)

Jesus never initiates a conference with me, and I have to force him to meet me about every other week. I poke and prod him when we confer and he reacts by agreeing with everything I say just to get away from me.

*Anne:* Read me what you have, Jesus, and then I want to ask you some questions.

*Jesus:* [He reads his piece to me. It's about a mouse named Itchy who has adventures traveling around the world. In each place, he makes a new friend and the friend joins him on his travels. He has been working on the same piece all term. He makes lots of starts, puts it away, starts again. It seems to me that he never commits himself to anything.]

*Anne:* What do you think of it, Jesus?

*Jesus:* It's good, I guess.

*Anne:* You don't sound too sure.

*Jesus:* What do you think?

*Anne:* I think I talk too much when we have a conference. I want to hear what you think about writing.

*Jesus:* I like it. [Long silence . . . He's waiting for me to say something.] I like this Itchy character. I have to use the globe to find the countries he'll go to next . . . and then I look up the country to find out about it and make up his friends' names and stuff like that. I keep getting new ideas for new places. It's fun.

*Anne:* That's what writers do all the time . . . They do research like you're doing.

*Jesus:* It takes time to do it . . . sometimes the whole writing period and I'm still not done. I read slow. Sometimes I have to ask Greg to help me with words.

*Anne:* I see. What do you plan to do with your Itchy stories?

*Jesus:* It's a chapter book. Every chapter is a different place. I have six places already. But it's taking me long to put it all together.

*Anne:* Read me the very first one you have.

*Jesus:* Why?

*Anne:* I don't remember hearing it. Don't you want to?

*Jesus:* Okay. [He reads the first draft he started months ago. He stumbles where sentences end and begin and has to go back to correct himself.]

*Anne:* Why is that happening?

*Jesus:* I don't have any periods. I can't use them when I write.

*Anne:* How come?

*Jesus:* It stops me from thinking so I put them in after. I haven't done it yet.

*Anne:* Oh . . . I see . . . It's good you know that about yourself.

*Jesus:* Yeah.

He continues reading his piece. It really is very funny. I realize I never asked him before why he was stumbling over words. I thought it was because he has difficulty reading and didn't want to embarrass him.

*Anne:* You're a great storyteller. Did you know that about yourself?

*Jesus:* Yeah. I was trying to write poems and mysteries and stuff like you wanted us to write, but it's too hard for me. I like to write funny stuff like this. It's easier to write about animals than about people too. You laughed at all the right places, Anne.

*Anne:* Was this a test?

*Jesus:* Yeah. [laughs]

*Anne:* What will you do now?

*Jesus:* I think I'll try to bring Itchy home again and go back and see what I can change from the beginning. It might take me a long time.

*Anne:* Should I wait for you to sign up for a conference when you're ready?

*Jesus:* Yeah. Sometimes I'm not ready when you call me.

*Anne:* Okay. Thanks, Jesus.

I felt bewildered after this conference. What made him think that I wouldn't value his piece because it wasn't as "hard" as a poem or a mystery? And why didn't he tell me before why he wasn't ready for a conference when I called him? And why didn't he object to being called in the first place? The usual procedure for a conference with me was to sign up when you needed one. The implication was that he couldn't be trusted to do that for himself. Why didn't I trust him?

Samantha never wants to confer with me or with other children. I have to seek her out. She's very noncommittal at a conference. She always makes me feel as though I'm intruding on her privacy.

*Anne:* What are you working on, Sam?

*Sam:* The same thing.

*Anne:* Read me some.

*Sam:* [She proceeds to read a piece she has started months ago. It's a "chapter book" about a brother and sister who decide to run away because their mother is getting married again and they hate their prospective stepfather and stepbrother. The first chapter is very well done. She has set up the characters very carefully. The second chapter, the one she is reading to me, is an elaborate explanation of how they plan to run away and where they're going to go, etc. She reads slowly and methodically, with very little expression or enthusiasm. She seems uncomfortable and angry at having to share it with me. She obviously wants to get it over with.]

*Anne:* I feel as if you don't want to share this, Sam.

*Sam:* Well, I wasn't ready.

*Anne:* Do you think I should wait until you sign up for a conference by yourself?

*Sam:* Yes. You don't call the other kids . . . just me. Why do you do that?

*Anne:* I guess because I'm afraid you're not writing anything and I need to find out what you're doing. You haven't published anything all year.

*Sam:* So what? You said authors take a year . . . sometimes two years to write a book. Nobody tells them they have to publish seven books a year. I don't think you're being fair.

*Anne:* How come you never told me that before?

*Sam:* Because nobody else seems to care about it.

*Anne:* Oh.

*Sam:* You let everybody else sign up for a conference when they need it. Why don't you wait for me to be ready?

*Anne:* Do you want to talk about your piece now?

*Sam:* Not really.

*Anne:* Okay.

*Sam:* I'll sign up when I'm ready.

*Anne:* Okay.

*Sam:* Maybe tomorrow or the next day.

*Anne:* It's okay, Sam . . . really. I'm glad you told me how you feel.

*Sam:* You see, when I write, it takes me a long time to figure out how something ends up. I try it different ways in my mind, but only one way fits right. I have to do it with every chapter because there's something that happens in each chapter that leads to something else in the next chapter. I have to think about things a long time without writing anything.

*Anne:* . . . and you don't need to talk to anyone to help you solve the problems.

*Sam:* No . . . it just interrupts me and I have to start thinking all over again.

*Anne:* Oh . . . so when I call you for a conference, it just interrupts you.

*Sam:* [big sigh] Yes!

*Anne:* Thanks, Sam . . . that's a big help to me.

*Sam:* Okay.

I've told my students so often that writers make many starts and sometimes take a long time to finally come up with a piece of writing that
satisfies them. By saying that, wasn't I giving them permission to take as
long as they needed? If I meant that, then why did I decide to require
seven published pieces? Is that why Samantha has seemed angry at me
all this time?

Ronnie does everything but write at Writers' Workshop. Mostly he draws
or reads or talks to other people about their writing. He loves to have peer
conferences and he'll confer with anyone who asks him. He has produced
one piece of writing, a fairy tale of some length that he worked on for
about six weeks. He made many revisions and was very proud of the
result. Since then, he hasn't produced anything.

*Anne:* What's happening, Ron?

*Ron:* I can't think of anything to write about.

*Anne:* I know . . . that's what you tell me every time we have a conference. Don't any of my suggestions help you?

*Ron:* No.

*Anne:* Tell me how you get an idea for a piece.

*Ron:* Myself?

*Anne:* Yes.

*Ron:* Why do you want to know?

*Anne:* I don't know . . . It occurred to me after listening to all the tapes
of our conferences that I never asked you that and I really want to know.

*Ron:* Well, it usually takes me a very long time. I never know when it hits
. . . it just comes to me . . . like that. Then I write and write and . . . like
my fairy tale. I got the idea from Andy when she was telling me about
this movie she saw then it just hit me . . . just like lightning.

*Anne:* Okay . . . so you get your idea and then you write and write and
then what happens?

*Ron:* After I publish, it's like I'm worn out . . . like when a balloon loses
its air . . . just flat. I don't feel like writing again for a long time . . . so I
do other stuff and just wait for another idea to hit me again.

*Anne:* Is there any way to make the ideas come faster?

*Ron:* I don't know. Do you know any?

*Anne:* I guess not . . . the ways I knew I shared with you and they didn't
seem to work.

*Ron:* I know. I guess writers all have their own way and nobody can
really help them.

*Anne:* I guess real writers know that about themselves.

*Ron:* What should I do now?

*Anne:* What do you want to do?

*Ron:* I think I'll read some more Shel Silverstein. I really like his poems.

*Anne:* Okay. Let me know when another idea hits you.

*Ron:* Okay. Thanks, Anne.

Ronnie was really happy with himself as a writer. So why was I feeling so frustrated all year? If he had been less independent and secure would I have felt more useful? What did all this have to do with Ronnie being labeled a reluctant writer?

As I looked over my transcripts of past conferences with these three children, I realized that my focus was constantly on ways to move them along to publish. I heard myself remind them over and over that they needed to publish seven pieces and they were nowhere near that number. I accused them, also, of doing nothing constructive at writing time, which, as you can see from these conferences, was the furthest thing from the truth. And most important, they knew themselves as writers much more intimately and intelligently than I did.

So then what is a "reluctant" writer? Is writing a social act for everyone? What drove me to require a particular number of published pieces? Where was the ownership of the writer in that decision? Are we talking about "writing" or about "composing?" And if we're talking about "composing," isn't it much more than "writing"?

It seems clear to me now that "writing" is only one piece of the puzzle that is "composing." I should have known that from my own experiences struggling to compose. Composing is the getting ready to take the risk; it's the struggling to develop an idea; it's the self-doubt, the inner critic constantly challenging you; it's all the revision that happens before you ever get a word down on paper. Composing is the thinking, the problem solving, the choices. It's the totality of every act that finally produces "writing." And this whole process is different for each one of us.

If all this is so, then what is the purpose and value of Writers' Workshop? Is it to help children to know themselves as writers, or to publish? (That question is rhetorical since one of the revelations that came to me "like lightning" is that Writers' Workshop time is for helping my students see themselves as writers and be secure with what they know.) Publishing is important if the writer thinks it's important, but it's no more important than any other piece of the composing process. It took these three children all term to get up the courage to tell me who they are. I read in a "teacher book" that children decide what is important not by what you say, but by what you do. My message to these children had been that publishing is writing, but they had the courage to resist me so that they could be true to themselves. There is nothing "reluctant" about them. There are other times of the day to be concerned about product. Writers' Workshop will be a time to be concerned about the process of composing.

There's clearly another issue that can't be avoided. If I really believe that the writer must have ownership of decisions about his or her writing, what drove me to establish a requirement for published pieces? Knowing what I know about my own writing process, I could never have met this requirement myself! I suppose it was my "easy way out." Evaluation of writing has always been impossible for me. Except for mechanics, everything else seems arbitrary. The final product is the end of a long road. I've never been able to simply look at the "finished" piece all by itself. Maybe setting a required number of pieces helped me to avoid the real issue: Why should writing be graded at all? How is this helpful to anyone?

As you can see, I have a few answers, but many more questions. Thinking about Tom, for example, I realize that he is much more afraid of writing than Jesus, Ronnie, or Samantha. He won't even talk about himself as a writer. It may be that he is whipping off all these pieces just to keep me happy and avoid having me ask him the questions I know now that I need to ask him. Would I call Tom a "reluctant" writer? He's reluctant to reveal himself, he's reluctant to share, he's reluctant to ask for help or admit he has needs. Maybe the real question is, why label him anything? It just gets in the way of knowing who he is. Schools shouldn't be for judging . . . they should be for listening, and respecting, and helping.

So . . . how do I help Tom? And how do I break it to the class that there is no required number of published pieces?

## Reflections on a Teacher's Reflection

Alpert's research starts from a teaching problem: How can she motivate children in her fifth-grade class who produce very little writing? Embedded in that problem are theoretical issues that her research eventually leads her to unearth and examine.

Her first clue comes unexpectedly from a conference with a prolific writer, Tom, an event she has not seen as useful to her inquiry and, thus, has not recorded, except in her memory. Perhaps because she's in research mode, she pays more attention to the uneasiness she's felt for some time about Tom as a writer, which leads her to question what she knows about her "reluctant" students as writers. In her next conferences she asks them questions about themselves as writers and truly listens to them as informants.

Her conference with Jesus leads her to a new set of questions about him and about herself:

> What made him think that I wouldn't value his piece because it wasn't as "hard" as a poem or a mystery? And why didn't he tell me before why he wasn't ready for a conference when I called him? And why didn't he object to being called in the first place? The usual procedure for a conference with me was to sign up when you needed one. The implication was that he couldn't be trusted to do that for himself. Why didn't I trust him?

Anne's conference with Samantha leads her to see a contradiction between the pedagogical beliefs she has asserted and her practice. Her awareness of this contradiction is a wedge that further opens up her inquiry. After completing her research, Anne reflects: "I've learned so much about myself from the writing of this chapter . . . about how easy it is to be a hypocritical teacher and not know it unless someone or something forces you to look at yourself and your practice and measure these against what you say you believe." As often happens in teacher research, the focus shifts from students to the teacher herself.

Her conference with Ronnie raises questions about her own expectations rather than, as originally, about her students' failure to live up to them. Recognizing that these students know themselves better as writers than she does forces her to redefine her research problem. Instead of asking how she can motivate these students to write more, she asks, "What is a 'reluctant' writer? Is writing a social act for everyone?" "Are we talking about 'writing' or about 'composing'?" "What is the purpose and value of Writers' Workshop?" Confronting the assumptions beneath her research problem as she originally framed it raises a host of theoretical questions.

## The Role of Research in Teaching

Anne's answers, explicit and implied, to these theoretical issues lead her back to her pedagogy—to her requirement that students publish a certain number of pieces—in light of which she had viewed Jesus, Samantha, and Ronnie as unmotivated. "Maybe setting a required number of pieces helped me to avoid the real issues: Why should writing be graded at all?"

All of these questions have been raised in the service of her teaching, and it is to her teaching that she returns in the end: "So how do I help Tom? And how do I break it to the class that there is no required number of published pieces?" When she wrote to me the following school year, Anne described further changes in her teaching:

> Writers' Workshop has been a lot more fun for me this year. Since I'm not requiring a set number of published pieces, my fifth graders are using the time to experiment, read, learn from each other, and share their attempts. Some have even published. I think they have the idea now that publishing five pieces in ten days is missing the point. The main thing for me is that I'm enjoying what each person is doing and thinking and trying at the moment—not feeling uneasy because they're not where I want them to be three months from now. That's a great relief.
>
> Some wonderful writers are emerging and just about all of them have moved on in some way from where they were when they came to me. You know I teach in an inner-city school. My class is completely heterogeneous—racially, economically, in every way. I really feel my kids are so willing to accept each other's efforts because I am and they see that I am.

What seemed like a straightforward, external question about motivating students turned into a critical analysis of Anne's practice and her theory. She hears both her students and herself with new ears. "By using the child as our curricular informant, we have a self-correcting device built into our model of curriculum and curriculum development," as Jerry Harste and J. McInerney point out (1990, 304–5). Teacher research enables Anne, like other teacher-researchers, to listen to her informants, to tune in to these self-correcting devices. Her inquiries into the meanings of student behaviors have turned the categories of her original research question upside down. Anne now sees important ways in which her "reluctant writers" were neither reluctant nor non-composers, and she redefines a prolific writer as "reluctant." Furthermore, she has posed questions on several levels—about these four students, about the relationship between her own principles and her practice, about the purpose of Writers' Workshop in her curriculum, and about the nature of writing.

Doing this research didn't suddenly give Anne a new way of thinking— she's probably always been a questioner—but it supported and confirmed the value of such thinking, validated the time to pursue it further, provided conversation with other teacher-researchers about her issues, and yielded the clarification that comes from writing and revising. Teacher-researchers are often amazed at how conscious and articulate even young students can be or become when their knowing is valued. The same is true for teachers.

What does Anne know as a result of her research? She knows her students more fully. And she knows herself, especially the principles on which her practice is based. Awarenesses rather than hypotheses may be the fruit of teacher research. An awareness is something I carry with me that changes how I see and interpret and thus how I respond and act. In this sense it's a beginning rather than an end, which is why teacher-researchers can never go back to teaching as usual. As Cora Five, who has done research for years in her fifth-grade classroom, told me: "Once you do teacher research, everything becomes something to investigate."

Another teacher-researcher, Carol Avery (1987, 15), put it this way:

> There are no big conclusions coming out of the classroom researching process but there sure are some very powerful learnings. The whole process is open-ended. Researching does not bring answers but rather raises questions. It keeps opening doors. When I was a child I had a book and on the cover of that book was a little girl reading a book and so on. I think teacher researching is like that book cover. It offers the potential to keep going on and on. That's exciting to me.

For experienced teachers, teacher research provides an avenue for professional renewal and growth; for all teachers, including those just beginning, it offers a way of learning with dignity from our experiences. Professors teach most education courses and write the texts—manage the domain of knowledge—while cooperating teachers are valued for contributing to the domain of practice, of doing. Teachers' knowing and teachers' thinking are missing links. Prospective teachers, beginning teachers—all of us—need models of courageous, inquiring teachers. We need to see teachers in the process of thinking and learning.

Researching as a teacher can bring about the critical consciousness of oneself as a meaning maker that Paolo Freire talks of, a consciousness that is liberating and empowering. We look at our knowledge, our assumptions, our interpretations as our practice renders them tangible, as re-searching makes them visible, and as critical consciousness opens them to questioning. What we see then are not merely faces or voices or events but meanings—which re-form our practice.

## References

Alpert, A. 1991. "Just Like Lightning." In *Teacher Research: Guess Who's Learning,* edited by G. Bissex, 1–10. Storrs: Connecticut Writing Project, University of Connecticut.

Atwell, N. 1991. *Side by Side.* Portsmouth, N.H.: Heinemann.

Avery, C. 1987. "Traci: A Learning-Disabled Child in a Writing-Process Classroom." In *Seeing for Ourselves: Case-Study Research by Teachers of Writing,* edited by G. L. Bissex and R. H. Bullock, 59–76. Portsmouth, N.H.: Heinemann.

Carson, T. 1990. "What Kind of Knowing Is Critical Action Research?" *Theory into Practice* 29:167–73.

Fox, P. 1988. Unpublished case study. Northeastern University.

Harste, J., and J. McInerney. 1990. "Whole Language: Starting New Conversations." In *Portraits of Whole Language Classrooms,* edited by H. Mills and J. A. Clyde, 301–7. Portsmouth, N.H.: Heinemann.

McKay, F. 1987. "Roles and Strategies in College Writing Conferences." In *Seeing for Ourselves: Case-Study Research by Teachers of Writing,* edited by G. L. Bissex and R. H. Bullock, 77–101. Portsmouth, N.H.: Heinemann.

North, S. M. 1987. *The Making of Knowledge in Composition: Portrait of an Emerging Field.* Upper Montclair, N.J.: Boynton/Cook.

Ockerstrom, L. 1989. Unpublished case study. Northeastern University.

Schon, D. A. 1983. *The Reflective Practitioner: How Professionals Think in Action.* New York: Basic Books.

Scudder, S. H. 1992. "Take This Fish and Look at It." In *Community of Voices: Reading and Writing in the Disciplines,* edited by T. Fulwiler and A. W. Biddle, 641– 46. New York: Macmillan.

Sheehan, P. 1987. "On Becoming a Teacher Researcher." In *Seeing for Ourselves: Case-Study Research by Teachers of Writing,* edited by G. L. Bissex and R. H. Bullock, 145–63. Portsmouth, N.H.: Heinemann.

# 7 Teacher Lore: Learning about Teaching from Teachers

William Ayers
University of Illinois at Chicago

William H. Schubert
University of Illinois at Chicago

*William Ayers and William H. Schubert suggest that teachers learn from each other. In this overview of the Teacher Lore Project, they describe how they have pursued, through professional autobiography and other qualitative methods, "the practical art and wisdom" of teachers. Teacher learning occurs in many ways. This chapter is a compelling reminder that to understand this learning we must listen to the voices of teachers.*

---

Who understands the peculiar demands of teaching, the mind-wrecking and back-breaking moments of it, the forests of paperwork that surround it, the endless preparation for it, the invasiveness of it into every corner of a life? Who knows the ecstasies of it, its specific satisfactions, its dazzling transformative possibilities—and these are not merely for the learners, but, in an elusive and wonderfully interactive way, at least as powerfully for the teachers themselves? Who can say what teachers think they are up to, what they take to be the point of what they are doing, what it means for teachers to teach? Who indeed. To say that teachers are the ones who understand, know, and can say seems so obvious that it is beneath reporting. But in the often odd, sometimes upside-down world of social research, the obvious news must be reported and repeated: The secret of teaching is to be found in the local detail and the everyday life of teachers; teachers can be the richest and most useful source of knowledge about teaching; those who hope to understand teaching must turn at some point to teachers themselves. (Schubert and Ayers 1992, v)

## Background

There is a long tradition of teachers drawing on the knowledge and experiences of other teachers in their struggles to develop a stronger, more complete

The authors wish to thank Marilyn Geron for carefully typing this manuscript, and Ann Lopez for proofreading and commenting on it.

teaching practice. This is typically an informal affair: teachers peeking into one another's classrooms, picking up bits and pieces of knowledge in the lunchroom or the hallway, passing along some practical art or wisdom that has been effective in teaching. In teacher education the knowledge of experienced teachers is sanctified to some extent in the structure of practicum and student teaching experiences—the embodied assumption being that the novice will learn to teach in part through taking on the skills, techniques, and approaches of a more experienced guide.

Sometimes drawing on the knowledge and experiences of teachers is more formalized—framed as a coherent approach to inquiry and formalized as a program of research on teaching. Action research or participatory research has a long if checkered history stretching back to some of the early work of John Dewey in Chicago, continuing in Alice Miel's (1946 and 1952) work at Teachers College, and being carried on today in the efforts of Ann Lieberman (1988) and Linda Darling-Hammond (for instance, Robinson and Darling-Hammond 1994) in New York. Action research conceives of teaching as experimental, always in search of better teaching, and of teachers as intellectual practitioners best suited to inquire into the subtle problems arising in their own complex and dynamic classroom settings. Action researchers assume that teachers have in many ways already developed a useful approach to inquiry, and think of themselves as tapping into, perhaps extending, and making public something that is already there—these researchers are in a sense following along in the footsteps of teachers. The goal of action research is linked directly and immediately to improved practice.

Similarly, the teacher-as-researcher movement identified with Lawrence Stenhouse (1975) in England assumes a thoughtful, inquiring teacher functioning in an excruciatingly complex world that she or he is best situated to understand. Again teaching is thought of as experimental, and research as most useful when it is infused with the teacher's sense of immediacy and commitment. The teacher-as-researcher approach began by pairing practicing teachers with university researchers; they posed questions and reflected on problems and possibilities together. This led to formal meetings and published accounts by teachers, for teachers—and to a spiraling effect in which experienced teacher-researchers paired with other teachers to continue the process.

There is a wide range of other approaches—sometimes complementary to one another, other times contradictory—that draw upon teachers as a valued source of knowledge about teaching. Cognitive psychologists have tried to capture teachers' thinking through close observations, interviews, videotapes, and stimulated-recall interviews (Calderhead 1981), sometimes comparing expert, novice, and postulant teachers (Carter, Sabers, Kushing, Pinnegar, and Berliner 1987). Other researchers have conceived of teaching as a "reflective practice," as an "art," or as a "narrative," and have developed research programs based on autobiography (Pinar and Grumet 1976), on story or narrative

(Connelly and Clandinin 1988; 1991), on "connoisseurship" and artistic criticism (Eisner 1985; 1991), and on co-biography (Ayers 1989).

Teachers' first-person accounts are another source of knowledge about teaching. Such books as *Thirty-Six Children,* by Herb Kohl (1968), *How Children Fail,* by John Holt (1964), and *Teacher,* by Sylvia Ashton-Warner (1963) remain classics. There is also a worthwhile literature about memorable teachers, for example, *A Teacher at Work,* by Margaret Yonemura (1986) and *Education as Adventure: Lessons from the Second Grade,* by John Nicholls and Sue Hazzard (1993). There are useful fictional accounts of teachers teaching like *Goodbye, Mr. Chips,* by James Hilton, and important phenomenological renderings like Max van Manen's *The Tone of Teaching* (1986) and *The Tact of Teaching* (1991).

The Teacher Lore Project fits into this overarching tradition. In 1985 a group of experienced teachers and principals, each a doctoral student at the University of Illinois at Chicago, asked Bill Schubert to organize a study group focused on progressive educational philosophy and practice. As participants discussed John Dewey, George S. Counts, William H. Kilpatrick, L. Thomas Hopkins, and others, their interest and attention turned and returned to contrast the power of experiential, practical knowledge with the lack of teacher participation in most sanctified research on teaching. They wondered: Where are the voices of teachers? What knowledge and experiences do teachers consider most worthwhile? Why do great classroom teachers typically retire into obscurity, without being asked what they learned? What wisdom is being missed, what lessons lost?

As a first step, this group decided to seek out experienced teachers who were acknowledged by colleagues, students, or supervisors to be outstanding. A broad group of Chicago-area educators was asked to name teachers who inspired them, who were effective with a range of students, who stood out among their peers, who found ways to bring teaching and learning alive in classrooms. There was no attempt to define "outstanding" in a precise operational sense, nor to determine quality beyond reputation.

Teacher lore differs from the larger corpus of teacher research in that it gives great credence to the insights, ideas, and tentative conclusions that guide teachers' lives. This includes their repertoires of teaching strategies and approaches and the more intangible aspects of personality that grow out of and influence their teaching (Millies 1989). Traditionally, the study of teachers has been more akin to the *study of* or *study about* others, as interesting phenomena to be reported on, in much the same way that ethologists might study baboons. In contrast, the Teacher Lore Project holds that teachers are more than curious objects; instead, they are considered to be complicated human beings who seek to create meaning and purpose through interaction with and reflection on the contexts of their experiences. We assume that by sharing insights they have derived from experience, teachers and the researchers who interact with them will benefit from that collective reflection. The sharing of stories and insights will help others reflect upon and perhaps reconstruct their own teaching and conception of teaching.

The term "lore" was selected because we see our work as part of a long tradition in many fields of acquiring knowledge from experience and its context. The work on the lore of children by Opie and Opie (e.g., 1959) is a salient example. While the Teacher Lore Project seeks lore in the form of knowledge that has guiding power in teachers' lives, we have also collected extensive bibliographical material on a whole range of different types of writing on teaching and teachers—from biography and autobiography, to histories and sociologies of teachers and teaching, to artistic portrayals of teachers in stories, novels, and films, and even to "how to" advice books for teachers (see chapter 9 of Schubert and Ayers 1992).

When the Teacher Lore Project began, we interviewed the teachers who had been identified by others (e.g., administrators, fellow teachers, union representatives, professors, parents) as among the best teachers they knew, or who had won awards for their teaching. Nominated teachers were interviewed concerning their assumptions and beliefs, their approaches and techniques, their experiential knowledge and accumulated wisdom about teaching. An archive of teaching has been growing and developing ever since. Participants in the original seminar as well as other doctoral students and colleagues have continued to contribute to this archive, and to supplement it with observations, further interviews, and deep reflections. In some cases these have been shaped into more disciplined and formal studies, for example, a special issue of the *Kappa Delta Pi Record* (Summer 1990), articles and chapters (e.g., Schubert 1990, 1991), and several dissertations (Hulsebosch 1988; Jagla 1989; Koerner 1989; Melnick 1988; Millies 1989; Ponticell 1991; Stanford 1991).

Our book, *Teacher Lore: Learning from Our Own Experience* (Schubert and Ayers 1992), is one milepost in this ongoing project. The heart of the book is a set of chapters that closely examines teachers' values, knowledge, and experiences. One chapter portrays a single teacher and highlights the way teaching saturates her being, forging dimensions of personality, beliefs, approaches, and repertoires (drawn from Millies 1989). Another chapter focuses on images teachers have of themselves and their work, images that range from the mundane to the ideal (drawn from Koerner 1989). A third chapter examines the use of intuition and imagination by exemplary teachers (drawn from Jagla 1989), while a fourth looks at the uses teachers make of their students' out-of-school lives (drawn from Melnick 1988). Finally, another chapter inquires into teachers' perspectives on parents, and the relationships teachers hope for and build with families (drawn from Hulsebosch 1988). Following are highlights of some of the studies that have contributed to the Teacher Lore Project to date.

## Sampling the Studies

Initially, our interviews of teachers identified assumptions that were progressive in character. For instance, many teachers could be categorized as holding, implicitly if not explicitly, assumptions or basic beliefs and orientations that characterized their work as involving:

1. holistic, situational problem solving;
2. enjoyable interaction with students;
3. an interest in students' non-school experiences;
4. love and compassion for students;
5. a sense that teaching holds great importance;
6. a search for students' strengths;
7. a desire to continuously revise one's sense of meaning;
8. a quest for the worthwhile and just;
9. a search for developmentally appropriate teaching;
10. ongoing self-education.

These generalizations point to directions that may open a range of productive possibilities for other teachers and would-be teachers, and yet we realized that our attempts to construct abstract generalizations about our early findings were less powerful than the concrete stories themselves, stories that were infused with urgency and immediacy. One conclusion we drew from our initial study was that we should describe the concrete experience, the context, and the situations from which teacher comments grew. We also concluded that as interpretive researchers who assume that we are each instruments of our own inquiry, we must look again and again at our own assumptions and experiences as well as comments we deem insightful. Because of the distinct orientations each of us has developed from the unique contexts of our lives, we bring different notions to bear, we interpret the same data (or interview conversations) differently. For instance, from the same tapes that yielded the above generalizations, Mari Koerner derived some additional themes. Among the themes she found were the following:*

1. a deep sense of responsibility for student learning and motivation;
2. high expectations for students and themselves;
3. self-blame if students fail or are unmotivated;

---

*A longer version of this list and another similar to the list presented above appears in Schubert 1991, 220–22.

  4.  an academic task orientation;
  5.  the desire to create a warm, supportive environment;
  6.  excitement that spurs student excitement about learning;
  7.  eagerness to learn from any resource that might be available;
  8.  wariness of the value of theory;
  9.  dissatisfaction with teacher education courses;
 10.  belief in the importance of student interest as a basis for teaching and
      learning.

A central point here is that it may be quite important to provide more than one interpretation for qualitative data sets, especially for interviews. This could give new meaning to the term "secondary data analysis," typically reserved for quantitative studies of large data sets or tapes. In the case of qualitative research, such as the Teacher Lore Project, the purpose of having other sets of interpretive lenses is not so much to confirm or disconfirm previous conclusions, nor to achieve replication of observations, nor to provide inter-rater reliability. Rather, it is suggested because it provides multiple perspectives. The analogy of film criticism may be helpful: one might read what several film critics say on any one film in order to enrich the range of viewpoints one has for interpretation and discussion. Thus, Mari Koerner's experience enabled her to see dimensions of the interviews that were not perceived by earlier interpreters. This provided a seedbed for further discussion of the issues, such as whether contradictions were present or whether they were only apparent, and indicative of greater complexity in teachers' lives than we had earlier imagined.

The experience of and dialogue about multiple interpretations led those who designed dissertations on teacher lore to seek others to join the interpretive process. Sometimes that took the usual form of submitting interpretations and data (interviews and observations) to faculty members who were members of doctoral committees. More novelly, student researchers would ask other doctoral students to read and comment on their interpretations, and a kind of research collective emerged. Further, most of these researchers involved the teachers studied by asking them to respond to the interpretations as well. The dialogue that ensued from such sharing led to more complex, integrated, and subtly nuanced interpretations.

Each of the dissertations thus far completed deals with a different aspect of teacher lore. More accurately, each dissertation contributes a dimension to what teacher lore has now become. We suspect that future dissertations on the topic will continue to expand and refine the image of what teacher lore is. It is intended to be an evolving image.

Suzanne Millies (1989) developed a conceptual scheme that could be utilized by others who engage in teacher lore or related research. Investigating and contrasting a veteran and a novice English teacher, she established three primary foci: (1) pedagogical personality, (2) pedagogical assumptions, and (3) pedagogical repertoire. These have helped us reflect on major features of teacher lore. A dimension of the pedagogical personality of the veteran teacher (less developed in the novice) was her capacity to use the literature she taught as a basis for insight into her own relation to students. She commented:

> If you look back to *The Scarlet Letter,* there are always facets of society that are making value judgments on other facets; we have to find some way to cope with all of this around us. Adolescents are very conscious of being judged. Most often they're hard on themselves; they judge themselves daily. The rest of us as adults are always showing kids faults, not virtues . . . the one thing they did wrong and the one thing they forgot, and they don't get a lot of stroking . . . although I have a very strict moral background, . . . I can listen to their problems and not judge them. (Millies 1989, 54)

The need to know students has been a powerful finding in the Teacher Lore Project. Teachers speak of the need to build teaching upon knowledge of student experiences, both in and out of school. Carol Melnick's (1988) dissertation has informed her published writing about teachers' use of non-school experiences in students' lives. In a book devoted to encouraging teachers to be more reflective, Melnick quotes an English teacher she identifies as Eugene Meyers:

> Some teachers think it's okay to throw in some occasional student participation, just a few crumbs. What I'm saying is that the student has to be fully integrated into the process, even into the goals of the process. I teach English and my goals are English Goals. But I know that my students want to communicate effectively. Once they admit that they want to communicate effectively, I try to suggest ways in which they can do that. But they start out believing in their goal, and they're involved in the process. That's the only way they're going to learn anything. (Melnick 1992)

In an attempt to demonstrate that good teaching makes valuable linkages between student lives and academic work, Melnick again draws upon Meyers:

> When Eugene teaches narrative point of view, he tries to show that this perspective allows the author certain strengths and limitations. In order to help students understand first- and third-person narration conceptually, he gives two assignments. He has them write a fairy tale, such as *The Three Bears,* from a first-person point of view. This changes their perception because the reader does not know what the three bears are doing; [the reader] only knows what goes on in Goldilocks' mind. In the second assignment the students write an autobiographical story from a

third-person point of view. While this perspective is unnatural, he is using students' autobiographical experience to teach them literary concepts. (Melnick 1991, 207)

Such involvement of students in imaginative activity invokes the topic of teachers' own uses of imagination. Virginia Jagla (1989), for example, interviewed and observed teachers who have reputations for imaginative teaching. An award-winning teacher whom she calls Erica, one of several studied, describes imagination thus:

> Imagination is picturing in your mind what will transpire or is likely to take place. I think teachers do that when they are planning ahead, making lesson plans. . . . I actually picture more images in my mind than I used to and I think that's helpful. I image when making the plans and then when evaluating them afterwards. . . . Some people don't visualize at all. I usually have a dialogue with myself. I have a conversation about the possibilities of what could happen. (Jagla in Schubert and Ayers 1992, 64)

While Jagla's imaginative and intuitive teachers reflected from quite varied perspectives, each perspective added enrichment to our notions of imagination and intuition. It is also interesting to juxtapose imagination in the lives of teachers with teachers' images of their work. This is the subject that Mari Koerner (1989) investigated. Recurrent themes include such images as hard workers, guides, professionals, creators of the body electric (drawing a classroom community variation of Walt Whitman's metaphor), collaborators, and perquisitors. The latter, the thorough searcher, captures the laudatory implications of each of the foregoing. These images contrast vividly with other images these same teachers felt just as strongly represented their work: ciphers, subordinates, jugglers, and cattle. Regarding the latter, a teacher called Pat said, "It's very degrading. You feel sort of like a bunch of cattle, you know" (Koerner 1989, 108). Koerner continues, "The image of a herd erases the individual differences which may exist. . . . It takes the notion of crowd and makes it inhuman and inhumane. Cattle are prodded, they are not talked to or with. Their needs are irrelevant compared to the needs of the people who own them and direct them" (Koerner 1989, 109). Contrast this image with Bob's under the perquisitor image:

> What I do, day to day, is wonderful. It's exciting. It's always different. I make it change. I like it to be considerably different each year. I enjoy being on my feet, being forced to be imaginative. . . . I find that environment to be very exhilarating. (Koerner 1989, 101)

It is interesting to note that the cattle metaphor and the perquisitor image are from the same profession, sometimes even the same person, and that the complexity of teaching can embrace wide contradictions.

The contradictions and compatibilities between the images of excellence that teachers have for their work and their sense of possibilities are portrayed by Judith Ponticell (1991). Based on essays written by twelve high school teachers who varied considerably in years of experience, expertise, and school location, and two follow-up interviews each with nine of them, Ponticell's study weaves teacher commentary and interpretation to categorize their beliefs about excellence and possibility in terms of (1) substantive knowledge, (2) human relations skills, and (3) transformational skills. She found the relationship between excellence and possibility to be highly complex, requiring an understanding of five interactive systems:

1. beliefs about self;
2. beliefs about teaching;
3. beliefs about students;
4. beliefs about learning;
5. beliefs about school contexts.

The ways in which teachers reconceptualize their images of excellence and begin to see the possibility of their actualization has been and is being explored as parts of several studies of teacher education, parent-teacher relations, and supervision. Grace Stanford's (1991) dissertation studied sources of student teachers' knowledge of teaching, in a sense testing the old adage that we teach the way we have been taught. As might be surmised, she discovered that these sources include examples from teachers that student teachers once had, and other sources as well, such as experiences with family, with subject matter as learners, in student teaching, and with children in such activities as coaching, babysitting, tutoring, scout leadership, and camp counseling, among others.

Realizing that much of teacher education occurs on the job and that much of that stems from interaction with parents, Patricia Hulsebosch (1988) drew upon feminist literature and focused on communication between mothers and women teachers. By relating interviews with teachers to extant literature on parental involvement in schools, she was able to sketch profiles of high-involvement and low-involvement teachers. Her study suggests that high-involvement teachers have more of several characteristics that have traditionally been considered feminine, such as granting primacy to childhood, emphasizing relationships, being nurturing, being responsive, and seeing the potential in differences.

The active involvement of supervisors is still another standpoint from which the lore of teachers might be investigated. Marilee Ewing, a school principal, is developing a study of teachers' images of (i.e., preferences for) good supervisors, and Richard Best, also a principal, is looking at the role of the principal as teacher educator. These studies contribute in different ways to a related dimension, one that might be dubbed "supervisor lore." Related to this, and even less examined, is a study of high school department chairs and their work, by Jill Wettersten (1992). The education of teachers whose education is from a considerably different orientation (both preservice and inservice) was developed by Wayne Carroll (1992), in a study of the basic beliefs of Waldorf School teachers, whose education derives from the work of Rudolf Steiner. Another principal, Yvonne Minor (1992), has reconstructed cases of mentoring in which she has been involved. These and numerous other studies that are currently in stages of conception and incubation continue to give new shape and direction to the Teacher Lore Project and its varied offshoots.

## Some Conclusions

All of these studies are based on teachers' own words and ideas, sometimes on autobiographical reflection and on telling stories about teaching, frequently on interpreting teachers' perspectives. The studies confirm the power of the voice of the teacher, a voice that is often urgent, full of investment, hope, and passion. We are convinced that outstanding teachers are thoughtful, caring people who reflect continuously on their work, and yet are seldom tapped as valued resources for an understanding of teaching. These teachers build upon experiences as a basis for crafting responses to new problems and as a framework for imagining different, more effective approaches. They continuously monitor progress and adjust practice to meet unique demands and needs. These teachers told us frequently that, far from being an intrusion into their work, the experience of the interviews themselves provided an opportunity they longed for but usually lacked—the chance to formally "debrief" their teaching practice.

While we are not overly concerned with the problem of perimeters and boundaries—we embrace a wide range of approaches and methods and forms of inquiry—what distinguishes teacher lore from many other projects focused on teacher thinking or teacher knowledge is its hearty regard for teachers' own insights and opinions. Much of the study of teachers out there is *about* teachers and *of* teachers, but seldom *for* or *by* teachers (Schubert and Lopez-Schubert 1981). In teacher lore we are interested in what teachers have learned, or what they think they have learned. We are not seeking the truth of teaching exactly, but more modestly, perhaps, the meaning of teaching to those who have lived it and practiced it. Teacher lore, like many other interpretive and qualitative approaches to inquiry, is in part an "experiment in equality" (Portelli 1991).

Teacher lore is storytelling. It is a living thing—a work-in-progress—which is by its nature unfinished, provisional, and partial. This is in part because of the complexity and diversity embodied in teaching, but also be-cause stories of teaching (and living) are always being revised in light of current choices, understandings, and experiences. In other words, a particular teacher's story of a teaching past is never immutable, solid, and fixed—even memory and myth are in the service of an ever-changing present. Teacher lore is an unfinished business—inexhaustible, open, fluid.

Teacher lore is subjective (but not in a pejorative sense); our goal is not to replace an old orthodoxy with a new one, to substitute some discredited truth with an imagined new one. As we see it, the truth of teaching is elusive. Teacher lore focuses on meanings for actors in situations. Context is impor-tant; meaning, intention, and action are crucial. Teacher lore, then, is not constructed on a base of whim, prejudice, or passing preference—a focus on meaning makes its own demands. Teacher lore hones in on meaning, and in this regard unlocking the hopes and dreams and passions of teachers is not a digression—it is essential science (in the European tradition of human sci-ences). If readers wish to turn to a body of literature to bolster theoretical defensibility, much of the Teacher Lore Project has been influenced by the philosophical writings of John Dewey.

Consonant with its origins in a graduate student study group that grew out of a course on John Dewey and other theorists of progressive education, the Teacher Lore Project has evolved with Deweyan principles. Perhaps the best way to describe Dewey's central principles is to look at the larger corpus of his work, both including and beyond his work on education. Since the idea of education writ large penetrates all of Dewey's work (from metaphysics to epistemology, and from aesthetics, ethics, and axiology to logic and politics), it is impossible to treat these perennial dimensions of philosophy in Dewey's work without addressing education.

In *Logic: The Theory of Inquiry* (1938), Dewey argues for a logic or sense of reason that grows out of the context of inquiry. Much to the chagrin of logicians who saw logic as syllogistic études or even propositional arguments, Dewey's emphasis on logic embedded in lived experience seemed anathema. Nonetheless, it persisted, to become an intellectual pillar of pragmatism's epistemology. Dewey holds that we come to know a situation, not by detached induction from it nor even by hypothetical deduction about it, but principally by interacting with it. From such interaction we gain insights about situations encountered, and are not duped into the tenets of research, misappropriated from the physical sciences, that put credence in the will-o'-the-wisp of certain knowledge, laws, and overblown generalizations (see Dewey 1929b, 1929c).

In the Teacher Lore Project we share these assumptions of Dewey's, noting that the teacher is a neglected and necessary source of insight about education, even about teaching. Who, more than the teacher, has learned about teaching from the standpoint of interaction with the phenomenon under inquiry? In most cases we have discovered that teachers' interactions with the problematic aspects of their situations has resulted in insights which serve as a basis for decision and action in continuing their work. Issues of decision and action obviously invoke ethics, and Dewey's works on ethics are legion (e.g., Dewey and Tufts 1908; Dewey 1922). Dewey expanded Charles Sanders Peirce's founding principle of pragmatism, that the truth value of any proposition resides in its consequences in action. Any inquirer must attend to the overt and covert consequences of his or her decisions and actions, with special note given to ethical and political consequences. Teachers, then, we assume, are both creators and repositories of experience in decision making and action.

In his *Sources of a Science of Education* (1929c), Dewey develops a broad image of educational science or research that encompasses teachers' inquiries throughout their everyday experience. He concludes by saying:

> The sources of educational science are any portions of ascertained knowledge that enter into the heart, head, and hands of educators, and which by entering in, render the performance of the educational function more enlightened, more humane, more truly educational than it was before. But there is no way to discover what is "more truly educational" except by the continuation of the educational act itself. The discovery is never made; it is always in the making. . . . Education is by its very nature an endless circle or spiral. It is an activity which *includes* science within itself. In its very process it sets more problems to be further studied, which then react into the education process to change it still further, and thus demand more thought, more science, and so on, in everlasting sequence. (Dewey 1929c, 76–77)

To capture the discoveries of teachers, their insights "in the making," is a central mission of teacher lore. To enable these insights to be shared with other teachers is its further mission. These missions require a sensitivity to the kind of flowing, ever-changing metaphysics of nature in which human nature and educational experience are caught up (Dewey 1922, 1929a). Moreover, such sensitivity is largely aesthetic. Dewey contends that "art has been the means of keeping alive the sense of purposes that outrun evidence and of meanings that transcend indurated habit" (Dewey 1934a, 348). Teacher lore, then, is in part a portrayal of teachers as they exercise aesthetic imagination to give pattern and meaning to their experience. Such portrayals are only partly sketches of what teachers have come to understand; they are illustrations of their wonderings as well. Dewey said: "Philosophy is said to begin in wonder and end in understanding. Art departs from what has been understood and ends in wonder" (Dewey 1934a, 270).

To claim that teachers' wonderings are worth sharing requires a faith in human nature that is indeed rare, yet it is a faith that can become the kind of "common faith" (Dewey 1934b) that is the basis of Dewey's religious philosophy. Such faith is a foundation stone of democracy because it leads to the continuous reconstructing of a public space (see Dewey 1927). The capturing and sharing of teachers' reflectivity (in its aesthetic, moral, and political dimensions) is what we in the Teacher Lore Project value as a resource for teachers that will enable them to more fully realize Dewey's definition of education, as stated in his magnum opus on education, *Democracy and Education*:

> We thus reach a technical definition of education: It is that reconstruction or reorganization of experience which adds to the meaning of experience, and which increases ability to direct the course of subsequent experience. (Dewey 1916, 76)

To enable teachers to realize this image of education more fully requires teacher lore and more. It necessitates explorations of a wider context of lore, which would further the Deweyan notion of integrating the many subsystems of educational life, in and out of school. Some examples of further explorations follow.

**Foreground**

Sometimes we find that the most useful knowledge is already there, and we are in this sense merely following ahead as we tap into and make public this knowledge. Justice Holmes spoke of small children who "follow ahead"; they run ahead of their parents, looking back frequently because they are actually following. Spinning off from the Teacher Lore Project is a wide range of activities and projects involving research, scholarly reflection, teacher education, staff development, and school improvement. Perhaps we, too, are following ahead as we recommend the need to study them.

*Student lore.* What can children and young people tell us about teaching and teachers, about curriculum and the purposes of schooling, about the place of school in their larger life patterns? This is the subject of a new book series at the State University of New York Press, the Student Lore series (William Schubert, series editor). Several dissertations are being developed on this general topic, and we are working on articles and books that reveal more about the educational experience of students in school and society. For example, Norman Weston is concluding a dissertation that investigates the ways in which seven- and eight-year-old students actually experience curriculum in an inner-city school and in an affluent suburban school, and Marie Mason is beginning a dissertation on the way junior high school students in a predominantly African American inner-city school develop their dreams and aspirations. At a much different level of student life, Ray Olesinski (1992) has investigated student selection of learning experiences in a self-designed medical education program. Nicholls and Hazzard (1993) have developed insights gleaned from becoming carefully attuned to what second graders have to say about their school experiences. Moreover, Bill Ayers is working on a manuscript with several teachers that is tentatively titled *Go Back and Circle the Verbs: Moral Classrooms in an Immoral Society*. As these teachers tried to come to grips with pressing moral and political problems, one of them perceptively used the "circle the verbs" phrase to exemplify schools' too-frequent lack of response to fundamental social issues. We are working on other collections of students' stories, particularly in urban areas, some of which we hope to have written by students themselves (such as those students described by Sally Hampton in chapter 8 of this volume).

*Family lore.* How does education occur in the context of family life, the concrete realities of the range of actual families we find in our communities? How do families, including those that educate their children at home as an alternative to schooling, develop their learning environments (Schubert, Schubert, and Schubert 1986)?

*Community lore.* What does the wider community expect of schools, and what impact do other community institutions (juvenile court, church, media) have on educational experiences? The work of Bernardine Dohrn (1992) and colleagues at Northwestern University is exploring aspects of juvenile court, the contexts of lives surrounding it, and implications for the rights of children. We feel strongly that curriculum and teaching need to be explored in the many non-school spheres of life (Schubert 1986, 1981; Schubert and Lopez-Schubert 1981).

*Educational lore in literature and the arts.* What has been lost in educational research by neglecting stories and other artistic renditions that enhance understanding of teaching and curriculum? This is beginning to be explored in theory (Coles 1989), in educators' autobiographies (Willis and Schubert 1991), and in proposals for curriculum design and development (Egan 1986).

*Professor lore.* What do professors of education learn from reflecting on their own teaching? A major step in this direction in the field of curriculum has been taken by Sears and Marshall (1990), who enabled author-teachers to focus critically on four salient dimensions of their teaching: self, teacher, community, and field. Such reflective learning by professors of education is also revealed vividly in the new journal *Teaching Education*.

*The lore of inservice teacher education.* How do teachers become educated after college, apart from graduate school? What kinds of relationships develop for their growth through formally designed and informally evolving forms of education in their lives as teachers? We have explored this question by offering teachers in the Chicago area opportunities to design inservice learning experiences around two questions: (1) What would you like to work on that could enhance your life with students? (2) What would you like to learn that you believe would help you become a more fully developed person? Teachers who worked on such projects claimed that pursuit of each question enabled both personal and professional growth.

*The oral tradition of lore in teaching.* All of the above are skewed in the direction of written lore. To develop a greater repertoire of written lore on different aspects of teaching (and education generally) is a large part of our goal. However, to stop at that point may be elitist. It may exclude those who have neither the time nor the inclination to write. Instead, many practicing teachers need opportunities to share, interpret, analyze, and evaluate the lore at their disposal on a daily basis. We encourage the development of networks and other situations wherein teachers and other educators share orally the lore within them. We are convinced by our explorations of lore among educators that the surface has barely been scratched. We need to work together to reopen oral traditions that once dominated human interchange, and enable teachers, students, families, communities, literary and artistic sources, professors, and inservice educators to teach one another, through both the written and the spoken word.

## References

Ashton-Warner, S. 1963. *Teacher.* New York: Simon and Schuster.

Ayers, W. 1989. *The Good Preschool Teacher: Six Teachers Reflect on Their Lives.* New York: Teachers College Press.

Calderhead, J. 1981. "Stimulated Recall: A Method for Research on Teaching." *British Journal of Educational Psychology* 51, no. 2:211–17.

Carroll, W. M. 1992. An Inquiry into the Nature of Waldorf School Teachers: Gaining Perspectives through Teacher Lore. Ph.D. diss., University of Illinois at Chicago.

Carter, K., D. Sabers, K. Kushing, S. Pinnegar, and D. C. Berliner. 1987. "Processing and Using Information about Students: A Study of Expert, Novice, and Postulant Teachers." *Teaching and Teacher Education* 3, no. 2:147–57.

Coles, R. 1989. *The Call of Stories: Teaching and the Moral Imagination.* Boston: Houghton Mifflin.

Connelly, F. M., and D. J. Clandinin. 1988. *Teachers as Curriculum Planners: Narratives of Experience.* New York: Teachers College Press.

———. 1990. "Stories of Experience and Narrative Inquiry." *Educational Researcher* 19, no. 5:2–14.

Dewey, J. 1916. *Democracy and Education.* New York: Macmillan.

———. 1922. *Human Nature and Conduct: An Introduction to Social Psychology.* New York: Holt.

———. 1927. *The Public and Its Problems.* New York: Holt.

———. 1929a. *Experience and Nature.* 2d ed. New York: Norton.

———. 1929b. *The Quest for Certainty: A Study of the Relation of Knowledge and Action.* New York: Minton, Balch.

————. 1929c. *The Sources of a Science of Education*. New York: Liveright.

————. 1934a. *Art as Experience*. New York: Minton, Balch.

————. 1934b. *A Common Faith*. New Haven: Yale University Press.

————. 1938. *Logic, the Theory of Inquiry*. New York: Holt.

Dewey, J., and J. H. Tufts. 1908. *Ethics*. New York: Holt.

Dohrn, B. 1992. Leastwise of the Land: Children and the Law. Paper presented at the Children at Risk Conference, May, Bergen, Norway.

Egan, K. 1986. *Teaching as Story Telling: An Alternative Approach to Teaching and Curriculum in the Elementary School*. Chicago: University of Chicago Press.

Eisner, E. W. 1985. *The Educational Imagination: On the Design and Evaluation of School Programs*. 2d ed. New York: Macmillan.

————. 1991. *The Enlightened Eye: Qualitative Inquiry and the Enhancement of Educational Practice*. New York: Macmillan.

Holt, J. C. 1964. *How Children Fail*. New York: Pitman.

Hulsebosch, P. L. 1988. Significant Others: Teachers' Perspectives on Parent Involvement. Ph.D. diss., University of Illinois at Chicago.

Jagla, V. M. 1989. In Pursuit of the Elusive Image: An Inquiry into Teachers' Everyday Use of Imagination and Intuition. Ph.D. diss., University of Illinois at Chicago.

Koerner, M. E. 1989. Teachers' Images of Their Work: A Descriptive Study. Ph.D. diss., University of Illinois at Chicago.

Kohl, H. 1968. *Thirty-Six Children*. New York: Signet.

Lieberman, A., ed. 1988. *Building a Professional Culture in Schools*. New York: Teachers College Press.

Melnick, C. R. 1988. A Search for Teachers' Knowledge of the Out-of-School Curriculum of Students' Lives. Ph.D. diss., University of Illinois at Chicago.

————. 1991. "Linking the In- and Out-of-School Curriculum." *International Journal of Educational Research* 15:201–14.

————. 1992. "Two Stories of Reflective Teaching and Educational Inquiry." In *Reflective Teaching: Becoming an Inquiring Teacher,* edited by J. G. Henderson. New York: Macmillan.

Miel, A. 1946. *Changing the Curriculum: A Social Process*. New York: Appleton-Century.

————. 1952. *Cooperative Procedures in Learning*. New York: Bureau of Publications, Teachers College, Columbia University.

Millies, P. S. G. 1989. The Mental Lives of Teachers. Ph.D. diss., University of Illinois at Chicago.

Minor, Y. S. 1992. Three Case Studies on Teacher Mentoring. Ph.D. diss., University of Illinois at Chicago.

Nicholls, J. G., and S. P. Hazzard. 1993. *Education as Adventure: Lessons from the Second Grade*. New York: Teachers College Press.

Olesinski, R. L. 1993. When Students Construct Curricula: The Selection and Organization of Learning Experiences. Ph.D. diss., University of Illinois at Chicago.

Opie, I., and P. Opie. 1959. *The Lore and Language of Schoolchildren*. Oxford: Clarendon Press.

Pinar, W. F., and M. R. Grumet. 1976. *Toward a Poor Curriculum.* Dubuque, Iowa: Kendall/Hunt.

Ponticell, J. A. 1991. What's Possible: Teachers' Beliefs about Teaching Excellence and Possibility. Ph.D. diss., University of Illinois at Chicago.

Portelli, A. 1991. *The Death of Luigi Trastulli and Other Stories: Form and Meaning in Oral History.* Albany: State University of New York Press.

Robinson, S. P., and L. Darling-Hammond. 1994. "Change for Collaboration and Collaboration for Change: Transforming Teaching through School-University Partnerships." In *Professional Development Schools: Schools for Developing a Profession,* edited by L. Darling-Hammond. New York: Teachers College Press.

Schubert, W. H. 1990. "Acknowledging Teachers' Experiential Knowledge: Reports from the Teacher Lore Project." *Kappa Delta Pi Record* 26, no. 4:99–100. The entire issue, edited by G. Ponder, is devoted to teacher lore, including essays by V. Jagla, P. Hulsebosch, C. Melnick, S. Millies, and M. Koerner.

Schubert, W. H. 1981. "Knowledge about Out-of-School Curriculum." *Educational Forum* 45, no. 2:185–98.

———. 1986. *Curriculum: Perspective, Paradigm, and Possibility.* New York: Macmillan.

———. 1991. "Teacher Lore: A Basis for Understanding Praxis." In *Stories Lives Tell: Narrative and Dialogue in Education,* edited by C. Witherall and N. Noddings. New York: Teachers College Press.

Schubert, W. H., and W. C. Ayers, eds. 1992. *Teacher Lore: Learning from Our Own Experience.* White Plains, N. Y.: Longman.

Schubert, W. H., and A. L. Lopez-Schubert. 1981. "Toward Curricula That Are of, by, and Therefore for Students." *Journal of Curriculum Theorizing* 3, no. 1:239–51.

Schubert, W. H., A. L. L. Schubert, and H. A. Schubert. 1986. "Familial Theorizing and 'Literatures' That Facilitate It." *Journal of Thought* 21, no. 2:61–73.

Sears, J. T., and J. D. Marshall, eds. 1989. *Teaching and Thinking about Curriculum: Critical Inquiries.* New York: Teachers College Press.

Stanford, G. C. 1991. Learning to Teach: A Descriptive Study of Prospective Teachers' Knowledge of Teaching. Ph.D. diss., University of Illinois at Chicago.

Stenhouse, L. A. 1975. *Introduction to Curriculum Research and Development.* London: Heinemann.

van Manen, M. 1986. *The Tone of Teaching.* Portsmouth, N.H.: Heinemann.

———. 1991. *The Tact of Teaching: The Meaning of Pedagogical Thoughtfulness.* Albany: State University of New York Press.

Weston, N. 1993. The Experienced Curriculum in Two Primary Classrooms: An Exploration of Student Lore. Ph.D. diss., University of Illinois at Chicago.

Wettersten, J. 1992. Successful Leadership Practices of High School Department Chairs in a "Loosely Coupled System." Ph.D. diss., University of Illinois at Chicago.

Willis, G., and W. H. Schubert, eds. 1991. *Reflections from the Heart of Educational Inquiry: Understanding Curriculum and Teaching through the Arts.* Albany: State University of New York Press.

Yonemura, M. V. 1986. *A Teacher at Work: Professional Development and the Early Childhood Educator.* New York: Teachers College Press.

# 8 Teacher Change: Overthrowing the Myth of One Teacher, One Classroom

Sally Hampton
Fort Worth Independent School District

*Teacher thinking does not develop, nor do teachers learn, in a vacuum. Too often our discussion of teachers and teaching neglect the real constraints under which they labor. Sally Hampton, herself a school administrator, describes the seemingly impenetrable barriers to teacher—and student—learning. Then she inspiringly describes how a teacher and a group of low-achieving inner-city students have succeeded in overcoming the constraints to arrive at real learning.*

---

Few would argue with the idea that our schools do a poor job of educating many students—poor students and students of color especially. Our schools also fail a great many mainstream learners who graduate with acceptable grade-point averages and high standardized test scores but with a very limited understanding about what they have studied. Schools fail because of their inability to change. In spite of a wealth of research about learning and thinking that should have fostered innovation, in spite of blue-ribbon commissions that have collectively wrung their hands over lack of student achievement, in spite of politicians elected to office on school reform platforms, American education today looks pretty much as it has for the past hundred years.

As those who work in teacher education increasingly send into the schools bright, dedicated professionals, we must be aware that these people face a tremendous challenge. They go to work in a hostile environment which will not nurture their professional development but, in fact, will subvert it. I worry that these new teachers will leave the profession—and the students who need them badly—because they are overwhelmed by the obstacles that school systems place before them. Yet, if we are to reform schools, these new teachers are our best hope. I would argue that we must all become more realistic about the challenge we are preparing these people to take on, and I would argue further that we must work to guard these new teachers against the inertia and apathy which characterize public school systems. Most important, we ourselves, as educators, must be prepared to support new teachers in very aggressive ways. We must become actively involved in school reform.

122

I read a good deal about how we might reform our nation's schools; and I am always amazed when people argue that the best way to change schools is to focus our efforts on changing individual teachers (or small groups of teachers). Obviously school reform requires teacher change but it shocks me when someone suggests that one teacher/one classroom at a time is enough to make an impact. The idea of one teacher at a time assumes that the power of the classroom is such that it can overcome problems created by the system of which the classroom is only a part. Yet research tells us different. We know that each level of the school organization produces results that affect the next lower level. The next *lower* level—the shock waves move down, not up. The theory is that the energy created by one highly committed, innovative teacher is sufficient to inspire other teachers to embrace new views of teaching and learning that eventually will permeate the entire system. The reality is that things don't work that way.

Schools reward certain kinds of students and certain kinds of teachers, and the culture of the schoolhouse does not typically nurture change. Only in theory is the teacher as an agent of change viewed in a positive light. In most schools, in practice, there is reverence for the status quo, and the system has both overt and covert methods of subverting the efforts of those who challenge traditional concepts of learning and teaching.

School districts, organized like factories of the industrial age, are characterized by a very controlling central office system (and sometimes an equally controlling school board); by lockstep, disconnected learning; by arbitrary, discrete blocks of time; and by very rigid and mechanical lesson designs. Teachers are expected to conduct their classes along fairly standard guidelines, and an entire structure—from textbooks to testing to report cards—exists to support those guidelines. It is myth that a teacher may close a classroom door and conduct learning in ways independent of and different from what tradition establishes. Sooner or later, the central office or other teachers will, either directly or indirectly, undermine or trivialize the work of the nonconformist. Calkins and Harwayne (1991) say as much when they warn that we cannot ignore the ecology of the rest of the school and expect an innovative classroom to flourish. Let me offer a few examples of how innovative teaching methods are routinely undermined.

## Situation One: Teacher Pressure

Innovative teaching methods are threatening to classroom teachers who are vested in the status quo, and those teachers react very quickly to any and all who might unsettle the routine of the schoolhouse. One effective way advocates of the old order move against change is to discourage the innovator by alienating him or her from the community of other teachers. The alienation is often accomplished simply by labeling the innovator a "hot shot," "hot dog," "star," or some other term which serves to identify this individual—often a new teacher—as different. (Notice that at the same time that the label sets the innovator apart, it slightly disparages the motives behind the difference.) We must remember the isolation that characterizes teaching in a public school system before we can appreciate the power of labeling as a strategy. Most public school teachers are isolated all day long in their classrooms. Their only contact with other adults may come briefly at lunch or—if they are lucky—during a conference or planning period. To be denied the sense of community with other teachers, in effect, denies them the support any teacher needs to meet the pressures brought both by students and by the job of teaching itself. New teachers are especially vulnerable to this tactic because they rely almost entirely on the community of other teachers to help them become established in their careers. Rather than risk alienation, many teachers allow themselves to adapt to old ways of doing business.

Another way for teachers to subvert an innovative teacher is to call into question the academic value of the kinds of learning going on in the innovator's classroom. After all, so the reasoning goes, what is in place, such as standard curriculum and conventional instruction, has served very well for all these years and represents the accumulated wisdom of the past. Anything different represents a lowering of standards or yet another experiment that won't work. Parents are particularly susceptible to this kind of reasoning because any attack on traditional curriculum or methods can be perceived as an attack on what they know, since they are products of the old order. And parents can be counted on to raise concerns with administrators about practices seen as different or experimental.

## Situation Two: Administrative Intervention

Principals may inadvertently penalize innovation when their loyalty to students is such that it causes them to overburden an innovative teacher in an attempt to help more students. For example, I know a particularly good teacher who several years ago began her career with about 130 students charged to her care, not an unreasonable load in an inner-city district. This teacher was determined to be successful with her at-risk students and was convinced that the all-pervasive rote drill was not the answer. She, therefore, created a rich learning experience in her classroom, altering the traditional curriculum and abandoning the emphasis on direct instruction and drill typical in her school. So successful with students was this young woman that her principal increased her student load to over 200 by midyear. He valued what this young teacher was doing, and he recognized that students responded positively to her methods; but in his effort to help kids who were genuinely in need of a good teacher, the principal caused this teacher to work with an unreasonable number of students, and predictably, her instruction deteriorated.

A different kind of administrative interference happens when a principal assigns large numbers of students with behavior problems to innovative teachers. Because innovative teachers are often assumed to be the most capable and committed, or because they are trying something new which might engage those students who are disenfranchised by traditional methods, principals often assign to them those students other teachers find impossible to control. With too many of these students on the class roll, no teacher—regardless of ability or energy level—can be truly successful. In fact, teachers must question why they should experiment with change if the only reward for good teaching is either the most difficult student population or the largest number of students per class.

## Situation Three: Administrative Reassignment

Sometimes a teacher tries something new and is so successful with it that central office staff become aware of the value of whatever it is that this teacher is doing. Encouraged by what seems to be a promising practice, the central office removes the successful teacher from the classroom, rewarding him or her with the title of "specialist" or "staff developer." The intent is that this assignment will allow the innovator to show other teachers new methods. The assignment, however, puts the innovator in a kind of limbo between central office staff and the classroom teachers, who often despise them for having what is perceived as an easy job. Lacking either the power to mandate change or the credentials to speak from day-to-day experience in the classroom, specialists and staff developers are often dismissed by those very teachers they were intended to work with. Most important, they are removed from the students whose learning they were once influencing.

## Situation Four: Student Reaction

Students, too, often work against change—after all, both mainstream and at-risk students depend on the status quo. They have learned how the system works and how to work the system. They, for the most part, do not want to have to figure out new ways of being successful.

The system works to ensure that mainstream learners will be successful (make high grades) and will be rewarded with test scores necessary to place them in prestigious universities. Anything which unsettles this carefully orchestrated plan poses a threat to those students who count on the status quo to advance them. These students often react quickly to any innovation they perceive as threatening to their grade-point averages or to their expectations about teacher and student roles.

For example, last year a twelfth-grade fine arts class was offered the opportunity to put aside the textbook and, working in groups, to learn about architecture firsthand by interviewing local architects, photographing interesting buildings, and creating displays which would represent the range of architectural styles within their city. Let us remember that these were high school students, twelfth graders who—one might reasonably expect—would be delighted to have the freedom accorded by this project. On the contrary. The students complained that the work was too demanding, the scope too ambitious, the responsibility too great. As one student told me, it was unfair to ask them to be successful with this kind of learning after they had spent years getting better and better at taking notes and performing on multiple-choice tests. A number of these students, supported by their parents, actually forced the teacher to abandon the project, issue the textbook, deliver lectures, and measure student learning in much more traditional ways.

A class of middle school at-risk students was similarly unsettled by change, although for different reasons, when their teacher abandoned worksheets and computer-assisted instruction for a writers' workshop format. These were students who for years had been subjected to drills and very low-level learning tasks. They recognized that what their teacher proposed by way of a change would require more of them than had typically been expected. Moreover, they were frustrated by the rigor of the reading/writing tasks and the lack of predictable classroom-management structures. Initially, these students rebelled through unruly behavior. In this case, however, the teacher prevailed and eventually the students proved to be capable of very good work. This classroom was ultimately a success, but not without a prolonged struggle to determine who was in control.

So the system—teachers, principals, central office personnel, and students—all have ways of undermining innovation. Given the collective power of these groups, the notion that change can be brought about by one teacher at a time is clearly a myth. In fact, one must wonder if change is possible on any terms!

## The Roots of Change

Research, however, suggests that there is hope. Teachers and schools can change, but only under very specific circumstances.

First of all, change, it seems, is most likely when it involves what Greenwood, Mann, and McLaughlin (1975) call a "critical mass" of classrooms. When this critical mass—whatever the actual number—is simultaneously involved in a new program, the new program is more likely to succeed than if it is carried out by a single classroom working in isolation. That is to say, teachers and students are reassured about innovation and are likely to be accepting of change when a significant number of faculty members are involved with making the new methods work. When a critical mass of teachers is involved in change, they (and their students) know that their efforts will not be ignored in future classrooms. We need, then, a "critical mass" to bring about any significant change in the way schools work.

However, even as we are aware of the "critical mass" theory, we will have to acknowledge that there are some teachers we simply will not be able to affect. Regardless, it seems, of anything we might do, certain teachers will be resistant. In fact, public school lore acknowledges as a given what it calls the "law of thirds": One-third of the teachers look for ways to change; simply show them a better way, and they will do it. Another third will change, but they may need some staff development to incorporate new methods or to give up old ways of doing things. The last third, however, those teachers remaining, will *never* change. Period.

To give them credit, many of this last group are simply burned out. Over time they have become cynical and disenfranchised victims of the callousness of the public education system. They have seen innovative methods come and go, and they have come to believe in very little—if anything—when it comes to new ideas for the classroom. Moreover, these people are often rewarded for what they do: they are praised by parents who are naturally suspicious of innovation; they are inspired and guided by textbook publishers, workbook skill-sheets and standardized testing efforts; they are honored in the images which represent our profession (such as the schoolmarm or schoolmaster standing at a chalkboard in front of students sitting silently at attention—working hard, keeping order, "teaching").

Let me say that these are not necessarily "bad" teachers in the sense of excessively punitive or intellectually substandard. They do what has traditionally been honored and, believe me, they work very, very hard to do it. The classroom teacher who spends six or seven hours a day, every day, leading resistant youngsters through a series of low-level textbook activities must maintain order by virtue of his or her personality. Such a teacher can never let down—must constantly provide busywork for youngsters—is ceaselessly "on," controlling, going from activity to activity until the dismissal bell rings. We cannot assume these people don't work—they work exhaustively. But they do irreparable damage to our students at all ability levels, and they perpetuate many of the problems within public education. Furthermore, because these teachers are not going to change and are not going to go away, either, they will work to keep in place those practices that innovation challenges.

Just for the sake of argument, let us put aside worrying about these teachers. Let us assume we could jump the first hurdle and draw together a critical mass of teachers—say two-thirds of the population of a school (or district). What then? What would we have to do to bring about the large-scale teacher change necessary for school reform?

Well, we'd have to be cognizant, of course, of what Fullan (1982) says about change: that is, we'd have to accept the fact that (1) one-shot workshops, without any follow-up, are ineffective; (2) topics must be absolutely relevant to those for whom the workshop is planned; (3) ongoing follow-up must be available; (4) the workshop must address *individual* needs and concerns (that is, the "but *my* kids, *my* parents, *my* district" arguments must be accommodated); and (5) we must find a way to deal with *both* teachers and systems. So if we take Fullan into account we must accept the fact that we are going to have to be involved with change for a very long time and to a very large degree. But let's assume we are still committed to change. What then?

We must acknowledge that on an individual basis teacher change is no easy task. Larry Cuban (1984) points out that teachers, after all, have absorbed lessons on their craft by watching, over the lifetime of their own educations, approximately fifteen thousand hours of classroom practice from kindergarten through university. In short, teachers have learned, first from their own teachers and later from colleagues, what works and what doesn't, and thus have developed a set of beliefs about teaching. These lessons have been molded by the American educational system, a system which, according to Goodlad (1984), has remained largely unchanged for one hundred years. When we ask teachers to change, we have to confront that vision of teaching and learning and ask teachers to create classrooms for which they have no personal experience—not their own schooling, not their teacher training, not what they currently see in the rooms around them.

And we must not underestimate the power that "business as usual" has over people. Every day in every classroom in this country teachers project images that perpetuate particular views of teaching and learning. These images define for people—among them future teachers and parents—a sense of what it is to teach. So if, for example, children see classrooms where students sit quietly in straight rows, answer questions when called upon, and otherwise remain relatively quiet and passive, this image becomes their sense of school. They see teachers as people who control and give out information. This image is reinforced day after day. Furthermore, it is reinforced across grade levels and content areas. At a very profound level, these images create our belief system about what teachers should do and what students should do.

Our belief systems—George Kelly (1963) calls them personal constructs—are the basis for our expectations about how things will/should happen in the future. They form the basis for a person's actions; they "channelize" a person's choices, actions, and decisions within particular areas of experience (Kelly 1963, 13). These beliefs are not necessarily conscious. Often they are "implicitly held." Daniels and Zemelman (1985) describe them as "semiconscious," second nature, so to speak. Although they are implicit rather than explicit, these personal constructs are, nonetheless, extremely powerful. Some constructs are permeable; that is, they are open to change or modification if they are articulated, examined, and found wanting. However, other constructs are impermeable and difficult or impossible to change. (A construct may be classified as impermeable if it is continuously reinforced and reconfirmed by events or if it is a superordinate construct, one which subsumes numerous other constructs and which, therefore, is rarely articulated and consequently rarely examined.)

To make explicit how teachers' beliefs or constructs can influence teaching, Harste, Woodward, and Burke (1984) examined a rather standard first-grade activity that called for students to draw a picture of themselves and to copy a short text, "Here I am. My name is _____." There are several teacher assumptions underlying this activity. Assumption one: one must be able to "discriminate visually between the letters of the alphabet." Assumption two: letter discrimination is best taught by activities such as underwriting which force the learner to "attend to the distinctive features of each letter." Underlying these two assumptions are yet more beliefs: for example, the belief "that children need to be able to note differences between the various letters of the alphabet in order to read and write" and the belief that "visual discrimination of letters must be formally taught" to students not already possessing the ability to discriminate between letters of the alphabet (Harste, Woodward, and Burke 1984, 4–7). Harste and his colleagues contend that some fifteen further beliefs about teaching and learning are also inherent in this single instructional activity. Inarguably, what a teacher believes strongly affects the choice of instructional activities and the handling of such activities.

The notion of beliefs or personal constructs often works to undermine educational innovations; unconsciously teachers are likely to adapt innovative materials and approaches to make them fit their implicit theories of teaching. This is especially true when there is a strong "clash" between the theories of curriculum reformers and the personal constructs of teachers. How many teachers undermine whole language programs by insisting on worksheets to focus on skills development? How many teachers encourage students to construct meaning as long as the meaning constructed matches standard literary interpretations?

Fortunately, there is some indication that teachers' personal constructs can be changed and so allow for classroom innovation. Research indicates that one way to accomplish this is to make implicit theories explicit. Sarason (1982) found that when he helped teachers become aware of the personal constructs underlying some of their teaching these teachers often found that they disagreed with their own constructs and were able to recognize the need to change. Similarly, Diamond (1982) found that making personal constructs explicit allows teachers to clarify and refine their individual theories and to recognize the possibility for change. Indeed, Sarason claims that teachers' constructs must become explicit; he warns that so long as these assumptions and conceptions remain unverbalized and unquestioned, there is little chance of substantive teacher change. Teachers must experience new ways of teaching and learning in order to reformulate their beliefs and go on to invent new constructs, and what we must construct for teachers, then, is a view of what is possible apart from what the system currently honors.

## Changing the System

The Fort Worth, Texas, superintendent of schools, Don Roberts, has committed his district to large-scale change. Disturbed because many who enter school drop out, and because many others who stay and graduate do not have the knowledge and skills necessary for employment, Roberts and his staff—both administrators and teachers—collaborated with Fort Worth community members and with representatives from area businesses to reinvent a vision of what school should look like. The vision redefines learning and teaching. It also causes major changes in the way schools are structured. These are fundamental changes that Roberts orchestrates. His position of authority gives assurance that large numbers of teachers (remember the law of thirds) will feel compelled to support the change. Further support for change comes from both the businesspeople and the community members involved in the endeavor. This breadth of support does two things: first, it reassures teachers as they give up old ways of doing things that their efforts are endorsed both up the administrative ladder and across the community, and, second, it gives teachers a sense of being part of a major undertaking, one that has high prestige and high visibility. Supported at every level of the administration, Roberts's vision is called "C3" in acknowledgment of its coming from the collaboration among Fort Worth classrooms, the community, and local corporations. It involves massive and ongoing staff development efforts, continuous interaction between school personnel and businesspeople, and access to classrooms which offer a view of teaching and learning representing a clear departure from the status quo. The view began with twenty teachers in twenty classrooms; four months later, twenty had grown to thirty-seven. Six months later, thirty-seven had grown to a hundred and ten. Most of these classrooms are clustered in schools across the district so that groups of teachers—rather than a single teacher—promote change at the building level. Fifteen of these classrooms make up the Alice Carlson Applied Learning Center, an elementary school serving grades K–5, which is characterized both by innovative staffing procedures and by an uncommon vision of teaching and learning.

To realize their visions, teachers across the city drew from Shirley Brice Heath's work with community-based organizations, from Eliot Wigginton's Foxfire Project, from Dixie Goswami's Writing for the Public Project, from the work done by the Secretary's Commission on Achieving Necessary Skills (SCANS), and from ideas generated in innumerable classroom writers' workshops. And they all reread John Dewey. In short, this vision builds on the images of others who work(ed) to rethink schooling. What I want to do now is to describe how this system-wide vision plays out in one ninth-grade English classroom. In so doing, I hope to help you see how our vision is affecting students.

### Changing Ninth-Grade English

The ninth-grade class I describe is taught by a very able teacher. The students who make up the class are typical of many inner-city kids who survive, but barely, in large urban school districts. Teachers assigned to such students work very hard to make learning meaningful and to engage students so that disruptive behaviors are kept to a minimum. This is a tough teaching task, but we began here, reasoning that if change could succeed in this sort of situation, we would have created a very powerful image, powerful enough to cause many teachers to question their constructs about student expectations and teacher behaviors.

In our particular ninth-grade English class, there were at any given time an average of twenty-eight students, plus or minus five students, on the class roll. (Class enrollment figures varied throughout the school: the high was thirty-eight; the low, twenty-two.) Several students were taking the course for the second or third time; one student was enrolled for the fourth time. More than one student had had problems with the law; several had been abandoned by parents and were living in shelters; two students were classified as special ed.; six to eight were second language learners. Many students had long histories of truancy and tardiness; several were known to be highly disruptive. There were on average fifteen boys and thirteen girls. (All of these numbers are somewhat inexact because enrollment was *never* stable. They do represent as much as possible, however, the general composition of the class.)

For the first several weeks of the school year the students "prepped" for a state-mandated test. This test requires students to write a persuasive essay and to answer forty multiple-choice questions about sentence structure, usage, and mechanics. Although the test is not particularly rigorous, it represents an obstacle for students who are traditionally unsuccessful in school; therefore, several weeks of prep time is not altogether excessive, and this form of instruction (i.e., test prep), represents business as usual for these students. On the day after the state test, however, the teacher announced that from that point forward the class was going to operate differently. (Predictably this announcement was met with little excitement. These kids, after all, have been in school long enough to have seen almost everything; and they are, therefore, somewhat cynical about change.) Rather than working in either grammar or literature textbooks, the students were asked to read *What Work Requires of Schools* (the SCANS report). This document, published by the Department of Labor, has as its major premise the idea that students must be educated differently if they are to compete in a changing labor market. The document is not lengthy—fifty-three pages—but the teacher kept the assignment minimal, allowing the students to work in groups and asking each group to read only a small number of pages and then to teach the content of those pages to the rest of the class. She accomplished several things with this assignment. First of all, she made the task doable. By restricting the number of pages and letting the students work in groups, she was assured that all students would be successful. She had also sent a clear signal that students were encouraged to work cooperatively when she agreed to their request that they be allowed to work in groups. And, finally, she used an out-of-school document rather than a standard textbook, clearly indicating that she had broken away from business as usual.

The teacher counted on the documents' holding the students' attention because she knew it was relevant to their interests. And it did interest them, so much so that they listened attentively as their classmates taught them its various sections. In fact, the students spent three weeks talking about the skills and competencies valued in the workplace. Somewhat surprisingly, the class felt confident of their ability to measure up to workplace standards, whereas they were somewhat less confident about their chances for academic success. In order to appreciate the import of the students' reaction to the SCANS competencies and skills, we must realize that these competencies and skills are quite demanding.

The SCANS document proposes that students need various foundation skills: the basic skills of reading, writing, arithmetic, mathematics, speaking, and listening; thinking skills, including the ability to learn, to reason, to think creatively, to make decisions, and to solve problems; and personal qualities such as responsibility, self-esteem, self-management, sociability, and integrity. Moreover, students should learn how to allocate such resources as time, money, materials, space, and staff; students should gain interpersonal skills so they can work on teams, teach others, serve customers, lead, negotiate, and work well with people from diverse backgrounds; and students must learn to acquire and use information, organize and maintain it in files, and interpret and communicate it. They must learn to use computers to process information. They must also learn to use systems productively: this skill involves being able to understand social, organizational, and technological systems; monitor and correct performance; and design or improve systems. Finally, they should be able to select equipment and tools, apply technology to specific tasks, and maintain and troubleshoot equipment.

Let me say, here, that what the Department of Labor puts forth as a list of prerequisites for successful employment would overwhelm many. These ninth graders, however, were reassured that they could see the worth of these skills and were confident of their ability to develop them. They could not, on the other hand, see the relevance of most of their academic tasks.

The students constructed charts displaying the SCANS competencies and skills and hung them around the room so that these necessary abilities would be constantly before them. At this point, the teacher had planned for the students to do an audit of the ninth-grade curriculum in order to determine the extent to which it addressed the SCANS skills and competencies. But first everyone agreed that it would be valuable to interview local businesspeople to make sure that what the Department of Labor asserted was, in fact, true. The students, therefore, contacted a local businessperson and created a list of questions. They came to the interview prepared and conducted themselves in a manner that would impress any adult. They asked very pointed questions and received reassuring answers.

Once assured about the validity of the SCANS document, the students were anxious to do the curriculum audit. Again, working in groups, the students read through the curriculum document. As might be expected, they immediately raised issues. The curriculum guide specifies that the students should engage routinely in writing "for a variety of purposes and audiences in a variety of modes." Obviously, the intent of this goal is to foster students' ability to write. The class argued that this goal did not address the SCANS competencies because as it had been translated into their previous classroom experience this goal prepared them to do little more than write themes on a variety of literary topics for a teacher. Students quite rightly could not see how this kind of writing could prepare them to write adequately beyond the high school classroom.

In large measure, these students had a point. There are major differences between traditional in-school writing and writing in nonacademic settings. For example, in-school writing usually has as its central purpose to display mastery of knowledge, skills, and format. Workplace writing, by contrast, has a range of purposes including to inform, to persuade, to clarify (or obscure), to soften the blow, and to tell others how to do something, and soon. Students in school write essays, book reports, poetry, stories, research papers, and letters. In the workplace, people produce reports, brochures, letters, proposals, planning documents, memos, minutes, instructions, surveys, and logs. Students in the classroom write for a single audience and their writing has no social or political ramifications. Workers write for a range of audiences— often at the same time within highly charged political situations. These differences could easily be addressed, of course, by creating writing situations in which students would have authentic purposes for real-world documents.

It was more difficult to manipulate the curriculum goal which specified that students "respond to various genres and themes of our diverse literary heritage." It must be remembered, here, that these students—many of them at least—had no real appreciation for literature, owing in large part, probably, to the very traditional ways literature had been "taught" (often for simple recall of information or memorization of features). Students felt the literature component should be compressed—it had previously spanned the entire school year with literary analysis essays their only opportunity to write. The class decided that the curriculum should exist primarily to ensure that students develop the skills and competencies necessary for employment and *then* offer enrichment (literature). This opinion was so strongly felt that the class decided to write a proposal for curriculum change.

At this point something very significant happened in this classroom. The teacher had intended to send the curriculum audit forward to her supervisor as a summary statement reflecting the work done to date in her classroom. The students, however, were intent on change, on making their voices heard. Therefore, they insisted on carbon-copying the proposal to this superior's own two superiors.

This decision on the part of the students was important for a number of reasons. First of all, it speaks to the fact that the students valued the work they had done—so much so that they insisted it be recognized beyond the classroom. Next, these students were taking responsibility for what they learned, signing off on it and presenting it as an action item for a real audience. Perhaps most important, by carbon-copying the document (and sending it) to people higher up on the administrative ladder, these students gained access to the system, ensuring that their work would not be patronized or overlooked.

The document went forward and received the hoped-for attention. When an administrator visited the class to discuss their proposal and elicit suggestions for a course of action, the class suggested that they be allowed to write and produce a video to be shown to all ninth-grade students in the district. The focus of the video would be the information contained in the SCANS document. The class determined that costs for this production would be covered by funds secured through a proposal the students would write. All text produced in conjunction with the video and the proposal would reflect what the students had learned about real-world writing and could be used to show that students had met the course requirements for writing. The administrator encouraged the students to begin these tasks at once.

Several weeks into these endeavors—after the district had funded the video proposal—the students were offered the opportunity to write for publication about their experiences. Although the class realized that committing themselves to this project would require a good deal of work, they were excited about the opportunity. They wrote a proposal (their third) to their principal asking to remain together as a class during the next school year and requesting the same classroom teacher. Once their requests were honored, they asked a lawyer to draft a contract that would make explicit each student's responsibility in the two projects. Furthermore, they agreed to make a presentation at a summer literacy conference where they would unveil their video.

In order to appreciate all that this class has accomplished, we must remember that for much of their school careers, these students had had only limited success. In addition to all the very successful writing they did as ninth graders, these kids proved themselves highly successful in terms of what the SCANS document values. Furthermore, within a few short months, they learned how to work within the system in very adroit ways. I do not suggest that this one experience is sufficient to change these students into scholars—but it did change them into learners, and that is the necessary first step.

Let's take a careful look at this one classroom and examine the ways in which it differed from other classrooms. First of all, we have derived six maxims from educational research. These maxims inform us that students

- value making immediate connections between academic concepts and real-world applications;
- are challenged by ill-defined problems more closely similar to those that people grapple with outside of school;
- are capable of complex thinking and group effort sustained over long blocks of time;
- respond well to agents and settings of learning that are not limited to teachers and classrooms;
- value knowledge associated with the everyday life of people not traditionally associated with the school and school learning;
- can engage in student-initiated, student-regulated tasks and projects.

We built classrooms where students were expected to meet certain goals. These goals included students' being able to

- understand disciplinary concepts and processes;
- learn to solve ill-defined problems;
- work collaboratively in groups;
- use documents/sources of information other than textbooks;
- produce something people can *use*;
- relate the work of the class to the world outside of school;
- influence/shape the course of their own learning.

Learning was organic to both short-term and long-term projects, designed around authentic questions and needs. Assessment procedures were in harmony with the principles of learning; that is, they called for students to work through ill-defined problems; they encouraged students to work in groups; they required students to use a range of sources of information—both academic and nonacademic; they were relevant to the world outside of class; they promoted learning as much as they assessed learning; and they encouraged students to produce knowledge and to reflect on their own learning processes.

The *students* took responsibility for what and how they learned. Their progress was determined by the problem solving they engaged in at various stages of their task. For example, they determined that a video would be a good thing; it would make widely known what this one class had learned— and, of course, it would be fun to produce. *But* they had no money—so they wrote a proposal. This required that they learn about proposals, how to write them effectively, whom to appeal to, and what arguments would be well received. Okay, they got the money. Now they needed a budget and a long-term plan; ultimately they had to submit a product and a fiscal accounting, and demonstrate clear evidence that what they had learned met the course description. Moreover, they learned that few things in life have closure and they learned that what they learn in school can serve them well beyond the classroom walls.

Now let's look at the *teacher*.

She slowly transferred responsibility to the students, providing scaffolding experiences for them, ensuring their success by allowing them to work in groups on manageable projects (or stages of a project) that were important to them. She allowed students to build upon previous successes. (The students' reading and discussion and reciprocal teaching led to an understanding of the necessary SCANS skills/competencies. This led to reading the curriculum document through the lens of the SCANS document, which led to conclusions about the value of the current curriculum. This led to a proposal for curriculum change. This led to suggesting viable alternatives, which led to negotiating the status quo. This led to informing others by way of a video, which resulted in one proposal for staying together another year, and another proposal for funding the video. This led to a long-term plan with carefully spelled-out responsibilities and consequences.) Obviously, this teacher's job was planning and orchestrating students' progress through these events. True, she acted as a resource (no doubt, she talked through the strategy of carbon-copying a document to ensure attention to its contents) and she may even have made use of textbooks on occasion, but she did little else that is typically a part of "teaching." What she did do was allow events to grow naturally out of preceding events, making sure that students' learning was rigorous and explicit but engaged in an overarching task, in a larger narrative or context from which the students will, ideally, be able to draw long after their memory of specific information has gone.

This teacher kept a diary during the year. Her voice in the diary is reassuring because it is not the voice of some stellar change agent; it is the voice of a classroom teacher, tentative about how things are going, unsure that students will learn, worried as much about the lives of her students as she is about their educational progress:

> I want this classroom to really belong to the students, well, to belong to us. . . . I want to work collaboratively with them and I'm scared they won't want to work collaboratively with me.
> They seem to work so slowly . . .
> I couldn't see any results as I looked at their papers. . . . I feel compelled to rush them to do more work and to work more quickly but I know that one of the reasons so many of them are repeating first-year English is that they have been rushed through the system.

She writes honestly about her students, who they are and what they can and will do.

> I spoke to X about his language yesterday. I think we've reached an understanding.
> Today Y told me that she hasn't been feeling well because of morning sickness.
> It's so frustrating to me to hear the noise and not see the results I want in their work.
> [These three girls] get very little on paper in class. They talk things over and make notes but most of their work is done outside class. I wonder why some students can work so effectively in the class and some can't. I'm glad that I've given them the opportunity to work outside class. There was a time, not so long ago, that I wouldn't have allowed it if I couldn't see more on paper during class.
> Thirteen students were absent today and eighteen were present.
> Valentine's Day began with a fight.

The *materials* are neither standard nor commercially prepared. All are the stuff of real life and so will probably be impossible to reproduce for other classes, whose needs and interests no doubt would be different. These materials do not fit into lesson plan cycles, shape themselves easily into multiple-choice questions, or align themselves with traditional course objectives. They are messy and often ambiguous, and they concern themselves with ill-defined problems which have no simple solutions. The teacher's diary describes how the *materials* she works with come both from the real world (SCANS) and from variations on the traditional curriculum:

> I made reading logs for the students. . . . Their assignment consists of two entries a week for the next two weeks . . . they can read whatever they like and write about it as long as what they read is appropriate to be brought to class and read aloud there. . . . I think some of them liked the fact that they could read their biology assignment and write about it for credit in English class.
>
> They could choose any topic [to write about] as long as they wrote on both sides of the topic. I suggested old friends—new friends; advantages of gum in class—disadvantages of gum in class. Then I asked them for suggestions of topics which had two sides and the suggestions blew me away. The first was abortion. Then these followed: firing teachers, attending class, continuing to go to school after having a child, legalizing currently illegal drugs; having a gun in the home; the rights of AIDS victims; and wearing seat belts. These kids have so much on their minds and we stupidly ask them to do these artificial kinds of writing that don't really prepare them for much.

The *culture of the school* is problematic. There is pressure to calculate grades at traditional grading cycles—even though the work may be too unformed as yet to evaluate. Students discover mid-class the need for something and must be allowed to leave the room to make phone calls, get materials, leave campus—in order for work to continue. Ideally, working materials should be left undisturbed so that precious time is not lost the next day as kids return to get started. But, of course, this is totally unrealistic. Time, interruptions that call kids out of class (class meetings, assemblies, pep rallies), six- or nine-week tests, teacher work days, arbitrary grading procedures, transferring in new kids and losing core group members to other teachers and programs: nothing in the school culture works to serve this classroom.

Again the teacher's diary gives us a sense of how the *system* is just as the system always is:

> [September 9]
> Today my class dropped from thirty-eight to thirty-two. The students who had their schedules changed were not happy about it, and although I know that the numbers needed to be smaller, I hated to see them go as

well. So now I have thirty-two on roll, but only twenty-three were present. Where are the other nine? Will they be lost? I am worried about some. The attendance rule states that each student must be present eighty days a semester in order to receive credit. One young lady has already missed six days, and there is a young man who is not far behind her.

I began to read the story to the class. I got about halfway finished when drums started pounding. Thinking the band was about to march through the halls to fire everybody up for the Friday night football game, I looked into the hall. Nothing but vibrating lockers. We all went to the windows and there was the percussion section, practicing just outside the window. I did finish the story [I was reading] and I think the kids enjoyed it, but it lost a little of the effect due to the distraction. That's life at school!

## A Last Word

Finally, a word about "site-based management" and "shared decision making," two strategies many currently propose for "school reform." The reasoning behind these strategies is that change must take place at the campus level and that such change must work to meet the particular needs of individual student populations on each campus. Probably this reasoning makes sense under particular circumstances, but it also has the potential to create havoc. What site-based management does is to put into the hands of principals—and maybe into the hands of "building-level teams"—all the decisions affecting the education of the children. To the extent that the campus-level people are informed and well-intentioned, site-based management should work. However, many building principals are held accountable primarily for test scores that do not always reflect student learning. Therefore, in states where high-stakes testing is in place, it would serve us to be skeptical about the kinds of teaching and learning decided on at the campus level. We should also remember the reverence for the status quo that often prevails and the law of thirds, and should question exactly which teachers—and whose agendas—are represented on "building-level teams." Finally I would argue that even highly qualified people are exhausted by performing the very demanding day-to-day teaching and managing tasks that schools require. And to ask these people to reconceptualize what schools might look like, while they are in the process of working at their jobs, places an incredible burden on their energies. Unless we are willing to work with these people to change schools, unless we can create so compelling a vision that it overcomes the entrenched indifference to real learning, we will be guilty of yet another pseudo-reform that will waste much money and time and effort; and we will bankrupt another generation of students and teachers.

## References

Calkins, L. M., and S. Harwayne. 1991. *Living between the Lines*. Portsmouth, N.H.: Heinemann.

Cuban, L. 1984. *How Teachers Taught: Consistency and Change in American Classrooms, 1890–1980*. New York: Longman.

Daniels, H., and S. Zemelman. 1985. *A Writing Project*. Portsmouth, N.H.: Heinemann.

Diamond, C. T. P. 1982. "Teachers Can Change: A Kellyian Interpretation." *Journal of Education for Teaching* 8:163–73.

Fullan, M. 1982. *The Meaning of Educational Change*. New York: Teachers College Press.

Goodlad, J. I. 1984. *A Place Called School*. New York: McGraw-Hill.

Greenwood, P. W., D. Mann, and M. W. McLaughlin. 1975. *Federal Programs Supporting Educational Change* 3, Santa Monica, Calif.: Rand Corporation.

Harste, J. C., V. A. Woodward, and C. L. Burke. 1984. *Language Stories and Literacy Lessons*. Portsmouth, N.H.: Heinemann.

Kelly, G. 1963. *A Theory of Personality*. New York: Norton.

Sarason, S. B. 1982. *The Culture of the School and the Problem of Change*. Boston: Allyn and Bacon.

U.S. Department of Labor. Secretary's Commission on Achieving Necessary Skills. 1991. *What Work Requires of Schools: SCANS Report for America 2000*.

# II Further Reflections on Teachers Knowing: The Commentary and Discussions

# 9 What's Effective Inservice?

Richard Beach
University of Minnesota

*One discussion group focused primarily on issues concerning the role of inservice education in teachers' growth and development. Richard Beach, in his summary of the discussion, provides reasons that inservice education so often fails to help experienced teachers, along with a rich collection of practical theory about how inservice might be made more beneficial.*

Our discussion group focused on issues related to the topic of inservice education for teachers. In our discussions, we shared our experiences with conducting or participating in various forms of inservice—graduate courses for teachers, inservice workshops in schools, or training programs for teaching assistants in composition programs.

Based on our collective experiences, most of us agreed that much of what occurs in inservice education fails to have any measurable impact on teachers' everyday instructional practices. Given the fact that many veteran teachers are, often for financial reasons, staying longer in the classroom before retirement, their participation in inservice programs may be their only exposure to new ideas or innovative teaching approaches. If they receive inadequate or inferior inservice, then it is unlikely that they will keep abreast of new developments in the field.

We also noted that we have no clear theoretical framework for defining what constitutes inservice instruction. While we can intuitively judge a good from a bad workshop or training session, we have no clearly defined criteria for evaluating inservice instruction. Lacking any clearly defined theoretical framework for assessing inservice, it is difficult to address the question, "What is effective inservice?" In order to begin to define such a theoretical framework, the group devoted its discussions to describing the nature of standard inservice methods and reasons these methods often fail. We then turned to examples of alternative inservice methods that show more promise for changing instruction than is the case with existing methods.

## Reasons for the Failure of Inservice Education

In our discussions, we noted a number of reasons for the dysfunctional nature of inservice education.

### *The One-Shot Format of Inservice Workshops*

Many school workshops are one-shot affairs featuring an inspirational outside speaker. While these speakers may provide a momentarily uplifting inspirational message, the effect of that message on classroom instruction is generally minimal. For change to occur in instruction, teachers themselves need to articulate the need for change, develop plans for making changes, and implement and evaluate these efforts toward change. Simply sitting and listening to a speaker involves none of these processes, and given a limited amount of time for a workshop, teachers may not have an opportunity for hands-on experimentation with the methods proposed. Without trying out activities themselves, teachers may have no clear sense of how they work or what their own attitudes toward the activities are. Moreover, without any follow-up, there is little incentive for teachers to try out new approaches in their own classrooms.

In some cases, one-shot workshops are driven by a single model or theory —"whole language," "outcome-based education," "process writing," "holistic education," and so on. While these workshops provide teachers with useful theoretical perspectives, they often assume that shifts in theoretical perspectives or attitudes precipitate changes in behavior. Others suggest, however, that changes in behavior precede changes in attitude. Without experiencing changes of behavior in the classroom, teachers may not change their attitudes and beliefs. This possibility points to the value of participation in long-term projects which focus on change in both attitudes/beliefs and behaviors, each feeding the other.

Rather than simply accepting a single model, teachers need to openly acknowledge a range of competing theories and paradigms of English language arts instruction. By unpacking their own assumptions regarding the larger purposes of instruction, teachers begin to grapple with alternative perspectives on their teaching. A teacher who believes in teaching "correct forms" may begin to examine his or her own assumptions when confronted with teachers who subscribe to a whole-language approach. This suggests the need for opportunities within inservice instruction for teachers to continually examine and debate the theoretical assumptions underpinning the methods being promoted.

### *Lack of Relevance to Particular Subject-Matter Concerns*

Many schoolwide inservice workshops are highly generic; they may not be clearly related to teachers' specific content-pedagogical interests. I recently sat through a workshop presentation on "outcome-based education," an approach mandated for use in the schools of Minnesota. While I learned some of the general tenets of outcome-based education, I had difficulty connecting to the topic because the facilitator did not relate it to the specifics of English education/language arts instruction. For example, much of outcome-based education relies on testing or evaluating whether individual students have achieved certain specified outcomes, an improvement over the norm-based grading system. However, when questions arose regarding the move—in English/language arts education—to replace testing with alternative forms of assessment, the facilitator, certainly not an expert in all subject-matter areas, was not able to connect the larger theory to these specific subject-matter concerns.

## The Disparity between University and School Attitudes

Another problem with inservice, particularly university coursework, has to do with the disparity between the world of the university and the world of the school. In their work with undergraduate teacher education, Athanases, Caret, Canales, and Meyer (1992), drawing on Feiman-Nemser and Buchmann (1985), describe this disparity as the "two-worlds pitfall." The university world rewards theory and research, while the school world rewards concern with practice. As group members noted, it is common knowledge that teachers often find that university coursework does not readily translate into practice or address teachers' particular needs and concerns. Again, as with the inspirational workshop speakers, a course may be intellectually stimulating, but bring about little or no change in teachers' behaviors. At the same time, teachers need to be open to the theoretical and research perspectives provided by university courses, perspectives that may yield new insights on their practice.

University instructors can better bridge the "two-worlds" gap by giving teachers time to apply theory and research through engaging in activities. For example, rather than simply talking about the theory and research associated with portfolio assessment, teachers in a course would construct their own portfolios. If teachers actively rehearse the very behaviors they may implement in their classes, their attitudes and beliefs may change.

## Mandated Inservice Workshops

Another limitation of workshops is that they are often mandated *by* administrators *for* teachers—with little or no input as to the nature and direction of the inservice. Just as students may balk at writing on assigned topics about which they have little or no interest, so teachers may resist the imposition of assigned workshops. If teachers have some say in planning, on the other hand, they may be more motivated to participate. Moreover, if they are offered a smorgasbord of options, teachers can choose those most relevant to their needs.

### *Lack of Incentives/Resistance to Change*

As previously noted, inservice programs are, ideally, designed to promote change. However, there are a number of factors that serve to limit the potential for change, thus undercutting the value of such programs. The culture of the school system, for example, may not serve to foster change. As dramatized by Samuel Freedman (1990) in *Small Victories,* a portrait of a successful high school English teacher in a lower-East-Side high school, teachers have difficulty going it alone, without strong support from administrators and teacher organizations. The often bureaucratic, legalistic climate of the large contemporary secondary school does not serve as a culture of change. Without the supportive community ethos often found in smaller schools, teachers rely on their own energies and personalities to motivate students within their own classrooms, only to burn out eventually. Without rewards or incentives for collective change by the entire community, teachers may perceive little need to risk changing only themselves.

As Sally Hampton documents (see chapter 8), there are a number of constraints in the school system that inhibit change. Colleagues, administrators, and students who are more comfortable with business as usual often resist or undermine teachers' innovations. Students who are accustomed to filling out worksheets in all of their other classes, for example, may resist a teacher's attempts to encourage them to use journals to express their own opinions and ideas. Moreover, teachers may create a number of rationalizations for resisting change, dismissing innovative ideas as "just another new gimmick or fad." Such rationalizations assume that their own tried-and-true instructional methods are a norm against which to judge innovations.

There is also little financial reward for innovation. Under the current system, teachers receive automatic salary increases regardless of their propensity to improve. While taking additional graduate coursework and inservice workshops may boost salaries, these experiences, as previously noted, do not necessarily lead to change. In examining alternative methods for recognizing and rewarding innovation, the group discussed large-scale efforts such as the National Board for Professional Teaching Standards review of middle school language arts teachers, which will begin in 1994 (see Petrosky, chapter 2). According to the board's current plans, teachers would "stand" for board certification by demonstrating their knowledge and skills at assessment centers located throughout the country. They would bring portfolio documentation and videos of their teaching to these centers, where they would undergo a number of assessment procedures. They would be evaluated on their ability to fulfill a set of standards that represent current theory and methods of language arts instruction. By becoming "board-certified," they might then be recognized as "accomplished teachers." However, if there are no rewards within the district or state for becoming board-certified, then there may be no incentive for teachers to expend the effort.

## Techniques for Effective Inservice

Given some of these obstacles to effective inservice, and based on their own experience, the group shared some techniques for conducting effective inservice workshops and courses.

### Ascertaining Teachers' Particular Needs and Concerns Beforehand

In conducting inservice courses and workshops, we often make assumptions about what teachers need or want. We may thereby launch into a workshop or course without acknowledging teachers' own particular needs and concerns and the constraints inhibiting potential change. As a result, we invite a "Yes, but . . . " reaction that undercuts our message.

Here's an ideal scenario. In an English department meeting, a number of teachers note that their students are having difficulty responding effectively to each others' writing. They know that their students need some instruction in conducting peer conferences, but they are not sure how to provide that instruction effectively. One of the teachers knows a teacher, Michelle, in another school who has developed an effective peer-conference program. With that particular need in mind, they contact Michelle, communicating to her their concern—lack of effective peer conferences, and their particular need—instruction in how to use peer conferences more effectively. Knowing the teachers' needs and concerns before the workshop, Michelle then organizes a series of hands-on activities that directly address those needs and concerns. In this case, the work was carried out by a teacher. It could have been conducted by a university professor. The key isn't who works with the teachers, but whether the facilitator can be as sensitive and responsive to teacher needs and concerns as Michelle was.

### Involving Teachers in the Topic

Rather than beginning with their own message or pitch, facilitators should begin a workshop with an icebreaker activity that involves teachers in actively discussing the topic or subject. For example, in conducting a workshop on writing across the curriculum for an entire secondary school staff, the facilitator might invite teachers to discuss—in small groups—the kinds of writing they do in their classes, and questions and concerns associated with using writing in the classroom. The small groups then report back their questions and concerns, reports that serve to set the stage for the workshop. Based on prior investigation or on feedback from the icebreaker activity, the facilitator can then visually display on a flip chart or overhead the group's questions and concerns. This visual display is a concrete demonstration that the teachers' questions and concerns are driving the workshop. At the end of the workshop, the facilitator can then return to their list to make sure that the various questions and concerns have been addressed. By initially involving teachers, the facilitator lets the teachers, as adult learners with particular needs, set the agenda for the workshop.

## *Exploiting the Insights and Experiences of Veteran Teachers*

Rather than posing as the sole expert in the room, a facilitator's job is to *facilitate* expression of the insights, experiences, or "teacher lore" (see Ayers and Schubert, chapter 7) of veteran teachers. Often by brainstorming in small groups and reporting back to the large group, teachers can generate a wealth of ideas or approaches similar to those the facilitator might have intended to impart. If the facilitator is introducing a new theoretical perspective, teachers may be asked to brainstorm possible implications of that perspective. And, when confronted with a challenge, rather than responding directly to the challenge the facilitator may turn to other teachers and ask them if they share the same perceptions or difficulties. By tapping teachers' own perceptions, facilitators convey the idea that it is teachers who ultimately shape the direction of change in their classrooms.

## *Incorporating Problem-Solving Activities*

A facilitator can continue to address real-world concerns and needs by incorporating problem-solving activities throughout the workshop. If teachers are encouraged to define their own problems or difficulties, they can then begin to link the methods or strategies proposed as solutions to their problems. For example, in her workshop on peer conferences, Michelle asked teachers to describe specific problems they had observed. One teacher, Bill, noted that students often said only "nice things" about each others' papers for fear of jeopardizing friendships or offending peers. Rather than providing an answer for Bill's problem, Michelle turned the problem back to Bill and the group, asking them what they might do. The group then brainstormed some possible solutions that were consistent with some of Michelle's previous ideas: create a context in which students perceive each other as "writers" versus "students"; train students to give concrete, descriptive, "reader-based" feedback that goes beyond vague "nice" comments; or discuss the usefulness of specific comments in fostering revision. As teachers are formulating their solutions, the facilitator is recording their comments on flip charts that can serve as ideas for action plans at the end of the workshop. By linking specific problems to specific solutions, the teachers may then leave the workshop with action plans based on their own concerns and needs.

### Ensuring Development of Action Plans for Implementing Change

At the end of the workshop, the facilitator can help teachers develop specific action plans for applying what they have learned to their everyday practice. For example, a teacher may write a "to do" list that includes such things as, "I will begin each class with a freewrite" or "When I respond to students' writing, I will avoid judgments and provide descriptive reader-based feedback." Teachers can share their plans with one another as well. They could then turn in their plans to the facilitator, who can return them at a later date as a reinforcer. Facilitators can also provide teachers with "job aids"—posters or tent cards that list key points, strategies, or prompts for use in the classroom.

### Conducting Follow-up Sessions or Reunions

To provide continuing support for and discussion of applications, successes, frustrations, and further questions, the facilitator may conduct follow-up sessions or reunions, at which teachers can share their experiences in applying the action plans developed in the original workshop. They can discuss reasons the action plans work well with some students but not others and they can discuss ways to assess their own effectiveness in implementing the action plans.

## Inservice Techniques for Fostering Reflection

While these various inservice techniques may serve to enhance teachers' involvement, the group noted that they may not by themselves foster reflection. Without teachers' reflections on their own teaching, no beneficial change may occur. A number of additional inservice techniques were discussed that serve to foster reflection.

### Ongoing Support Groups

In order for teachers to reflect about their teaching, they need ongoing support groups that serve as open-ended forums for such reflection. A number of the group members who had participated in the Iowa Writing Project, for example, described the ways that the National Writing Project's inservice education model serves to foster reflection. As part of that model, teachers have opportunities to share and exchange ideas in support groups over a long period of time. While they may attend an intensive summer school orientation, they also meet throughout the school year to review and reflect on changes they are making in their teaching. Moreover, their efforts are recognized and legitimized by newsletters and annual meetings. Assuming that substantive change occurs only over a long period of time, such ongoing support mechanisms help sustain the incentive for change.

## Cases and Narratives

As Grossman and Shulman argue (see chapter 1), rather than deal with theory in a vacuum, cases present concrete instances of problems that allow teachers to discuss how they might react in specific hypothetical situations. Cases also serve to ground discussions in specific contexts, requiring consideration of how certain methods vary according to the constraints of different situations.

There was some discussion in the group regarding the utility of cases. In response to Grossman and Shulman, Petrosky argued that cases often represent artificial situations removed from the realities of teachers' own classrooms. He suggested that teachers should construct their own cases, based on narratives about their own teaching. To do so, they may audiotape or videotape a class, and then use the tape to construct a narrative of what happened in the class (Beach and Tedick 1992). Consistent with Bruner's (1986) notion of narrative as a way of knowing, constructing the narrative itself serves to precipitate reflection on the events. In framing classroom behaviors in narrative form, teachers are organizing their perceptions of those behaviors according to the unusual or extraordinary nature of an event. In doing so, they render the event as "tellable"—as worth telling (Labov 1972).

As if they were readers responding to a story, teachers then reflect on the meanings of their narratives in terms of what they learned from the events. They could also discuss what knowledge and beliefs they draw on in reflecting on their narratives. For example, a ninth-grade teacher, Maureen, constructs a narrative about a large-group role-playing activity that she carried out with her students, based on a school board censorship hearing. In that hearing, some parents have lodged a complaint about *I Know Why the Caged Bird Sings,* by Maya Angelou, a book the students are reading. She recalls specific instances in which students were and were not able to assume their roles. And, she recalls arguments about cause-and-effect relationships between reading and attitudes/behaviors. She then reflects on reasons for student difficulties in assuming roles and on the quality of the students' arguments. Drawing on her knowledge of role playing, she notes that she should have given the students more time before the role play to caucus and plan out their roles. In this way, her reflection points to potential changes in how she conducts the role play in the future.

## Group Discussion of Classroom Tapes

Teachers could also meet in groups to share their reactions to one another's tapes of their teaching (Dunstan, Kirscht, Reiff, Roemer, and Tingle 1989). For example, having viewed a tape, teachers might share the disparities between what they intended to have happen and what actually happened. In explaining intentions to other group members, teachers may realize the extent to which their own intentions were not fulfilled. As one teacher in such a group noted:

> By the time I finished explaining to my colleagues all my purposes in moving students from their own stories, through group responses (popularity polls) on myths and fairy tales, and back to their own stories, I had had a thorough education. I heard all the unclear signals, the unmade distinctions, the downright misleading emphases coming from the tape. . . . I think you can only come to such painful realizations in a group that is listening to your intent as well as watching the result. (Dunstan, Kirscht, Reiff, Roemer, and Tingle 1989, 45)

That teachers in this group were all viewing the same tapes meant that they could discuss the particulars of specific classroom behaviors. And, they were able to watch for recurring patterns, patterns that suggested underlying scripts or scenarios shaping teachers' behavior, scripts or scenarios that differed from what those teachers intended to accomplish in the classroom. As Gutierrez (1992) found in her analysis of teachers' composition instruction, while teachers may espouse a student-responsive, writing-process approach, they often fall back on routine classroom scripts that are inconsistent with these beliefs.

## Peer-Dialogue Journals

Keeping a journal as part of a course or workshop also serves to foster reflection. As with narrative writing, keeping a journal invites teachers to stand back and mull over classroom events. The extent to which teachers reflect on events may be enhanced by having them exchange entries with peers, who react by posing questions or by citing their own related experiences. Reactions from peers serve to encourage teachers to further reflect on their teaching, reflection that may not occur with solo journals. For example, in her journal, Kathy describes a conflict with a student who is continually disrupting her class. In her description, she provides little or no explanation for why the student is being disruptive. Her partner, Ray, responds by asking a series of questions regarding reasons for the student's disruptive behavior. In answering these questions, Kathy begins to define reasons that have to do with the student's social relationship with his peers (i.e., his need for attention). Having defined these reasons, she then explores some possible solutions, a problem-solving process precipitated by her partner's questions.

Having kept a journal for a period of time, teachers might review their entries and reflect on the underlying attitudes, roles, and assumptions about teaching and learning revealed there. And, adopting Britzman's (see chapter 4) poststructuralist perspective, they could examine the ways in which their discourses or underlying power relationships reflected competing or multiple selves and sensibilities. For example, Linda Brodkey (1989) examined an exchange of letters between teachers and students in an adult education course. She found that the teachers often distanced themselves from directly addressing the students' emotional needs. For Brodkey, the teachers' often condescending letters were shaped by a bureaucratic "discourse of education" that prevented authentic communication between them and the students. By analyzing the limitations of their own categories and discourses, teachers may realize how they are shaped by those categories and discourses. And they may also see themselves not as single "individuals," but rather as "conflicted selves" each of whom represents a multitude of different selves and sensibilities. As Britzman dramatically illustrates with the case of the self-deprecating student teacher, by recognizing that we are a multitude of selves and sensibilities, we avoid the tendency to blame "ourselves" (as individuals) for the inevitable difficulties teaching entails.

*Peer Cross-Visitation*

Another inservice method, suggested by Susan Lytle and Robert Fecho (1991), involves peer cross-visitation. Over an extended period of time, teachers visit each others' classrooms and provide each other with helpful comments. Lytle and Fecho distinguish "cross-visitation" from peer coaching, which they perceive to focus more on providing "technical training" than on fostering support and reflection. The success of cross-visitation hinges on establishing an authentic collaboration, as opposed to contrived, artificial, assigned relationships. Based on their research on cross-visitation in the Philadelphia public schools, they found that, from working with other teachers, teachers recognized the fact that they were interdependent on one another—that their students were shaped by experiences with other teachers within the school community. By garnering alternative perspectives from their partners, they adopted different perspectives on their own teaching. In the process, they discovered that they had to break out of the roles and techniques associated with traditional "outside expert" inservice models. They learned not to perceive each other as "outside experts" who would conduct "demo lessons" on how to teach, but rather as partners who collaboratively shared their experiences. Although the teachers in the study learned to alter their perceptions of themselves, others, and "the system," Lytle and Fecho are unsure about the long-term impact of such methods on instruction and curriculum. "When asked about what they have learned from the experience of cross-visitation, teachers most often responded with what they had learned about working with adults, about understanding and coping with the system at large, and/or about their own self image as a teacher" (25).

## Teacher Research

Another basic approach designed to foster reflection is that of teacher research involving some systematic investigation of teaching and learning (Bissex and Bullock 1987; Carr and Kemmis 1986; Cochran-Smith and Lytle 1990; Daiker and Morenberg 1989; Goswami and Stillman 1987; Patterson, Stansell, and Lee 1990; see also Moss, chapter 5, and Bissex, chapter 6, in this volume). Such research differs from university educational research in that the questions or problems addressed are based on practitioners' own particular concerns or interests (Cochran-Smith and Lytle 1990). Rather than simply making casual reflections on teaching and learning, teachers employ a systematic set of research procedures for studying their own or others' teaching or their students' reading and writing processes. In conducting a research project, a teacher poses a set of questions; gathers information to answer those questions through observations, interviews, analysis of students' and teachers' writing or talk; analyzes that information; and draws some conclusions.

There is considerable debate as to whether a teacher can conduct research on his or her own teaching. Some of this debate is related to the question of stance. In order to examine his or her own teaching, a teacher needs to adopt an alternative stance associated with being a "researcher." Teachers may be more likely to adopt such a stance if they collaborate with colleagues. Through collaboration, teachers gain alternative perspectives from one another that encourage different ways of reflecting on the same data. Inservice workshops or courses can provide teachers with qualitative research methods for observing classrooms and the school culture, interviewing students and colleagues, and analyzing data. And teachers can collaboratively plan projects with peers and university faculty, a process that itself fosters a considerable degree of reflection.

While the group, in a brief series of meetings, did not have the time to formulate a definitive theoretical model for what constitutes effective inservice, it initiated a dialogue about something we spend a lot of time doing but little time talking about. This suggests that those of us who advocate teacher reflection in our inservice courses and workshops may need to spend more time reflecting on our own efforts.

## References

Athanases, S. Z., E. Caret, J. Canales, and T. Meyer. 1992. "Four against 'The Two-Worlds Pitfall': University-Schools Collaboration in Teacher Education." *English Education* 24, no. 1:34–51.

Beach, R., and D. Tedick. 1992. Teachers' Reflection in Journal, Case-Study, and Narrative Writing. Paper presented at the annual meeting of the American Educational Research Association, April, San Francisco.

Bissex, G. L., and R. H. Bullock. 1987. *Seeing for Ourselves: Case-Study Research by Teachers of Writing*. Portsmouth, N.H.: Heinemann.

Brodkey, L. 1989. "On the Subjects of Class and Gender in 'The Literacy Letters.'" *College English* 51, no. 2:125–41.

Bruner, J. S. 1986. *Actual Minds, Possible Worlds*. Cambridge: Harvard University Press.

Carr, W., and S. Kemmis. 1986. *Becoming Critical: Education, Knowledge, and Action Research*. London: Falmer Press.

Cochran-Smith, M., and S. L. Lytle. 1990. "Research on Teaching and Teacher Research: The Issues That Divide." *Educational Researcher* 19, no. 2:2–10.

Daiker, D. A., and M. Morenberg, eds. 1990. *The Writing Teacher as Researcher: Essays in the Theory and Practice of Class-Based Research*. Portsmouth, N.H.: Boynton/Cook.

Dunstan, A., J. Kirscht, J. Reiff, M. Roemer, and N. Tingle. 1989. "Working in the Classroom: Teachers Talk about What They Do." *English Education* 21:39–52.

Feiman-Nemser, S., and M. Buchmann. 1985. "Pitfalls of Experience in Teacher Education." *Teachers College Record* 87, no. 1:53–65.

Freedman, S. G. 1990. *Small Victories: The Real World of a Teacher, Her Students, and Their High School*. New York: Harper and Row.

Goswami, D., and P. R. Stillman, eds. 1987. *Reclaiming the Classroom: Teacher Research as an Agency for Change*. Upper Montclair, N.J.: Boynton/Cook.

Gutierrez, K. 1992. The Effects of Contexts on Writing Process Instruction for Latino Children. Paper presented at the annual meeting of the American Educational Research Association, April, San Francisco.

Labov, W. 1972. *Language of the Inner City: Studies in the Black English Vernacular*. Philadelphia: University of Pennsylvania Press.

Lytle, S. L., and R. Fecho. 1991. "Meeting Strangers in Familiar Places: Teacher Collaboration by Cross-Visitation." *English Education* 23, no. 1:5–28.

Patterson, L., J. C. Stansell, and S. Lee. 1990. *Teacher Research: From Promise to Power*. Katonah, N.Y.: Richard C. Owen.

# 10 Issues Emerging from the Teacher-Researcher Discussion Group

Christine C. Pappas
University of Illinois at Chicago

*Christine Pappas provides an interpretive account of the conference discussions that centered on teacher inquiry and research. Here she shares insights about the role of theory in teacher inquiry and the implications that such research has for existing power relations in the educational community.*

This paper is based solely on my own recollection of ideas and issues that emerged in the teacher-researcher small-group discussions that took place throughout the weekend of the conference. Although I had not yet been asked to summarize the proceedings, and so I had not kept formal notes or audio recordings, I hope that this rendition will seem familiar to the other participants in our small-group sessions—even with the influence of my own personal interpretive frame on the topic of teacher research.

Two sets of concerns stood out for me as causing the most heated and lively discussion, so I will focus on them. One had to do with the development and use of teacher "cases" in language and literacy education, and the other centered on the role of theory in teacher research. A brief summary of the kinds of questions that emerged in our group on each of these two topics is presented first, and then issues of power and knowledge that necessarily undergird these questions are discussed.

## The Development and Use of Teacher Case Studies

Much of the discussion in our group about the role of teacher case studies in teacher education was sparked by the Grossman and Shulman presentation (see chapter 1). They argued—toward the end of that paper—that the "knowledge base" of teaching must consist, in large part, of carefully collected and analyzed cases of teaching and learning, and that the use of these case studies could be extremely helpful in teacher education. In other words, principles could be derived from the analysis of these accounts that could then be compared to accounts of teaching from other, traditional, forms of educational investigation, and this process would offer a new and better way to educate teachers in university methods courses.

Most comments in our group concerned issues and questions regarding the use of these case studies—in terms of teacher research. Much discussion revolved around the notion of "case" itself. What exactly is a case? It seemed to be a "hot" topic for secondary teachers/educators, but many of us—perhaps because a majority of the group members were involved primarily in elementary education—did not know what it meant. Many questions arose. What was the purpose of a case? How was a particular case initiated or selected? That is, in the development of these cases, does the teacher pose the questions, which would be a hallmark or distinguishing feature of teacher research? Or is a case someone else's description of a teacher's teaching? And, when a researcher writes a narrative of the teaching of a particular teacher, does the methodology used in developing that case involve opportunities for that teacher to respond to what has been written about him or her? If so, how is that response incorporated into the final representation of the teacher's thinking and knowledge about his or her teaching?

Another set of questions asked about issues involved in actually using these cases in teacher education. When university professors choose particular sets of teacher cases for their students to read and study, aren't there problems of selection? That is, won't their own interpretive frames be reflected in what narrative cases they present to students, and how they present them? And, if only short excerpts of cases are provided, on what criteria will these abbreviations be based? In other words, in choosing particular cases, university-based teachers are making certain points, and there may be danger of an "agenda"— a hidden curriculum—operating that is not explicit. Participants wondered: Why don't university educators just use teachers' own personal narratives written by themselves?

## The Role of Theory in Teacher Research

The role of theory in teacher research was debated in our group discussion, especially after Glenda Bissex's talk (see chapter 6). Many in the group felt that she was arguing that teacher research is atheoretical—that what teachers are investigating in their own classrooms is generated and influenced exclusively by their practice, not theory. Participants' questions included: Aren't there some theoretical notions—even if they are implicit or tacit—that have led to particular teacher inquiries into teaching, learning, and schooling? Maybe when teachers initiate a study to know more about something that has surprised or puzzled them in their teaching they are discovering or gaining insights into their underlying theories, and in the process making those theories more explicit.

Others suggested that what is at the root of our views about the importance or even the existence of theory in teacher research may have to do with what is meant by "theory." Perhaps the problem is that we may conceive of a theoretical grounding based on a teacher's practice and research as something qualitatively different from a theory adopted from someone else. Why can't the conceptions that result from the teacher's own interpretive frame or stance toward teaching and learning be theoretical? Maybe we err when we view theory as that which must be somehow "proven," rather than as a way to understand or construct teachers' own sense of things happening in the classroom.

Related to these concerns were questions from university-based educators. If we are going to recognize and accept the importance and validity of teachers' constructions of their own theories or interpretive frames, what is the role of these university teachers in the process? Moreover, how can university teachers foster and support inquiry in beginning teachers in teacher preparation programs, as well as throughout teachers' professional lives?

## Knowledge, Power, and Teacher Research

As the above summaries indicate, mostly questions, not resolutions or conclusions, emerged in our teacher-researcher group discussions. I believe that underlying all of these questions are issues of knowledge and power.

The questions about the development and use of teacher cases or narratives reflect certain epistemological and methodological issues. According to Gitlin (1990), traditional educational research rarely involves a level of question-posing from teachers. As a result, this research silences teachers-as-subjects and "strengthens the assumptions that practitioners do not produce knowledge, that their personal knowledge is not useful" (444). Although teacher case studies are seen to be narratives of how teachers have constructed their knowledge and beliefs about teaching, many of the group's questions addressed the extent to which these teachers were given opportunities to initiate their own questions about their teaching, or to respond to what had been written about them. In other words, from the perspective of teacher research, participants in our group discussions were concerned as to whether teacher case study research has been done *on* teachers or *with* teachers. Heron (1981) has expressed such concerns and how they entail issues of power:

> For persons, as autonomous beings, have a moral right to participate in decisions that claim to generate knowledge about them. Such a right . . . protects them . . . from being managed and manipulated . . . [T]he moral principle of respect for all persons is most fully honored

> when power is shared not only in the application . . . but also in the
> generation of knowledge. (155)

It is impossible to do research and represent teachers' knowledge without being concerned with matters of power; it is an unresolvable paradox (Oyler and Pappas 1992). In the words of Nespor and Barylske (1991), "To represent others is to reduce them and to constitute relations of power that favor the representers [the university researchers] over the represented (such as the teachers we write about)" (806). But we can begin to be more aware of the problematic nature of representation and power inherent in approaches of narrative interviewing, upon which many of these teacher cases rely, and we can begin to reevaluate and perhaps modify our methodologies to make sure that we are presenting, as clearly as we can, teachers' own voices. As our questions indicated, a similar awareness is also necessary in using cases in teacher-education programs. As Foucault (1971) wrote: "Every educational system is a political means of maintaining or modifying the appropriateness of discourses with the knowledge and power they bring with them" (3). Being explicit about the issue of knowledge/power in the ways in which teacher cases are developed, as well as in how these cases are selected for use in particular courses, seems critical.

Teacher research, or the inquiry that makes possible *learning from teaching* (Cochran-Smith and Lytle 1992), involves issues of knowledge and power no less. Debates about the role of theory in teacher research are concerned with the nature of the knowledge that both spawns, and is generated by, teacher research. Power issues are raised when many university researchers view teachers' knowledge generated from teacher research, or teachers' practical theories of teaching, as somehow having "second-class" status.

The current interest in and visibility of teacher research (for example a recent international conference held at Stanford University that focused solely on teacher research) is in many ways integrally related to new definitions of literacy and how literacy should be, and is being, taught. These new ideas in language education—what Willinsky (1990) calls the New Literacy—involve making reading and writing more personally meaningful, making the processes of the formation of literacy more powerful for students. These new directions in literacy require changing the relationships of control in classroom activities for both teachers and students alike. In Willinsky's words:

> The New Literacy speaks directly to teachers reasserting control over the
> work that goes on in the class, even as it attempts to hand a greater part
> of the locus of meaning over to the student. It represents a taking hold of
> the curriculum by the teacher at a fundamental level by challenging the
> meaning of literacy in the classroom as well as the nature of a teacher's
> work with the students. (19)

Thus, the New Literacy calls for teachers to have more autonomy with regard to what happens in their classrooms, and, as Willinsky's remarks imply, has teachers reevaluating the everyday structural patterns of their interactions with their students. At the root of these changes are changes in basic issues of power and authority as teachers take on more of a collaborative style of teaching. Moreover, it is these changes, I believe, that have prompted many teachers to initiate the study and analysis of their own teaching.

Just as teachers struggle to recognize their students as meaning makers ("constructors of their own knowledge") by sharing power and control with them through collaboration, many of the questions in our group sessions indicate how university educators are also struggling to construct new collaborative relationships with teachers. Adopting a constructivist stance to teachers' knowledge, assuming that teachers have the authority to know, means that university educators must find new ways to share power with them in both teaching and research. How do we develop preservice and inservice programs that both respect and foster teachers' constructions of knowledge? How can we make our knowledge in our university classes problematic so that it can be seen as rich and generative, not as received wisdom (Cochran-Smith and Lytle 1992)? How can we demonstrate inquiry in the ways we conduct our courses so that teachers can develop skills to do inquiry into teaching and learning in their own classrooms, schools, and communities (Pappas, in press)? How can we do research *with* teachers and not *on* them (Miller 1990)? How can university-based and teacher-based researchers collaborate so that we can challenge each other, from our respective social networks (Nespor and Barylske 1991), to make our practice fit our theories, and change our theories as they are informed by our practice (Oyler and Pappas 1992)? These are some of the implications and challenges that the conference engendered for those who participated in the teacher-researcher discussion group.

## References

Cochran-Smith, M., and S. L. Lytle. 1992. "Interrogating Cultural Diversity: Inquiry and Action." *Journal of Teacher Education* 43:104–15.

Gitlin, A. D. 1990. "Educative Research, Voice, and School Change." *Harvard Educational Review* 60:443–66.

Heron, J. 1981. "Experimental Research Methods." In *Human Inquiry*, edited by P. Reason and J. Rowan, 153–66. New York: John Wiley.

Miller, J. L. 1990. *Creating Spaces and Finding Voices: Teachers Collaborating for Empowerment.* Albany: State University of New York Press.

Nespor, J., and J. Barylske. 1991. "Narrative Discourse and Teacher Knowledge." *American Educational Research Journal* 28:805–23.

Oyler, C., and C. C. Pappas. 1992. Collaborative Research on Authority and Power with Teachers in Transition. Paper presented at the International Conference on Teacher Research, April, Stanford, Calif.

Pappas, C. C., in press. *Teacher Research in Integrated Reading-Writing Instruction.* White Plains, N.Y.: Longman.

Willinsky, J. 1990. *The New Literacy: Redefining Reading and Writing in the Schools.* New York: Routledge.

# 11 The Role of Universities in the Professional Development of Practicing Teachers

James Marshall
University of Iowa

*Another group met to discuss what role, if any, universities should play in the professional development of practicing teachers. James Marshall, in a careful synthesis of those discussions, provides an analysis of the problems and possibilities for collaboration. He calls for the establishment of a new relationship between universities and schools that would better support teacher learning.*

What should be the university's role in the development of practicing teachers? That is the question that anchored a series of small-group discussions in which I participated at the NCRE/NCTE Research Assembly conference in Chicago, and the question that I would like to explore in this essay. Before going further, though, it seems important to recognize that the question is askable only because of two assumptions that may themselves require exploration. The first is that there should indeed be a role for universities in the development of teachers in the field. We don't often ask, after all, what the role of universities should be in the ongoing development of journalists in the field, or accountants, or filmmakers, or software authors. We assume, rather, that such professionals may be provisionally trained in the universities, but that they will learn much if not most of what they need to know on the job. Practicing teachers, our question assumes, need or deserve more from the universities than that. But the second assumption implicit in our question is that we aren't sure what kinds of service those teachers need or deserve. In other professional fields—medicine, dentistry, law, engineering—the university has a distinct and usually unchallenged role: to train practitioners and to conduct the research that will make practice more effective. But such a straightforward and easily defined role for universities has eluded professionals in education, and for that reason the question of what service universities can provide for practicing teachers remains before us.

I will explore that question here by examining the traditional roles universities have assumed with regard to teachers in the field as well as some of the alternatives that have recently been suggested. I will close by offering a series of issues that need to be addressed if new and more productive relations between universities and teachers are to be realized.

What do universities do for practicing teachers? Perhaps coming first to mind is the research on teaching, learning, and schooling that is conducted in universities, usually in colleges of education, and then circulated through the rounds of professional conferences, journals, and books. In the field of literacy studies, the last twenty to thirty years have seen university-based research, for instance, on sentence combining, writing processes, small-group discussions, reading comprehension, and the teaching of literature, some of it supported by large funding agencies and all of it justified in some measure by the implicit assumption that the research would be used to improve the education of students in the schools. In fact, the "Implications for Teaching" section of almost any research report in education is a striking reminder of how sturdy are the expectations that educational research will have practical, if not immediate, benefits. The validity of those expectations may be arguable, but the conduct of research seems clearly to be a large part of the role universities see for themselves in teacher development.

In addition to research, there are at least three other ways in which universities can be said to be serving practicing teachers—all of them in some measure a function of the university's own teaching mission. Most obvious are the graduate courses designed specifically for teachers, offered usually in the summer or the evening, and meant to provide teachers with new understandings and new knowledge derived from new research. So important are these opportunities that some school districts have resisted moving to year-long school calendars precisely because teachers would then have fewer opportunities to read and reflect on professional matters.

The second service provided by universities, or, more commonly, by individuals within universities, is the kind of consulting or inservice work that brings university personnel to the schools for late-August professional development days, after-school workshops, or longer and more ambitious programs that call for daylong meetings, released time for selected teachers, and ongoing relationships between university and school staff. The cost and formality of such arrangements vary widely, as do the educational philosophies of those providing the service (from Madeline Hunter to Donald Graves). But what they have in common is the presence of someone from the university among teachers, and the expectation that that someone is going to help the teachers do their work more effectively.

And lastly, universities, or again, individuals within universities, are usually the ones who oversee, edit, or sometimes write the textbooks that will be made available to teachers and students in the schools. Whether such texts help or hinder teachers in their work undoubtedly depends on the books chosen, but the fact that there are almost always some university personnel working with textbook publishers suggests that this too is a way in which universities help shape the kind of instruction teachers can provide.

Such an overview of universities' role in teacher development is sketchy at best, but it can perhaps provide a point of departure for examining if and how that role might be changed. Of course, we might argue that there are no clear alternatives to these traditional relationships. Given the fact that university researchers who work with practicing teachers must still achieve respectability among their colleagues on campus, it would be unreasonable, we might say, to expect them to spend more time providing service to teachers and schools. Such work drains energy and resources that might otherwise go to academic scholarship, and it is that scholarship, after all, that leads to professional advancement. Providing courses over the summer, orchestrating workshops and inservices, consulting on textbooks—in one view, these represent the reasonable limit of what universities can do for teachers.

But such an argument is weak on at least two fronts. First, whatever the institutional convenience of current arrangements for university personnel, it seems obvious that those arrangements have not always been as helpful to teachers as they might be. We have volumes of studies documenting the fact that educational research has frequently not found a clear way into practice, and additional quantities of reports from teachers, both formal and anecdotal, that they are often impatient with and even distrustful of the research and service provided by university personnel. If university-based research and service as presently structured cannot be justified on the basis of their clear usefulness to schools, the traditional relationships between universities and classroom teachers will need to be reexamined.

But there is an even more compelling reason for such a reexamination. Even a cursory overview of university-school relations, such as that provided here, suggests an unequal distribution of knowledge and power among the stakeholders, with university personnel as the producers of discourse about education and classroom teachers as the consumers of that discourse. Teachers in this model are to receive university-based research, listen to inservice presentations, employ the textbook exercises provided to them. Knowledge flows from the university, in this view, to the schools and to the teachers who work in them. What makes such a model not only ineffective, but, ironically, inappropriate, is that it is precisely this "traditional" model of instruction that much of our research and scholarship about teaching has been working to dismantle.

The critique of that traditional model of teaching, of course, extends from Rousseau through Dewey, and has continued in our own field in the work of Moffett (1968), Britton (1970), Barnes (1975), and Elbow (1973), among others. The critique itself represents a tradition—a progressive tradition as sturdy, indeed as venerable, as almost any in educational thought. It has manifested itself in proposals for process approaches to writing instruction, reader-response approaches to literature instruction, and whole-language approaches to elementary reading and writing instruction. As part of its agenda for change, the progressive tradition has sought to valorize classrooms that are student-centered instead of teacher-centered, where students are not implicitly conceived as containers to be filled, but as producers of discourse, as makers of meaning. And in efforts to implement that agenda, progressive educators such as Donald Graves and Nancie Atwell have developed a wide range of classroom strategies that provide students with increasing opportunities to participate in the ongoing construction of knowledge.

The progressive critique of traditional instruction can be extended quite easily to the "traditional" relationship between universities and schools that I have been outlining, and when it is, clear changes seem called for. A new, more progressive model of that relationship would begin with a conception of teachers as skilled experts, equipped with an abundance of professional knowledge and hard-won classroom experience. In such a model, teachers do not need the outside expertise of university personnel so much as they need opportunities to develop and share their own perceptions and understandings. Instead of consumers of university-generated knowledge, teachers in this model would become producers of school-based, teacher-generated knowledge. The university's role with regard to teachers might shift in much the same way as a teacher's role shifts in progressive models of classroom learning. The university would become facilitative rather than directive, providing forums for teachers to set their own agendas and develop their own professional understandings of their students, their teaching, and their schools. We have already seen in the National Writing Project one highly successful effort to provide teachers with the time and opportunity to make knowledge for themselves, and other, more local, efforts—some of them described in this volume—are also demonstrating how powerful a reimagined model of teacher development can be.

But there are, I think, several issues that need to be addressed before we can move more fully into a new kind of relationship between universities and schools. I would like to examine three of those issues here.

First, what longstanding conventions of universities and schools may constrain efforts to redesign the relationship between them? Both institutions may have to confront fundamental questions of knowledge, power, and resources if new connections are to be made. On the one hand, universities will have to find a way to value the more facilitative role their personnel will assume and may, more critically, have to question their own privileged role as the most important producer of knowledge about teaching. What position will university-based research about teaching hold when teachers are themselves producing knowledge about teaching? What position will university-based researchers hold with respect to teachers who are newly empowered to conduct their own research? The political dynamics of a new relationship will clearly require new strategies and new assumptions on the part of universities.

But that new relationship will also require new policy directions in schools. More than anything, teachers who are empowered to produce and share knowledge about their work will require the time and the resources to do so. Are schools ready to consider reduced teaching loads, sabbatical leaves, and new rewards for teachers who are making efforts to extend their professional understanding? Is the public ready to fund a redesigned career for teachers—a career that may increasingly resemble that of university professors in its commitments and privileges? If we are serious about making teachers more central in the development of professional knowledge, then clearly some very basic changes will have to be made in the way teachers' professional lives are structured.

Second, in what ways will teacher-generated knowledge about teaching be different from university-generated knowledge about teaching? Lil Brannon (1989) has argued that teacher knowledge is fundamentally narrative in form, taking its shape from the time-and-space-bound contours of classroom life. In such a view, teacher knowledge might best be represented as a set of thought-ful stories that together would constitute an evolving body of case literature based on actual events. Stephen North (1987), on the other hand, has argued for a conception of teacher knowledge as "lore"—a fundamentally oral and always developing body of advice, strategy, and professional wisdom that comes directly from classroom experience and is, therefore, far more trust-worthy to teachers than the more distant and abstract forms of research provided by universities. And Miles Myers (1985) has presented a case for teacher research that is local and practical in its aspirations, but that resembles in many respects the kinds of inquiry undertaken by university research. All of these may be accurate descriptions of the knowledge teachers will make, or none may be, but the fact remains that we have encouraged so little teacher-generated discourse about teaching that we are not sure what it will look like when it becomes more widely available.

The third issue, and the most troubling, I think, is this: In what ways will providing opportunities for teachers to reflect on their work make that work more meaningful and more effective? Or put more bleakly: In what ways will the opportunity to think clearly about their work leave teachers with a more depressed sense of the inadequacy of current policies in schools? This last issue has been brought forcefully to my attention at my home institution, where for several years we have been encouraging practicing teachers to use newly available state and local funds to come back to the university for a semester or sometimes a full year. These teachers work as part-time instructors in the first-year composition program, take graduate courses toward their master's degrees or Ph.D.'s, and become for a time members of a community that reads about, talks about, and writes about teaching in critically reflective ways. When the teachers are with us, they have reported, they feel energized and renewed. But when they go back to their schools—to the five classes of thirty students each, to the assistant principal who doesn't understand their field, to the required basals and the required standardized tests—they often feel overwhelmed by what they formerly took for granted. Their testimony suggests that schools as they are currently structured may not reward the kinds of reflection a new model of teacher development would propose. In fact, in some respects, teachers' work may become even more challenging and politically charged when they are given the time to consider the extraordinarily complex nature of that work, and the opportunity to discuss alternatives.

None of the three issues I have raised here, of course, represents an insoluble problem in the renewal of the relationship between universities and schools. But they do not seem trivial or avoidable either. If we are to move forward in enfranchising teachers as producers of their own professional knowledge, then we need to assess realistically the obstacles that longstanding institutional conventions have left in our path. Finding a way to talk about those obstacles and those conventions may be the first step in beginning a new and different kind of conversation between universities and teachers.

## References

Brannon, L. 1989. *Teaching Literature in High School: A Teacher-Researcher Project.* Technical Report for the Center for the Learning and Teaching of Literature. Albany: State University of New York.

Barnes, D. 1976. *From Communication to Curriculum.* Harmondsworth: Penguin.

Britton, J. N. 1970. *Language and Learning.* Harmondsworth: Penguin.

Elbow, P. 1973. *Writing without Teachers.* New York: Oxford University Press.

Moffett, J. 1968. *Teaching the Universe of Discourse.* Boston: Houghton Mifflin.

Myers, M. 1985. *The Teacher-Researcher: How to Study Writing in the Classroom.* Urbana, Ill.: NCTE.

North, S. 1987. *The Making of Knowledge in Composition: Portrait of an Emerging Field.* Upper Montclair, N.J.: Boynton/Cook.

# 12 What Followed for Me

Michael W. Smith
Rutgers University

*Michael W. Smith coordinated discussions of preservice education at the conference. In this highly personal account of the impact of the proceedings on his own thinking, Smith provides a thoughtful analysis of the overall experience. He goes beyond the notion of simply summarizing or interpreting the conversations and shows how the issues raised in the papers and discussions have continued to percolate for him.*

In David Lodge's *Small World* (1984) the hero befuddles a panel of famous literary critics and causes a huge uproar at the MLA convention by asking what seems to be a very natural question: "What follows if everybody agrees with you?" That was also the question that our discussion group of people involved in preservice teacher education asked after each of the papers and that I've been asking myself in the months since the conference. I'm happy to be part of a discipline where asking such a question is to be expected. But ease of asking and ease of answering are not necessarily linked. And no important question has an easy answer. So what I'd like to share is how the question I have been asking has been evolving, and the kinds of thinking it's been forcing me to do.

During the conference my group talked about specific implications of each of the papers. For example, after Pamela Grossman presented the paper she wrote with Lee Shulman (see chapter 1) we discussed how we used or might use case studies in our methods classes. But in my subsequent reflection on the conference, rather than seeing the papers as a series of suggestions, I began to see them as all relating to a central issue, one that I now think is at the very center of teacher education, but one that I had not spent enough time considering. That issue, in Deborah Britzman's words (see chapter 4), is "the terrible problem of knowing thyself," a problem she illustrates by telling the story of Jamie Owl, a student teacher who is struggling "to construct and negotiate" her identity as a teacher.

In telling Jamie's story, Britzman makes an important distinction between a teacher's role, that is, the teacher's public function, and the identity of a teacher, that is, the values and beliefs one brings to teaching. Jamie's story illustrates what happens when playing the role of a teacher impedes inventing an identity. Jamie's struggle can perhaps be explained by psychologist Dan McAdams. He argues that

> a major goal in life—perhaps the major goal—is to compose the right story for one's own life. The person who is able to do so understands who he or she was, is, and will be, integrating past, present, and future into a meaningful life narrative. The person who has found a story to unify life has found what psychologists call "identity." (1989, 28)

Jamie could not compose a meaningful life narrative because her story could not accommodate both what she brought to teaching and what she did as a teacher. Jamie was having an identity crisis, a term that is too often used to dismiss a problem as an adolescent concern that will be outgrown. McAdams gives us insight into just how important such a crisis is.

In thinking about Jamie's story I've thought about my own. And I've wondered about how the differences in our stories would have affected the way I would have worked with Jamie. Unlike Jamie, I have always embraced the idea of being a teacher. Some years ago some friends and I played a parlor game that can only be played by good friends and even then only after a good dinner and a little wine. Someone asked, "If you could choose only one word to describe yourself, what would that be?" After some debate about whether hyphenations would be allowed, we all thought seriously about the single word we would choose to describe ourselves. I chose "teacher." The picture I had in my mind was not the picture of the authoritarian that so bothered Jamie. What I pictured instead was someone humane, and patient, and funny, and concerned, and open-minded (qualities that while I may not have I at least aspire to), someone who worked with others to bring out their best.

Because this was the picture that I brought with me to my methods classes, and because I assumed that my students brought with them similar pictures, I concentrated on working with prospective teachers on how to enact that picture, how to plan reading, and speaking, and writing activities consistent with the image of "teacher" that I held. But I too seldom articulated the vision behind my teaching, and even more important I too seldom asked my students to articulate theirs.

Jamie's story has helped me understand how important it is to provide opportunities for my students to elaborate what it means to them to be a teacher, the perspectives and metaphors that will guide their efforts (cf. Gere, Fairbanks, Howes, Roop, and Schaafsma 1992). I think that Jamie suffered in part because she had not done this. Instead of looking to her own conception of what it means to be a teacher Jamie talked about adopting the role "that has been designated teacher." The passive construction indicates that she was struggling against a vision of teaching that had been handed down to her from some unnamed source. If what Britzman says is true, and I am in large measure persuaded that it is, what follows for me as a teacher educator is that I must work to help my students develop their visions of themselves as teachers.

Jamie's equating "teacher" with "authoritarian" was at the center of her difficulty. And she is not alone in making that equation. Brian White, one of the participants in the conference, explained that his study (1992) of the questions that student teachers posed in their journals suggests that although students were struggling to understand their role, they saw being a competent manager as central to it. In fact, questions about management were more common than questions about any other aspect of a teacher's role. Of course, management is important, but it is little wonder that student teachers who see maintaining order as the *sine qua non* of teaching are uncomfortable stepping into that role. What they need, it seems to me, is a new vision of what it means to be a teacher. The papers of Judy Buchanan (see chapter 3) and of Glenda Bissex (see chapter 6) offer one such vision: the teacher as inquirer.

This vision of what it means to be a teacher is radically at odds with the one that Jamie and so many other student teachers hold. Three crucial differences stand out for me. In the first place both Buchanan and Bissex write of the teacher as inquirer, as what one *is* rather than as what one *does*. That is, unlike Jamie, who saw being a teacher as doing the things that teachers do, Buchanan and Bissex speak of teachers in terms of the habits of mind they bring to their teaching, their concern, thoughtfulness, open-mindedness, and courage. This shift in focus would certainly be important to Jamie. Jamie is disturbed because she cannot compose a coherent life story. Britzman argues that Jamie's effort is a mistake, that she is "attempting an impossible transcendence." But what McAdams (1989) describes is not a search for transcendence, but rather a search for coherence. He argues that what provides this coherence is the nature of the main character in the story that a person composes. (His discussion of generativity [160–64] is especially germane in this context.) If Jamie's conception of what it means to be a teacher had changed, her search for coherence would not have been thwarted by the interference of the role she was forced to play. Casting herself in the role of inquirer would instead have allowed her to create a more consistent vision of herself, for this role requires much of what Jamie sees in herself as a "human being," including the doubts.

Second, in the conception of teacher as inquirer, the locus of authority shifts from Jamie's unnamed others, who are dictating what a teacher should be, to the teachers themselves, who are the creators and disseminators of knowledge. Britzman notes that one of Jamie's problems is that she is working to create an identity in a situation in which she has little say. But as Smagorinsky and Jordahl (1991) conclude, the politics of the student-teaching experience change when the student-teacher is also a researcher, especially when the cooperating teacher is a co-investigator.

And third, instead of being paralyzing, the conception of teacher as inquirer brings with it a commitment to activism, a commitment by both student teachers and experienced teachers to change their classrooms, schools, and districts in accordance with what they have learned in their inquiries. (See Lytle and Cochran-Smith 1992 for elaboration of this point.) If what Buchanan and Bissex say is true—and I find their arguments very persuasive—what follows for me as a teacher educator is that I must work to make it more likely that my students will put inquiry at the heart of their practice.

The conference, then, presented me with two challenges: working to help my students articulate their visions of teaching and encouraging them to include inquiry as part of that vision. The other papers of the conference suggested ways to help me meet those challenges. Schubert and Ayers (see chapter 7), for example, argue that more attention could profitably be paid to educational lore in literature and the arts. They suggest that such study may enhance our understanding of teaching and the curriculum. What strikes me is that this study might also help my students understand their conception of teaching and the extent to which it has been influenced by the arts. How many of our students come to us inspired by the Robin Williams character in *Dead Poets Society?* More than a few, I would guess. But do we treat this inspiration seriously? Having prospective teachers write and talk about the artistic influences that have shaped their vision will help them explore the assumptions that underlie those visions, making it more likely, on the one hand, that they can put them into practice, or, on the other, that they can turn a critical eye on them.

Artistic renditions of teaching are to some extent cases. Grossman and Shulman (see chapter 1) argue that the knowledge base of teaching should largely be made up of case studies of teaching and learning, a principle that also guides the Teacher Lore Project about which Ayers and Schubert write. Grossman and Shulman contend that studying cases will help students understand the range of possibilities inherent in a given teaching situation. They argue further that through such study students can learn the "strategic and moral lessons" the narratives contain. Petrosky (see chapter 2) notes that the consideration of cases can provide the occasion for the production of discourse and that discourse can be interpreted for the kinds of knowledge it employs. It does not stretch Petrosky's argument much to see the discourse student teachers might produce about cases as texts that would help them read themselves by helping them understand the beliefs they are bringing to teaching.

When students are doing this analysis, they are doing research. The conference helped bring home to me that if I want my students to understand the benefits of inquiry, I have to do more than actively engage them in discussing the results of the research of others. I have to engage them in the collection and analysis of data. The ethnography projects that Beverly Moss describes (see chapter 5), for example, could be at the center of a methods class and give students lessons about sameness and diversity and about what inquiry can teach them.

The conference has made me think hard about my teaching. And my courses will be different because of it. But I don't want to give the impression that the papers provide easy answers. Although I think that it is important to have students explore their conceptions of teaching, I know that their explorations are likely to put me in a dilemma. I have to create an atmosphere in which students feel safe to say what they are thinking. But I don't believe that all conceptions of teaching are equal. I don't think much of the kind of teaching Robin Williams's character did in *Dead Poets Society,* for example. How can I communicate my thinking without making the project another version of "Guess What's on the Teacher's Mind"? I know that articulating a vision is important, but I also know that students need specific knowledge, what Grossman and Shulman call pedagogical content knowledge, to be able to put their visions into practice. I worry about finding a balance between seeing the big picture and studying the little things that make the big picture possible. I think I know some of those little things, but I wonder if sharing them makes my students passive recipients of my knowledge rather than creators of their own. I want my students to make inquiry part of their teaching, but, as Sally Hampton points out, schools are not set up to support that kind of inquiry.

As comforting as it would be to go away from a conference with definitive answers, going away with questions may be even more important. If I believe that the vision of teacher as inquirer offers my students an important way of imagining themselves, then what follows for me as a teacher is that I must be an inquirer too, that I must study my own practice. The conference has given me a place to start.

## References

Gere, A., C. Fairbanks, A. Howes, L. Roop, and D. Schaafsma. 1992. *An Integrated Approach to Teaching English.* New York: Macmillan.

Lodge, D. 1984. *Small World: An Academic Romance.* London: Secker and Warburg.

Lytle, S. L., and M. Cochran-Smith. 1992. Inquiry and Action: Interrogating Cultural Diversity. Paper presented at the University of Pennsylvania Ethnography in Education Research Forum, Philadelphia.

McAdams, D. P. 1989. *Intimacy: The Need to Be Close.* New York: Doubleday.

Smagorinsky, P., and A. Jordahl. 1991. "The Student Teacher/Cooperating Teacher Collaborative Study: A New Source of Knowledge." English Education 23:54–59.

White, B. 1992. Becoming an English Teacher: A Focus on Survival. Paper presented at the NCTE Annual Convention, November, Louisville.

# 13 In Search of Community within English Education

Renée T. Clift
University of Illinois at Urbana-Champaign

*Renée T. Clift was charged with the responsibility of being a commenta-
tor at the conference. She was asked to make sense of all of the papers
and proceedings and to share her insights with us at the final session. It
is apparent from what follows that at times she heard a cacophony of
discordant voices. Nevertheless, she provides a masterly and generous
account of some of the common themes that resonated throughout the
meetings. She places our "search for community" as a central force,
process, and fact of life in all teacher learning development.*

My remarks in this chapter are based on two assumptions about the nature of
knowing and learning how to teach. The first is that categories of knowledge
for teaching English are formed, reformed, constructed, reconstructed, and
rearranged as teachers interact with others in and out of classrooms. The
second assumption is that this process of knowing is profoundly affected by
teachers thinking about who they are and who they would like to be as persons
and, then, who they are and who they would like to be as teachers of English.
What counts as knowledge for the teaching of English, therefore, is both a
function of social negotiation and of individual biography. For those of us
who are educators, salient (or valued) knowledge within the larger domain of
English is a reflection of the communities created by drawing boundary
lines—those drawn to *exclude* categories of ideas, people, and items that do
not belong; those drawn to *include* categories that do belong; and those drawn
to illustrate the *intersections* among items that might properly belong to more
than one category.

What I might consider to be essential knowledge—an understanding of
reader-response theory, for example—another might consider either controversial, trivial, or impractically theoretical. As I interact with those who hold
different views, I may change my mind, adapt my position to accommodate
these different views, agree to disagree, or choose to withdraw from further
interactions. In this chapter I will argue that several diverse discourse commu-

nities are drawn upon as novice teachers move through university settings, into school settings, and (perhaps) into collaborations between the two. While one person might construe these communities as alike, possibly even the same, another might construe them as distinct and even antithetical to each other.

As Beverly Moss (chapter 5) reminds us, within and across communities there are similar and dissimilar values, norms, goals, and rituals. When one stands far from the perimeter of a community, one might not notice this. But when one begins to interact with community members, similarities and differences become more apparent, although how one interprets these may depend on whether one has a receptive or a hostile mindset. While we are beginning to learn more about the communities involved in learning to teach English, we have tended to focus more on the individual construction of knowledge than on the social, and we know more about the novice teacher's construction of knowledge in English than we do about those who affect that construction, whether they are university professors, graduate students, or field-based teacher educators.

I hold these assumptions, in part, because of my research with novice English teachers who are simultaneously labeled students and teachers, in what Britzman (see chapter 4) notes is the oxymoron of student teaching. In working with the novices I have come to understand how much we do not understand about the adults with whom they interact briefly, nor do we have sufficient knowledge of how individuals construct meaning when the messages from those adults are perceived to be discrepant or contradictory. But also, reflection on my experiences as an English teacher, a teacher educator, and a researcher has a very personal meaning as I think back on my experiences with and around communities defined by labels such as *drama teacher, speech teacher, advanced placement teacher, remedial teacher, English professor, education professor, teacher educator, psychologist, educational researcher,* and others. Moving into any of these communities requires both individual volition and acceptance by the community. While I have always labeled myself an educator, throughout the past twenty-plus years I have moved in and around numerous educational discourse communities—some with which I strongly identify, others in which I remain on the periphery, and still others to which I will never be accepted because I do not have the proper "credentials." And so I begin with a brief example of my own background as a prelude to speculating on others who are in the field of English education.

## A Personal Biography and Search for Community

For eight years I was a high school English teacher. Although I was primarily assigned to teach speech and drama, I also taught world literature, British and

American literature, and, for a few very special semesters, the literature of mystery, suspense, and science fiction. When I think back to those eight years in Florida I see one often confused high school teacher working with various groupings of white and African American students in work that was sometimes devoid of meaning for them, for me, and for us as a group. I wondered a lot about this issue of meaning. Why were my drama students usually involved and committed, while these same students in my literature classes were compliant, but unenthusiastic? Why was I able to help my speech students develop confidence, critical analytical skills, and a sense of self, while my students' writing never showed similar progress? And, finally, what did it mean to be a student in New Smyrna Beach Senior High School when racial tension was low? Or high? When drug use was the norm for some groups, but not for others? I realize now that I would have been a good member of the Philadelphia Teachers' Learning Cooperative (see chapter 3), but at the time I did not think in terms of research or action research.

I did think about my teaching and my students, although I never used terms like "reflection on action" or "reflection in action" (Schon 1983). I wasn't a perfect teacher; I made a lot of mistakes. But there were moments when I was a very, very good teacher. Those were the moments when the students and I had all worked hard to produce a play, to record student-authored mysteries, or to write poems to one another, or when we all became a community of learners as we investigated the meaning of a short story, poem, or novel—when "I" was a contributing part of "we." In making the decision to leave high school for full-time graduate work I opted for time to think, to reconstruct my experience as a high school teacher of white and African American children, and, then, to continue teaching somewhere, not to leave the classroom.

Graduate school was total immersion into the language of academic research. Experimental design, cognitive developmental comparisons, clinical interviews, connoisseurship, trustworthiness, positivism, probability sampling, triangulation, and other terms I had never encountered were made familiar and even comfortable as I read and worried and now tried to make sense of my reconstructed self—a teacher who was striving to be accepted as a researcher. But other terms also entered my awareness, such as process writing, new criticism, reader response, social construction, narrative unity. For just as I had never encountered research in my undergraduate education, I had never encountered theoretical orientations within the field of English. By the time I received my degree I had become aware of many concepts in English education that I hoped to take back to some classroom, some day.

My degree, however, is not in English education. In my first university position I taught foundations courses and general methods to prospective teachers in a collaborative program that crossed university departmental lines. With these colleagues I helped redesign an entire teacher education curriculum, and I wrote about reflective practice. I both wrote about and lived collaborative teaching and collaborative inquiry. I even began to categorize myself (carving out an identity as a scholar)—and the category was not English education. Although I maintained membership in NCRE and NCTE, I did not attend their conferences, because I identified more closely with the members of AACTE, ATE, and AERA. While I continued to read in some journals related to the teaching of English, I was consciously aware of the lines I was drawing—and the possibility that the community of English education would be closed to me.

I was also conscious of the continuing impact the discourse of learning to read and learning to write had on my own teaching. I had become committed to helping college students write more analytically and clearly, as well as to "debriefing" my students on their readings of texts with which I was already familiar. And, through their eyes, I learned that what I read into the "text" of an article, a book, or even an entire course, was not always the same as what they did. I recall one painful attempt to understand my students' perceptions better while working with Norm Kagan, a counseling psychologist. His counselors-in-training, using his technique of "interpersonal process recall," interviewed the prospective teachers in my class by discussing an audiotape of a lecture I had given. They expressed anger, pain, and hostility in recorded comments such as, "She didn't even thank us for turning in our papers." "She is lecturing about wait time and just asked a question [rhetorical, I thought] and didn't wait for an answer." "She doesn't care about us!" I also recall one student in an Introduction to Education course berating me for allowing multiple drafts of papers—because he felt it penalized students who had no time to redraft. Clearly, I had been influenced by my interactions with the English education community, but I had a lot to learn about translating my knowledge into the practice of working with adults.

In my present position at the University of Illinois, I have begun to shift my thinking about myself and my category. I am working within the context of a collaborative school-university teacher education program. I teach English methods; I also make numerous visits to observe my students and to talk with my field-based colleagues. I am a novice English educator, but an eager one. In my eagerness to improve my teaching and use my research skills I have conducted an action research project into my own teaching, in collaboration with prospective English teachers and our field-based teacher educators.

As is often the case with qualitative inquiry, the perspectives on meaning varied across role-groups. What I did not anticipate (but should have) was that the discourse community that shapes and is shaped by research values disconfirmation, while the discourse community that shapes and is shaped by teaching may see disconfirmation as harsh criticism. And so I bring to this chapter a biography shaped by walking and continuing to walk the boundaries among several professional discourse communities.

Increasingly, I have become aware of the "language with all its controls and desires" (Petrosky, chapter 2) that I and my academic colleagues use to maintain our status within our fields. It is entirely possible that the discourse that serves us well in academia oppresses our public school colleagues and, maybe, the teachers-to-be who are also our students. I have become increasingly aware that much of the discourse oriented toward teacher preparation in general, and English education in particular, is not shared by many of our university-based or school-based colleagues. Different groups have drawn boundaries around what is and is not requisite knowledge for learning English in elementary, middle, and senior high school. Each group has made decisions that some sources of knowledge are privileged and others are marginal. In reflecting on the NCRE/NCTE conference, the preceding chapters, and my current work with collaborative English education I will frame the remainder of this discussion around three questions suggested by the conference proceedings: Can we identify bases for creating community within English teacher education? Indeed, why might it be desirable to create a community of English teacher educators? And finally, will university-based educators be accepted as members of such a community?

## Bases for Creating Community within English Education

My use of the term "community" has been strongly influenced by Gee's (1990) analysis of the ideology in discourse.

> A discourse is any stretch of language (spoken, written, signed) which 'hangs together' to make sense to some community of people who use that language. . . . But making sense is always a social and variable manner: what makes sense to one community of people may not make sense to another. (103)

Communities may be defined by proximity, as with the teachers on the kindergarten team; by belief, as with the Amish; by commitment to a particular set of goals, as with the pro-choice movement; or by work role, as with professors of rhetoric. To belong to a community one may or may not be located near other members, nor do members even need to know one another (as is often the case with the NCRE/NCTE community). Proximity and acquaintance are less important than a shared worldview, or, to paraphrase from Gee, a shared ideology involving

- a set of values and viewpoints about the relationships between people and the distribution of social goods.

- the adoption of standpoints and positions defined, in part, by their opposition to other standpoints and positions.

- the advocacy of certain concepts, viewpoints, and values at the expense of others. (144)

Gee uses the term "discourse" as a count noun naming "a sort of 'identity kit' which comes complete with appropriate instructions on how to act, talk, and often write, so as to take on a particular social role that others will recognize" (142). To be accepted into a community one must not only master the discourse, but the discourse community must acknowledge that one has been accepted. Thus, while I may use concepts from social linguistics to frame one part of my construction of learning to teach, and while I may continue to study in this area, it is unlikely that I will be accepted into this particular discourse community because my training, my personal history, and my professional affiliations lie with teacher education and with English education.

I could, however, return to graduate school and retrain. Even then I might not be accepted as a sociolinguist, depending upon my performance in graduate school, my ability to integrate prior work with my new learning, and my ability to assimilate the values of the linguistic community. One barrier might be my strong conviction that educators, especially those who work with teachers, must consider how theories play out in practice in addition to developing and testing theoretical constructs. My emphasis on practice illustrates the power of individual biography on choice of community membership, but it also provides some insight into the fact that community within the university-based component of teacher education is rare.

Teacher preparation curricula are typically fragmented into courses taught by graduate students or by professors whose primary concern is education within a discipline, not the education of prospective teachers (Judge 1982; Goodlad 1990; Shuell 1992). In addition, many of these courses emphasize knowledge transmission within a narrow specialization (such as Victorian novels, or Eliot's poetry) as opposed to the individual and social integration of knowledge across domains (Ginsburg and Clift 1990). This fragmentation is often exacerbated by field experiences which may be miseducative (Feiman-Nemser and Buchmann 1987). Taken together, both university-based and field-based experiences often provide students who would be teachers with mixed messages about the status of education, the process of learning, and even the relative value of course content (Clift, Meng, and Eggerding 1992). As we move from issues in general teacher preparation to issues in English education in particular, Grossman and Shulman (see chapter 1) remind us that the term "English" is itself open to multiple interpretations and, therefore, that studying teacher knowledge in English is difficult, at best.

At least four discourse communities are embedded within Grossman and Shulman's discussion of teacher knowledge in English: (1) the community represented by Applebee, Elbow, and others who study the nature of English and English teaching; (2) the community represented by Shulman, Grossman, and others who study both the general nature of teacher learning and the distinctions that must be made when one focuses on learning within a specific content domain; (3) the community of researchers and professional educators interested in the potential of case-based learning for knowledge acquisition in complex domains; and (4) the community of novice English teachers who are in the process of constructing practical knowledge of teaching.

Ideally, the communities represented by 1, 2, and 3 would work in concert to influence and improve the learning experiences for 4. But if we were to create Venn diagrams representing intersections among these four communities would we find that this is the case? And, if we added additional communities—the university-based teachers of literature and writing and the school-based teachers of grades 6–12, would we be able to say that there is a community of English educators working in concert to optimize professional learning experiences?

Britzman's chapter (see chapter 4) suggests that the answer is "no." Her story of Jamie Owl's search for identity highlights the tension that results when a novice's personal identity confronts an experienced teacher's construction of classroom culture. While Jamie struggles to make sense of what is happening to her, she does not find a supportive group who could help her enter the discourse community comprising senior high school English teachers. There is no analogy to the child study group Buchanan describes for the student teachers in Britzman's study. Rather, while standing on the outside of the community, Jamie decides to reject the high school English teacher community and Britzman challenges us all to reconceptualize research on teacher thinking as a problem of language, as it influences the construction and reconstruction of identity.

Moss (chapter 5), who currently would not identify herself as a teacher educator, confronts issues of identity, language, and culture directly. She and her students acknowledge the tension that exists as personal identity and understanding of others' identities meet and interact. She argues persuasively that not only do her students reconstruct their understanding of similarity and diversity, but that her own understandings are reconstructed each semester she teaches composition to her first-year students. Her discussion of cultural differences as resources makes an important case for learning from both sets created by the hypothetical Venn diagrams referred to above—those communities that intersect as well as those that are disjoint. While her statement, "I want my differences to be recognized and celebrated, and I want my similarities to be recognized and celebrated," is embedded in a discussion of cultural and racial classroom issues, the words have meaning for any discussion of cultural and professional discourse issues. What are the similarities that we can celebrate across the discourse communities comprised in English education? What are the differences that we can recognize and celebrate without alienating one another?

The teachers who are, at the same time, researchers (see Bissex, chapter 6, and Buchanan, chapter 3) emphasize one potential similarity that is enjoying a resurgent prominence—the importance of teachers' learning from their own teaching. For Bissex, university teaching is at once a process of studying her own teaching, enabling others to learn from their own teaching, and creating a context in which this learning is shared and opened to discussion. For Buchanan, elementary school teaching is the same process. The Philadelphia Teachers' Learning Cooperative, through teacher-organized child study groups, provides a context for learning equivalent to that of a university course—but eliminates some of the political negotiations for power and authority that Jamie Owl experienced.

Judy Buchanan's is the only other chapter in this book to use the term "community" in its title. Buchanan acknowledges that there is some tension inherent in working across communities—especially the tension produced by talking about teachers as "they," while at the same time thinking through necessary reforms in American education. She also acknowledges that this tension is not always resolved, but ends her discussion with the observation, "It is having the opportunity to keep asking these questions that has contributed to my growth as a teacher, and it is the support of communities of teachers that makes asking these questions possible." Bissex has also noted that "a community of teacher-researchers is building—a community of teachers who are coming to see themselves as knowers." One item that we might all have in common is a commitment to continually learning, to asking the same questions in different contexts, and to growing as learners of English and learners of teaching.

A second possible base for community within English education is our interest in and fascination with the use of language in all its forms. Whether we are assessing facility and expertise in language use (see Petrosky, chapter 2), recording the oral language of teachers (see Ayers and Schubert, chapter 7), analyzing the political dimensions of language (see Britzman, chapter 4), or trying to find the right words in order to complete a book chapter, we are all fascinated with the power and beauty of oral and written communication. Too often, however, we draw a boundary line that separates our interest in language use from students' opportunities to share that interest.

Hampton's accounts (see chapter 8) of elementary and secondary school students using oral and written language to create their own curricula and to change the nature of English education in their schools is at once exciting and sobering. She reminds us many times that one teacher working in one class-room can have only a limited impact on educational change. Change is systemic; risk taking that is not supported throughout the system can result in disaster for teachers, students, and administrators. She reminds us, as do Britzman and Petrosky, that education occurs in a political context—one that we cannot escape even though we may wish to do so. And so, even though we may find bases for community in English education through our interest in language, our concern for personal and professional growth, our commitment to inquiry, and other possible similarities not discussed above, we may find that these bases are neither necessary or sufficient to promote structural or curricular change, given our differences in worldviews, especially those re-lated to the differing political and economic contexts of university systems and public school systems.

## The Potential for Community within English Teacher Education

For two years I have had the opportunity to work through an action research project with two student teachers wherein we all attempted to understand better, and to improve, our teaching. This experience has made me acutely aware of the social, political, and educational barriers that affect any attempt to redraw the boundary lines across the communities of college English, teacher education, and secondary teaching. It has also convinced me that redrawing boundaries to examine the intersections of these communities is an important task for all of us who are interested in improving instruction for students at all levels of the educational enterprise.

Scott Eggerding took his first teaching job in August 1992. As a student teacher and, later, as a graduate student in English literature, he analyzed and wrote about his experiences in both communities in an attempt to understand his own thoughts and feelings as he moved in and out of three student teaching assignments, balanced student teaching with methods instruction, and mapped the graduate study of literature onto his experiences in teaching.

> At Washington University I had expected small classes where I would be able, as I said in an interview, to "discuss literature on a higher level than I was able to do at the high school." What I found, as one of my professors put it, was "the end of my liberal education." After spending sixteen weeks of student teaching searching for any semblance of an educational philosophy or an image of myself as an educator and not an imitator, I was surprised to find that I was now supposed to shut up and learn. I found myself criticizing my English professors and the graduate program based on a set of ideal images I had formed of what a graduate instructor was supposed to be.

Creta Meng is a graduate student in English education. She is currently beginning a master's thesis tracing the philosophical heritage contributing to Louise Rosenblatt's theories of teaching literature. Her experiences have been somewhat different from Scott's and, unlike him, she is still not sure if she wants to make secondary school teaching a career.

> As I stated earlier, as an undergraduate student I considered education courses a necessary evil—something to be endured but not enjoyed. When I decided to go to graduate school, I was torn between an advanced degree in English and one in education. My English classes had been exciting and intellectually stimulating, while my education classes had been boring and, from a novice point of view, fairly commonsense. My decision to apply to the College of Education was pragmatic—acceptance was assured with only a minimal expenditure of effort. And yet I was unsure that I was making the right choice. A year later and a year smarter, however, I feel that my pragmatic decision was also a sound one.
>
> I can't imagine teaching without the knowledge that I have now. The opportunity to read, discuss, and reflect, in more depth, upon educational research literature, the social and philosophical foundations of education, curriculum design and development, and the theory and practice of teaching and learning has finally enabled me to begin to articulate a consistent theory of practice. From an intellectual point of view, my graduate course work has been both provocative and empowering. Perhaps most important, working on this project has enabled me to more fully understand myself.

Both students' writing illustrates the dynamic status of learning to teach as it has been affected by interactions across discourse communities. Their viewpoints on their separate graduate communities have been changed by their semester-long experience with student teaching—an experience that was not entirely pleasant for either student (for an extended discussion of their experiences see Clift, Meng, and Eggerding 1992). But their views on graduate school have been profoundly influenced by their interactions with secondary school students and their teachers. Neither was accepted as a member of the teaching community, and both chose to remain students for one more year. Within that time they were able to reflect on and examine the messages they inferred from coursework and from experience and to think through the controls they perceived on their thoughts, behaviors, and values.

When we began data analysis, seven months after completing student teaching, Scott and Creta still retained very negative attitudes about their experience—a feeling of being frustrated by a system over which they had little control and a sense that their student teaching semester had been uncommonly problematical. Through reading others' research, and through our long discussions while writing together, we had the opportunity to analyze, evaluate, and reconstruct our experience mediated by time. Scott has come to identify most closely with the community of high school English practitioners, although we will all be interested in his perceptions of his first year as a probationary member of that community. Creta still identifies with the university academic community, and all three of us wonder if she will ever attempt to be a secondary school teacher. We know that ours is an unfinished story. We also know that if we had not analyzed our data together our separate constructions would be very different from the one we have come to agree upon.

While all three of us have primary membership in different discourse communities, we know that our concerns and interests overlap. The context of collaborative inquiry has enabled all three of us to unlock and learn from the miseducative aspects of experience and to form a more positive attitude, not only about learning to teach but also about teaching as a profession. Based on our work we have argued in our joint writing for inclusion of the student teacher in the dialogue of learning to teach. Inclusion, we feel, would resolve much of the miscommunication we experienced and would help to reconcile the roles and relationships of the student teaching triad.

While conducting this research I have also had many opportunities to discuss our project with several field-based colleagues who teach middle school and senior high school English. Although they agree that the research has been beneficial to Scott, to Creta, and to me, my field-based colleagues are withholding a value judgment. They are currently working through the problems that result when student teachers voice their pain in a public forum. And, I must add, they would not label the problem as I would. The cooperating teachers with whom we worked were and are hurt that the students were not able to voice or to resolve communication problems at the time. They do not know why communication was a problem. They are also bothered that the students should choose to write openly about these problems with a university professor. For other teachers, the research has triggered discussions that had never occurred in a joint school-university forum before.

Why might we want to create community within English teacher education? In part the answer lies in the ongoing conversations produced by our action research. In addition to raising questions of research ethics and of giving voice to politically powerless student teachers, the cooperating teachers have expressed concern regarding the poor preparation student teachers received in English content—even though they were English majors! Other English teachers have begun to examine exactly what expectations they have for prospective English teachers—and how they might best convey these expectations. The program staff (both at the university and the schools) have begun to plan structures to encourage more joint planning for the teacher education courses and to build in stronger lines of communication that include computer networking among cooperating teachers, student teachers, and methods instructors.

We have also raised with the college administration our joint concerns regarding the time and stress associated with accepting student teachers—especially when one is attempting to be a concerned teacher, teacher educator, and parent all at once! And we have begun to restructure classes for experienced teachers that encourage knowledge construction within our joint field of teacher education. Finally, we have realized that we do not share a common set of values with regard to critical inquiry when that inquiry focuses on issues close to self and identity. We know that we operate within different discourses; we hope that we can use that knowledge to at least tolerate both our similarities and our differences, possibly even to celebrate them.

What we have not discussed is how we might bring our colleagues who specialize in literature, speech, rhetoric, and linguistics into our discussion. Recall that one of Gee's contentions is that becoming a part of a discourse necessitates the adoption of standpoints and positions defined, in part, by their opposition to other standpoints and positions. Student teachers, who walk the boundaries among discourse communities, are placed in an uncomfortable and powerless position. In the university English department it may be important to speak in the language of poststructuralism; in the high school English classroom it may be important to decry the irrelevance of English department ideology. In a teacher education program it may be important to criticize tracking or streaming students; in the high school it may be important to accord greater status and respect to the Advanced Placement teachers; in a liberal arts and sciences program these issues may be uninteresting. Which brings me to my last issue—one which was not directly raised by the preceding chapters, but was discussed often during small-group sessions at the NCRE/NCTE conference.

## Should University-Based Educators Be Part of a Community of English Teacher Educators?

This is not a rhetorical question. For many years the university community has debated and discussed this question in print (a few examples are Borrowman 1956; Haberman and Stinnett 1973; Clifford and Guthrie 1988; Goodlad 1990), and within the past decade we have seen a rapid proliferation of programs in which school districts certify teachers, several instances of states severely restricting university monopolies on certification preparation, and a few instances in which both public and private universities have abandoned teacher education completely. Today on many campuses the teacher education program is seen as having low status by professorial colleagues within colleges of liberal arts and sciences *and* within colleges of education (Ginsburg and Clift 1990; Goodlad 1990).

Although the Research about Teacher Education Studies (AACTE 1987) and other studies provide data suggesting that students are generally satisfied with their experiences in education classes, the folklore continues to tell us otherwise. One statement that we frequently encounter in our collaborative program is that students only learn to teach through experience, that education courses are too impractical. And, as I suggested above and as Grossman and Shulman argue, the content in university-based English courses is of contestable value when novice teachers begin to consider how to teach in school settings. One obvious example from Scott's experience is the expectation that he teach *Romeo and Juliet* while also teaching research skills. Another, from Creta's experience, is the expectation that she hold high school students accountable for independent reading and encourage them to appreciate *Spoon River Anthology* at the same time. The emphasis on accomplishing multiple objectives while teaching a district-required text to students who did not choose to be in class, but had no option to leave, was a major problem that university professors of literature never discussed and possibly never faced.

If the university community is ambivalent about the importance of their role in preparing people to teach English; if the classroom teaching community is a bit skeptical of the quality of university preparation; and if students feel unsupported by either community, then we have a social situation in which each community sends messages that marginalize the other. Recognizing this possibility, many teacher education programs have begun to restructure the social and the curricular domains of teacher education. For example, the University of Cincinnati has begun co-admitting students into liberal arts and sciences and education as a cohort and requiring that they attend seminars and other small-group sessions that enable them to bridge their learning among courses and between their courses and the public schools. The University of New Mexico pioneered a collaborative program in which classroom teachers are temporarily assigned to co-teach university methods courses with university faculty. College of Education faculty and Liberal Arts and Sciences faculty at the University of Dayton are co-teaching courses for both prospective teachers and students who are not necessarily prospective teachers. I could also mention innovative collaborations in Pittsburgh, Boulder, Milwaukee, Gainesville, and many other institutions whose faculty have made a commitment to creating teacher education communities.

Many of these programs were initiated by universities and enjoy the current support of both their respective institutions and the public schools—representing a significant commitment to collaborative program development. In several of the programs, there is also a commitment to collaborative inquiry. In other words, there are positive examples of individual and institutional commitment, places where change has moved beyond one teacher educator, one experimental program. And on that positive note I would like to return to the assumptions expressed in the first paragraph and turn them into questions.

If categories of knowledge for teaching English are formed, reformed, constructed, reconstructed, and rearranged as teachers interact with others in and out of their classrooms, what contexts facilitate knowledge construction within the field of English? How can we examine and evaluate the social, psychological, political, and personal forces that foster change or serve to maintain the status quo? Which of these inquiries are best conducted by participants? By those external to the situation? How does membership in a particular discourse (or group of discourses) affect the questions one asks and the evidence one counts as valid? Is a new discourse community likely to emerge if participants from diverse discourses work together?

Is the process of knowing profoundly affected by teachers thinking about who they are and who they would like to be as persons and, then, who they are and who they would like to be as teachers of English? Or does this assumption overly emphasize the individual and the impact of one's biography? Are the boundary lines that are drawn to exclude, include, or determine intersections a product more of history, of class, of ethnicity, or of other social forces? Is there a syntactic structure within English that provides a skeletal framework for knowing and coming to know? Or, is this too a social construction?

What is the impact of working with others whose discourses are different? Do negotiated understandings emerge, or do participants withdraw in misunderstanding, alienation, or admission that the potential outcomes are not worth the effort? These questions and many others are appropriate topics of study for NCRE/NCTE members and, also, for the many related groups who are interested in improving teaching and learning within the field of English. This implies thinking more globally than Buchanan's emphasis on classroom teachers meeting together, than Bissex's emphasis on university teachers and classroom teachers meeting together, and even than Hampton's reminder that change must be systemic, for we must begin to think across systems and across discourses as we raise the same questions over and over, in order to fashion temporally and situationally appropriate answers.

## References

American Association of Colleges for Teacher Education Research about Teacher Education Project. 1987. *Teaching Teachers: Facts and Figures*. Washington, D.C.: AACTE.

Borrowman, M. L. 1956. *The Liberal and Technical in Teacher Education: A Historical Survey of American Thought.* New York: Teachers College Bureau of Publications.

Clifford, G. J., and J. W. Guthrie. 1988. *Ed School: A Brief for Professional Education.* Chicago: University of Chicago Press.

Clift, R. T., L. Meng, and S. Eggerding. 1994. "Mixed Messages in Learning to Teach English." *Journal of Teaching and Teacher Education* 10:265–79.

Feiman-Nemser, S., and M. Buchmann. 1987. "When Is Student Teaching Teacher Education?" *Teaching and Teacher Education* 3, no. 4:255–73.

Gee, J. P. 1990. *Social Linguistics and Literacies: Ideology in Discourses.* London: Falmer.

Ginsburg, M., and R. T. Clift. 1990. "Hide and Seek: Researching the Hidden Curriculum of Pre-service Teacher Education." In *The Handbook of Research on Teacher Education: A Project of the Association of Teacher Educators,* edited by W. R. Houston. New York: Macmillan.

Goodlad, J. I. 1990. *Teachers for Our Nation's Schools.* New York: Longman.

Haberman, M., and T. M. Stinnett. 1973. *Teacher Education and the New Profession of Teaching.* Berkeley, Calif.: McCutchan.

Judge, H. G. 1982. *American Graduate Schools of Education: A View from Abroad.* New York: Ford Foundation.

Schon, D. A. 1983. *The Reflective Practitioner: How Professionals Think in Action.* New York: Basic Books.

Shuell, T. J. 1992. "The Two Cultures of Teaching and Teacher Preparation." *Teaching and Teacher Education* 8:83–90.

# Author Index

Agassiz, L., 93
Alcoff, L., 56, 71
Allen, J., 40
Alpert, A., 93–102
Amarel, M., 49
Anderson, D. K., 14
Apple, M., 72
Applebee, A. N., 4, 27, 177
Ashton-Warner, S., 107
Athanases, S. Z., 14, 145
Atwell, N., 90, 164
Avery, C., 102
Ayers, W. C., 105–21, 148, 170, 180

Bakhtin, M. M., 61, 72
Ball, D. L., 6
Barnes, D., 4, 163
Barylske, J., 54, 158, 159
Beach, R., viii, 143–54
Ben-Peretz, M., 5
Berliner, D. C., 106
Berriault, G., 17
Best, R., 113
Bevington, D., 7
Bhabha, H., 58
Bissex, G. L., 88–104, 153, 156, 169, 170,
     180, 186
Bodner, G. M., 13
Borrowman, M. L., 184
Brannon, L., 165
Brickhouse, N., 13
Britton, J., 163
Britzman, D. P., 53–75, 152, 167, 168, 169,
     174, 179, 180, 181
Brodkey, L., 54, 68, 152
Brophy, J., 6
Bruner, J. S., 6, 150
Buchanan, J., 39–52, 169, 170, 179, 180,
     186. *See also* Allen, J.
Buchmann, M., 145, 178
Bullock, R., 153
Burke, C. L., 129
Burke, S., 17

Bussis, A., 49
Butler, J., 58

Calderhead, J., 106
Calkins, L. M., 123
Canales, J., 14, 145
Caret, E., 14, 145
Carini, P., 41, 42
Carlsen, W. S., 11
Carlson, A., 131
Carr, W., 153
Carroll, W., 114
Carson, T., 92
Carter, K., 106
Cherryholmes, C., 67
Chittenden, E., 44, 49
Clandinin, D. J., 107
Clarke, S., 4
Clifford, G. J., 184
Clift, R. T., 12, 13, 173–87
Cochran-Smith, M., 41, 153, 158,
     159, 170
Coles, R., 118
Comeaux, M. A., 5, 13, 14
Connelly, F. M., 107
Coombs, R. H., viii
Coser, R., 5
Coulson, R. L., 14
Counts, G. S., 107
Cuban, L., 128

Daiker, D., 153
Daniels, H., 129
Darling-Hammond, L., 106
de Lauretis, T., 56, 70
Denyer, J., 6
Derrida, J., 27
Dewey, J., 3, 106, 107, 115, 116, 117,
     131
Diamond, C. T. P., 130
Dohrn, B., 118
Donald, J., 60
Dunstan, A., 151

189

# Subject Index

# Editor

**Timothy Shanahan** is professor of urban education at the University of Illinois at Chicago, where he is coordinator of graduate programs in reading, writing, and literacy, and director of the UIC Center for Literacy. His research focuses on the relationship of reading and writing, the assessment of reading ability, and the development of literacy. He is the author of more than ninety research articles, chapters, and other publications, including the books *Multidisciplinary Perspectives on Literacy, Reading and Writing Together,* and *Understanding Research in Reading and Writing.* His research has appeared in journals such as *Reading Research Quarterly,* the *Journal of Educational Psychology,* and *Research in the Teaching of English.* He has served as Director of Cooperative Research for the National Conference on Research in English, and as associate editor of the *Journal of Reading Behavior.*

Shanahan has received the Milton D. Jacobson Readability Research Award from the International Reading Association, and the Amoco Award for Outstanding Teaching. He was elected to the honors society, Phi Kappa Phi, and is listed in *Who's Who in the Midwest.* He received his Ph.D. at the University of Delaware in 1980. His research and development projects have attracted more than one million dollars in funding from federal agencies and the philanthropic community.

# Contributors

**William Ayers** is a school reform activist and associate professor of education at the University of Illinois at Chicago, where he teaches courses in elementary education, interpretive research, and urban school change. A past chair of the Alliance for Better Chicago Schools (a coalition shaping the Chicago reform), he taught young children for twelve years, and has taught teachers for the past eight. A graduate of Bank Street College of Education, and Teachers College, Columbia University, he has written extensively about the importance of creating progressive educational opportunities in urban public schools. His research interests focus on the political and social contexts of schooling, and the meaning and ethical purposes of teachers, students, and families. His articles have appeared in many journals including the *Harvard Educational Review, Journal of Teacher Education, The Nation,* and *Teachers College Record.* His books include *The Good Preschool Teacher,* and *To Teach: The Journey of a Teacher.*

**Richard Beach** is professor of English education at the University of Minnesota and former president of the National Conference on Research in English. He is author of *A Teacher's Introduction to Reader Response Theories,* co-author of *Teaching Literature in the Secondary School,* and co-editor of *Multidisciplinary Perspectives on Literacy Research.* He has chaired the Board of Trustees for the NCTE Research Foundation and is currently a member of the National Board for Professional Teaching Standards. His research focuses on the teaching of literatures and response to literature. He received his Ph.D. from the University of Illinois at Urbana-Champaign.

**Glenda L. Bissex** has worked with teacher researchers across the U.S. and Canada as well as in Northeastern University's Institute on Writing and Teaching. Her publications on teacher research include *Seeing for Ourselves: Case Study Research by Teachers of Writing,* co-edited with Richard H. Bullock. Her own research includes *GNYS AT WRK: A Child Learns to Write and Read* and many articles on children's literacy learning. She has been a trustee of the NCTE Research Foundation, where she helped establish grants for teacher researchers, and a member of NCTE's Commission on Composition. She was for many years a high school teacher of English and a teacher of reading in the elementary grades through college. She received her Ph.D. from Harvard University.

**Deborah P. Britzman** is associate professor in the Faculty of Education with cross appointments in Social and Political Thought and Women's Studies at York University in Canada. She is the author of *Practice Makes Practice: A Critical Study of Learning to Teach.* Her recent writing concerns what cultural studies offers to the study of education, with a focus on relations between narratives of sex, race, gender, and social identity and the practices of equality and inequality in education. Recent book chapters have appeared in *Race, Identity, and Representation in Education, Ninety-Second Yearbook of the Society for the Study of Education,* and *Continuity and Contradiction: The Future of Sociology in Education.*

**Judy Buchanan** is director of the Philadelphia Writing Project, working as a teacher on special assignment from the School District of Philadelphia. She has taught elementary school students for seventeen years and has been a member of the Philadelphia Teachers' Learning Cooperative, a teacher collective, since 1978. In addition to her articles in *The Voice* and *Work in Progress* (both Philadelphia Writing Project publications), she has written about her classroom in *Delicate Balances* and *Inside/Outside: Teacher Research and Knowledge.*

**Renée T. Clift** is associate professor of curriculum and instruction at the University of Illinois at Urbana-Champaign. She is co-editor of *Encouraging Reflective Practice in Education: An Analysis of Issues and Exemplars.* She has published articles on collaboration and teacher education in the *Journal of Teacher Education* and the *American Educational Research Journal.* Her research on learning to teach English has been published in *Teaching and Teacher Education,* the *Journal of Teacher Education,* and *English Education.* She has twice been a recipient of the Richard A. Meade Award for Research in English Education from NCTE's Conference on English Education.

**Pamela L. Grossman** is associate professor of curriculum and instruction at the College of Education, University of Washington. She is the author of *The Making of a Teacher: Teacher Knowledge and Teacher Education.* She received the Richard A. Meade Award for Research in English Education from NCTE's Conference on English Education in 1991, and the Outstanding Dissertation Award from the American Association of Colleges of Teacher Education. She was a Spencer Foundation Predoctoral Fellow, 1978–79, and received her Ph.D. from Stanford University.

**Sally Hampton** works in the Fort Worth, Texas, school system, where she is responsible for that district's writing and reasoning skills program. Her work involves designing assessments of literacy skills, making explicit in the curriculum the connections between in-class learning and out-of-school problems, and the developing of both teacher and student portfolios. She is currently involved in an assessment project focusing on specific linkages between writing in the world of work and the writing taught in schools. She is a language arts consultant to the New Standards Project and a member of the Performance Assessment Collaborative for Education Advisory Board. She has published chapters in *Theory and Practice in the Teaching of Writing* and *Educating Everybody's Children: Diverse Teaching Strategies for Diverse Learners.*

**James Marshall** is associate professor of English and English education at the University of Iowa, where he is director of the General Education Literature Program. Having taught high school English for six years, Marshall is especially interested in the relationships between writing and literary understanding among secondary students and in the ways that literature is discussed in English classrooms. His publications include research reports in *Research in the Teaching of English; Ways of Knowing; Research and Practice in the Teaching of Writing,* with James Davis; *Teaching Literature in the Secondary School,* with Richard Beach; and a wide range of book chapters on the teaching of writing and literature. He is currently chair of NCTE's Standing Committee on Research and executive secretary of the High School Task Force for the Standards Project in English Language Arts. He has won the James N. Murray Award for Faculty Excellence, and the Outstanding Teaching Award for Faculty Excellence from the University of Iowa.

**Beverly J. Moss** is assistant professor of English, specializing in composition theory and pedagogy and literacy theories and practices, at the Ohio State University. In addition to authoring several essays, she is the editor of *Literacy across Communities* (1994) and is currently working on a book-length manuscript on literate texts, community texts, and literacy traditions in African American churches. She received her Ph.D. in English from the University of Illinois at Chicago.

**Christine C. Pappas** is professor in the College of Education at the University of Illinois at Chicago. A major focus of her research has been on studying how young children learn various written genres. She (along with co-authors Barbara Kiefer and Linda Levstik) has just completed the second edition of *An Integrated Language Perspective in the Elementary School: Theory into Action.* Her current research (funded by the Spencer Foundation) involves collaborative work with urban teacher-researchers who are attempting to develop culturally and linguistically responsive pedagogies in various literacy curriculum genres in their classrooms.

**Anthony Petrosky** is the principal investigator and co-director of the Early Adolescence English Language Arts Assessment Development Lab for the National Board for Professional Teaching Standards. Petrosky holds a joint appointment as professor in the School of Education and the English Department of the University of Pittsburgh. Professor Petrosky was the past director of the Pittsburgh Public Schools' Critical Thinking Project. He has also served as co-director of the Western Pennsylvania Writing Project. He was a senior researcher for the MacArthur Foundations' Higher Literacies Studies, where he was responsible for conducting and writing case reports on higher literacy efforts in the school districts of Denver, Pittsburgh, Toronto, and Ruleville and Mound Bayou in the Mississippi Delta. He is past chair of the NCTE Standing Committee on Research and a past elected member of the NCTE Research Foundation. Along with David Bartholomae, Petrosky is the co-author and co-editor of three books: *Facts, Artifacts, and Counterfacts: Theory and Method for a Reading and Writing Course, The Teaching of Writing,* and *Ways of Reading: An Anthology for Writers.*

**William H. Schubert** is professor of education and chair of curriculum and instruction in the College of Education at the University of Illinois at Chicago, where he was given the Distinguished Scholar-Teacher Award in 1986. Author of more than one hundred journal articles on curriculum theory, history, inquiry, and development, he is especially concerned with the contribution of teachers, students, and families to education. He is author of *Curriculum Books: The First Eighty Years,* and *Curriculum: Perspective, Paradigm, and Possibility.* He edited *Teacher Lore* with William Ayers, and is editing a book series on *Student Lore: The Educational*

*Experience of Students in School and Society.* Schubert is currently president of the John Dewey Society, and former president of the Society for the Study of Curriculum History.

**Lee S. Shulman** is Charles E. Ducommun Professor of Education and professor (by courtesy) of psychology at Stanford University, where he has taught since 1982. He has been a Guggenheim Fellow, a Fellow of the American Psychological Association, and a Fellow at the Center for Advanced Study in the Behavioral Sciences. He is immediate past president of the National Academy of Education and is a past president of the American Educational Research Association (AERA). In 1989, he received AERA's award for Distinguished Contributions to Educational Research.

Professor Shulman's scholarship has investigated issues in discovery learning and processes of inquiry, medical decision making and problem solving, the psychology of instruction in science, mathematics, and medicine, and cognitive processes in teachers.

**Michael W. Smith** is assistant professor in the Literacy Education Cluster of Rutgers University's Graduate School of Education. He focuses on secondary English education, especially on identifying the knowledge that readers and writers employ and how teachers can help students develop that knowledge. His publications include *The Language of Interpretation: Patterns of Discourse in Classroom Discussions of Literature* (with J. Marshall and P. Smagorinsky); *Apprehension* and *Understanding Unreliable Narrators,* two monographs in NCTE's Theory and Research into Practice series; articles in journals such as *English Journal,* the *Journal of Educational Research,* the *Journal of Reading, Research in the Teaching of English,* and the *Review of Educational Research;* and numerous chapters in edited collections. He is currently co–associate chair of NCTE's Assembly on Research.

# About NCRE

The **National Conference on Research in English,** founded in 1932, is a professional organization committed to furthering research in the teaching of the language arts and to improving instructional practice through the dissemination of research findings. NCRE sponsors research, provides a forum for discussion of current and needed research, and disseminates research through conferences and publications.

## NCRE Publications

*Academic Libraries and Research in the Teaching of English.* Timothy Shanahan and Michael L. Kamil. Special Report of the Center for the Study of Reading, University of Illinois at Urbana-Champaign. 93 pp. 1994. Coll.

*Multidisciplinary Perspectives on Literacy Research.* Richard Beach, Judith L. Green, Michael L. Kamil, and Timothy Shanahan, editors. 418 pp. 1992. NCRE and NCTE. Coll. ISBN 0-8141-3219-7.

*Context-Responsive Approaches to Assessing Children's Language.* Jessie A. Roderick, editor. 137 pp. 1991. NCRE. Grades K–7. ISBN 0-8141-0853-9.

*The Dynamics of Language Learning: Research in Reading and English.* James R. Squire, editor. 425 pp. 1987. ERIC/RCS and NCRE. Grades K–Coll. ISBN 0-8141-1276-5.

*Research on Written Composition: New Directions for Teaching.* George Hillocks, Jr. 369 pp. 1986. ERIC/RCS and NCRE. Grades K–Coll. ISBN 0-8141-4075-0.

*Composing and Comprehending.* Julie M. Jensen, editor. 200 pp. 1984. ERIC/RCS and NCRE. Grades K–6. ISBN 0-8141-0802-4.

*Secondary School Reading: What Research Reveals for Classroom Practices.* Allen Berger and H. Alan Robinson, editors. 206 pp. 1982. ERIC/RCS and NCRE. Grades 9–12. ISBN 0-8141-4295-8.